Preven‌‌ ‌‌ld Sexual Abuse

Preventing Child Sexual Abuse

Evidence, policy and practice

**Stephen Smallbone,
William L. Marshall and
Richard Wortley**

WILLAN
PUBLISHING

Published by

Willan Publishing
Culmcott House
Mill Street, Uffculme
Cullompton, Devon
EX15 3AT, UK
Tel: +44(0)1884 840337
Fax: +44(0)1884 840251
e-mail: info@willanpublishing.co.uk
website: www.willanpublishing.co.uk

Published simultaneously in the USA and Canada by

Willan Publishing
c/o ISBS, 920 NE 58th Ave, Suite 300
Portland, Oregon 97213-3786, USA
Tel: +001(0)503 287 3093
Fax: +001(0)503 280 8832
e-mail: info@isbs.com
website: www.isbs.com

First published 2008

ISBN   978-1-84392-222-3 paperback
ISBN   978-1-84392-221-6 hardback

British Library Cataloguing-in-Publication Data

A catalogue record for this book is available from the British Library

Typeset by GCS, Leighton Buzzard, Bedfordshire
Printed and bound by T.J. International Ltd, Padstow, Cornwall

Contents

1 **Child sexual abuse: definitions, dimensions and
   scope of the problem**   **1**
   Defining child sexual abuse   2
   Dimensions of child sexual abuse   4
   Scope of the problem   17
   Summary   19

2 **Explaining child sexual abuse: a new integrated theory** **21**
   Biological foundations   23
   Developmental influences   29
   Ecosystemic factors   33
   Situational factors   39
   Summary   44

3 **Identifying prevention targets**   **46**
   Current approaches to prevention   46
   Implications of the integrated theory for preventing
     sexual abuse   54
   Offenders, victims, situations and communities   61
   Summary   63

4 **Developmental prevention**   **65**
   Conceptual and empirical foundations   65
   Developmental prevention of child sexual abuse
     offending   71
   Summary   86

5   **Criminal justice interventions**   89
    Detection, investigation and prevention   90
    The psychology of punishment   94
    Deterrence strategies   97
    Incapacitation strategies   104
    Summary   111

6   **Treating adult and adolescent offenders**   112
    General principles   113
    Treatment for adult child sexual abuse offenders   115
    Treatment for adolescent child sexual abuse offenders   123
    Treatment outcomes   130
    Summary   132

7   **Victim-focused prevention**   134
    Interventions with potential victims   134
    Interventions with known victims   142
    Summary   153

8   **Situational prevention**   155
    Conceptual and empirical foundations   156
    Situational prevention of child sexual abuse   161
    Summary   174

9   **Community-focused approaches**   176
    Community-focused approaches to crime prevention   176
    Community-focused approaches to preventing
       maltreatment   183
    Community-focused approaches to preventing sexual
       abuse   188
    Summary   194

10 **Towards a comprehensive prevention strategy**   197
    Primary prevention   198
    Secondary prevention   204
    Tertiary prevention   209
    Where to from here?   214

References   217
Index   253

Chapter 1

Child sexual abuse: definitions, dimensions, and scope of the problem

Although child sexual abuse (CSA) is generally referred to as a distinct and singular phenomenon, there is a remarkably wide range of circumstances and events that may constitute CSA. Wide variations have been observed in the characteristics, modus operandi and persistence of CSA offenders, in the characteristics, circumstances and outcomes for victims, and in the physical and social settings in which CSA occurs.

These multiple dimensions of CSA, and the wide variations within them, may at first seem to make the task of prevention overwhelmingly difficult, if not impossible. However, it is important to recognise that on virtually none of these dimensions is the incidence of CSA evenly distributed. Not all children are equally at risk of falling victim to sexual abuse, not all victims will be affected in the same way, not all adolescents and adults are equally at risk of becoming offenders, not all offenders are equally at risk of proceeding to a chronic pattern of offending, and not all physical and social environments present the same risk for CSA to occur.

The first step towards developing a comprehensive, evidence-based approach to preventing CSA is therefore to understand the patterns of variation within, and the interactions between, its key empirical dimensions. To the extent these patterns can be reliably identified, the focus of prevention strategies can be narrowed, and prevention resources can accordingly be prioritised. Notwithstanding the limitations of the current knowledge base, the main aim of the present chapter is to specify where, when, how, to whom and by whom CSA occurs. We will turn our attention to the equally important question of *why* CSA occurs in the next chapter.

We begin here by considering how CSA is defined. We then draw on available evidence to sketch out the key empirical dimensions of CSA, namely the characteristics of offenders, the characteristics of victims and the characteristics of the settings in which CSA occurs. We conclude the present chapter by considering what is known about the scope of the problem.

Defining child sexual abuse

Alongside physical abuse, neglect and negligent treatment, emotional abuse, and the commercial or other exploitation of children, CSA is one of the five types of child maltreatment recognised by the World Health Organisation (WHO 2006). While there may be broad agreement about the social justice principles underlying the need to protect children from all forms of abuse, neglect and exploitation, there is no clear consensus among researchers or practitioners about exactly what constitutes maltreatment, nor among legislators about where to draw the line between illegal and legally tolerated actions involving children. Indeed, in its 1993 review of child maltreatment policy and practice, the US National Research Council (NRC) concluded that despite vigorous debate over the preceding twenty years there had been little progress in the most fundamental task of establishing reliable and valid definitions of child maltreatment, including CSA.

The NRC pointed to problems specifically with: 1) a lack of social consensus about what constitutes child maltreatment; 2) uncertainty about the criteria that should be applied to defining maltreatment, and particularly whether the characteristics or behaviour of the perpetrator, the outcomes for the child, the circumstances of the maltreatment incident, or some combination of these, should be considered; 3) disagreement about whether definitions should rely on standards of actual or potential harm; and 4) confusion about whether the same standards should apply for scientific, legal and clinical purposes (National Research Council 1993). Although some commentators have argued that an increasing consensus has emerged in the period since the NRC review (see e.g. Herrenkohl 2005), the reliability and validity of maltreatment definitions are yet to be established.

Conceptual ambiguities arise with each term in the phrase *child sexual abuse* (Haugaard 2000). Researchers concerned with establishing the prevalence of CSA have defined the term *child* using chronological age thresholds of sixteen (Wurr and Partridge 1996), seventeen

(Finkelhor 1979) or eighteen years (Russell 1983; Wyatt 1985). Legal definitions of childhood vary even more widely, with the legal age of consent for heterosexual activity ranging from as low as twelve in some parts of Mexico and the Philippines, to as high as twenty-one in Madagascar. Age of consent is undeclared in Ecuador, North Korea, Oman and Pakistan, and male homosexual activity, regardless of age, remains illegal in some fifty countries worldwide (AIDS Education and Research Trust 2005).

Defining the term *sexual* is also problematic. While there may be little disagreement that behaviours such as genital stimulation or sexual intercourse constitute sexual behaviour, it is much less clear whether behaviours such as bathing or sleeping with children, kissing, massaging, and so on, might be sexual. Establishing whether the older person in these latter circumstances was sexually motivated is itself problematic, since sexual motivations are difficult to observe and unlikely to be frankly disclosed. Finally, it can be unclear whether the term *abuse* refers to the intent of the perpetrator or to the experience of the victim, to actual or potential harm to the victim, or even to the violation of social norms.

Early prevalence studies (e.g. Finkelhor 1979; Russell 1983; Wyatt 1985) used broad definitions of CSA that included behaviours such as being invited to do something sexual, being kissed, and nongenital fondling, alongside behaviours such as genital stimulation and sexual intercourse. Haugaard (2000) notes that these early prevalence studies were very influential in drawing public attention to the problem and suggests that the broad research definitions used in these studies may have subsequently influenced clinical and legal definitions. Research using broad definitions tends to produce high prevalence estimates, and to identify large proportions of CSA victims whose abuse experience is at the lower end of the severity continuum (Haugaard 2000) and which is therefore associated with a lower incidence of observable harm (Rind, Tromovitch and Bauserman 1998). A risk in using broad definitions is that the experiences of victims who have suffered more severe abuse may be obscured by more general findings. On the other hand, narrowing the definition of CSA may raise objections that the broader social problem is being minimised.

The World Health Organisation (WHO), together with the International Society for the Prevention of Child Abuse and Neglect (IPSCAN), defines CSA broadly as:

> … the involvement of a child in sexual activity that he or she does not fully comprehend, is unable to give informed consent

to, or for which the child is not developmentally prepared, or else that violate the laws or social taboos of society. Children can be sexually abused by adults or other children who are – by virtue of their age or stage of development – in a position of responsibility, trust or power over the victim (WHO 2006: 10).

Like most general definitions of CSA, the WHO definition seeks to describe the general features of the problem rather than to specify its dimensions and to clarify its boundaries. Nor does it resolve any of the definitional problems outlined above. Nevertheless, since it places CSA in an international context the WHO definition suffices as a general conceptual definition for our present purposes.

While it is important to acknowledge the problems associated with defining CSA, it is equally important not to overstate them. Little disagreement is likely to be found in prototypical cases; rather, it is at the boundaries of the problem where disagreement is likely to be the greatest. Although uncertainty about individual cases will no doubt continue to present serious challenges to those involved in CSA investigations and prosecutions, for example, it makes sense for prevention policy to prioritise those forms of CSA that are known to present the greatest risk of harm for the children concerned, and therefore about which there is least likely to be disagreement. Increasingly, researchers have recognised that the sequelae, and to some extent the causes, of CSA are likely to vary according to temporal factors (age of onset, frequency and duration), severity and the relationship with the perpetrator (Manly 2005), and it is therefore these dimensions that most need to be understood and targeted as priorities for prevention efforts.

Dimensions of child sexual abuse

Our main aim in the present chapter is to sketch out what is presently known about where, when, how, to whom and by whom CSA occurs. While there is an extensive empirical literature on CSA offenders and victims, our emphasis is given initially to the demographic, temporal, spatial and behavioural dimensions of the problem. The various approaches to prevention canvassed later in the book will require consideration of further evidence, which we will examine as required in subsequent chapters.

CSA offender characteristics

Gender

Criminal justice statistics and victimisation surveys consistently identify males as responsible for the vast majority of all sexual offences, including CSA offences. While males are over-represented in virtually all forms of crime, official crime data indicate that sexual offences are almost exclusively the domain of male offenders. By way of illustration, for the year 2004/05 reports to police in Queensland, Australia, indicated that females were involved in 37% of all fraud offences, 31% of theft offences (other than motor vehicle theft), 23% of property offences, 22% of assaults, 12% of robberies, 10% of unlawful entries, and less than 3% of all sexual offences (Queensland Police Service 2006).

Cortoni and Hanson (2005) recently reviewed prevalence studies of female sex offending in the US, the UK, Canada, Australia and New Zealand. Official data showed that the proportion of female sexual offenders ranged from 0.6% in New Zealand to 8.3% in the US, with an unweighted average of 3.8% across the five countries. The proportion of female sex offenders identified in victimisation surveys ranged from 3.1% in New Zealand to 7.0% in Australia, with an unweighted average of 4.8%.

While prevention of CSA by females may require special attention, available evidence suggests that prevention efforts should concentrate particularly on males as potential, undetected or known offenders. Indeed, there is no other identifying characteristic of CSA offenders that has been as consistently observed as male gender.

Age

Unlike all other forms of crime, the *age-crime* curve for sexual offences is markedly bimodal (Canadian Center for Justice Statistics 1999). As with nonsexual offences, participation in CSA offending peaks in adolescence and early adulthood. Although reliable prevalence data are notoriously difficult to obtain, international estimates are that adolescents and young adults may be responsible for between 30% and 50% of all CSA offences (Bourke and Donohue 1996; Finkelhor and Dziuba-Leatherman 1994).

However, unlike for nonsexual offences, a second, more prominent peak in involvement with sexual offences occurs in the mid- to late thirties. Some commentators argue that this represents adolescence onset and life-course persistence as the typical trajectory for sexual offenders, including CSA offenders (Abel, Osborn and Twigg 1993).

5

However, rates of observed sexual recidivism among adolescent sexual offenders rarely exceed 10% (Righthand and Welch 2001), and only a minority of adult sexual offenders report that they began their sexual offending as adolescents.

Abel and his colleagues' confidential self-report study (Abel *et al.* 1987; Abel and Osborn 1992) is commonly cited to support assumptions that early onset is typical for adult CSA offenders. However, a close examination of Abel's data shows that early onset was more characteristic of the victimless paraphilias (e.g. transvestism and fetishism) than of sexual offences themselves. The only subgroup of CSA offenders to report adolescence-onset of deviant sexual interests was nonfamilial offenders against males. For these offenders, who constituted about 20% of the CSA offenders in Abel *et al.*'s sample (and about 8% of the total sample), the mean self-reported age of onset of their deviant sexual interests was eighteen years. The mean age of onset for nonfamilial offenders (female victims) was twenty-two years, for familial offenders (male victims) twenty-four years, and for familial offenders (female victims) (who constituted 58% of all the child-sex offenders in their sample) twenty-seven years.

In a large-scale correctional survey, the average age of sexual offence convictions for Canadian, British and US adult incest offenders was reported to be forty years, and for adult nonfamilial CSA offenders thirty-seven years (Hanson 2002). However, since CSA offences are often not reported until many years after they have occurred, the age distribution of convicted CSA offenders may be a poor indicator of offending onset. Smallbone and Wortley (2004a) found that the average age at *first* sexual offence conviction for 362 Australian adult CSA offenders to be thirty-seven years. In the same study, confidential self-reports indicated that the average age at CSA offence onset was thirty-two years. The modal onset-age bracket, accounting for 37% of the sample, was thirty-one to forty years. The age distributions for both the official and self-reported first CSA offence were normal, with very wide ranges: fifteen to seventy-six years for official onset, and ten to sixty-three years for self-reported onset. These data indicate that, for adult CSA offenders, late onset appears to be as common as early onset, but that neither is as common as onset in early middle-age.

Among the implications of these data is that there are two distinct populations of CSA offenders – adolescent and adult offenders – and that different prevention strategies may accordingly be indicated. While there is undoubtedly some overlap between these populations (some adult offenders do begin in adolescence, and some adolescent offenders do proceed to a chronic pattern of sexual offending), available evidence suggests that this overlap is considerably smaller than has traditionally been assumed. It thus seems clear that there are two distinct risk periods for the onset of involvement in CSA offences – adolescence and early middle-age.

Persistence

Much more empirical attention has been given to patterns of CSA offending following initial detection, prosecution and in many cases serving a term of imprisonment, than to offending patterns prior to being arrested for the first time. We simply do not know how many people may commit one or two CSA offences, never get caught, and never repeat it, although presumably this happens. Among those who are caught and are included in research studies, pre-arrest persistence seems to vary systematically according to whether the offending occurs in familial or nonfamilial settings, and according to victim gender. Although Abel *et al.*'s study has been criticised for its unrepresentative sampling and other methodological problems (see e.g. Marshall and Eccles 1991), it nevertheless shows marked differences in self-reported persistence between familial and nonfamilial CSA offenders. For example, the mean number of victims disclosed by familial offenders in Abel *et al.*'s study was 1.8, whereas for nonfamilial offenders it was an astonishing seventy-three. The mean number of 'completed paraphilic acts' (i.e. the number of discrete incidents reported by the offender that were judged by interviewers to constitute sexual offences) for familial offenders was seventy-seven, and for nonfamilial offenders 128 (Abel and Rouleau 1990). Thus for familial offenders the mean number of incidents per victim was forty-three, and for nonfamilial offenders 1.8.

Abel *et al.* also found striking differences in victim gender patterns. For nonfamilial offenders, the mean number of girl victims per offender was twelve, while the mean number of boy victims was sixty-one. Male victims outnumbered female victims by 5:1. Notwithstanding the possibility that these were more serious offenders than would generally be encountered in criminal justice settings, the general pattern observed here is consistent with other clinical research findings: familial CSA offenders tend to have only one or two (usually female) victims but tend to offend against them repeatedly before being caught, whereas nonfamilial CSA offenders tend to have more (usually male) victims but tend to offend only once or twice against individual victims.

These high rates of pre-arrest persistence stand in stark contrast to generally low observed sexual recidivism rates among CSA offenders, which, taken together, suggest that being arrested has a major impact on persistence trajectories for CSA offenders. Studies of adolescent sexual offenders have generally reported average sexual recidivism rates ranging from 0% to 20% (Nisbet, Wilson and Smallbone 2004), with findings in the upper range associated with longer follow-up periods (up to ten years), more stringent measures of recidivism (e.g. new charges, rather than new convictions), and residential or custodial samples. In their meta-analysis of sexual offender recidivism studies involving more than 22,000 (mainly adult) sexual offenders from five countries (US, Canada, UK, Australia and New Zealand), Hanson and Bussiere (1998) reported an average sexual recidivism rate for CSA offenders of 12.7% over an average four to five years at risk. Even over the longer term (up to twenty years at risk), average sexual recidivism rates rarely exceed 50% (Hanson 2000; Janus and Meehl 1997). Emerging evidence suggests that the risk of sexual recidivism for CSA offenders declines substantially with age (Hanson 2002).

Hanson and Bussiere's (1998) meta-analysis showed that nonfamilial offenders were more than twice as likely to be reconvicted for new sexual offences (19%) than were familial offenders (8%). Of course, as with nonsexual offences, many sexual offences are never reported to police or child protection authorities, and official recidivism data will therefore under-estimate true recidivism rates. It is unlikely, though, that the extent to which official recidivism data under-estimate true recidivism is uniformly reflected in the discrepancies between official and unofficial victimisation. Rather, as with nonsexual offenders, a small group of persistent offenders may be disproportionately responsible for sexual offence recidivism. For example, Abel *et al.* (1987) reported that although their sample of nonfamilial CSA offenders (male victims) disclosed a mean number of 150 victims, the median number was 4.4. Thus a small number of offenders were disproportionately responsible for a very large number of victims. Similarly, when Smallbone and Wortley (2001) asked 180 Australian CSA offenders about the unofficial or 'true' extent of their sexual offending, almost half said they had only ever offended against one child. Ten per cent said that they had offended against more than ten children, including two offenders who reported more than 100 child victims. These data illustrate how the selective targeting of a relatively small group of persistent, serial CSA offenders should, at least hypothetically, produce a disproportionately large reduction in CSA victimisation.

Criminal versatility

Empirical evidence shows unequivocally that adult CSA offenders are about twice as likely to be convicted of nonsexual offences than of sexual offences, both before and after being convicted of a sexual offence. In our Australian study of CSA offenders (n = 362), 62% had at least one prior conviction recorded in their official criminal histories. All sixteen of the Australian Bureau of Statistics offence categories, including abduction, robbery and homicide (although rare), were represented in these offenders' criminal histories. The most common prior convictions were for theft (29.7%), traffic and motor vehicle offences (23.5%), sexual offences (22.3%), justice offences (20.7%), personal injury offences (18.9%), burglary (14.4%) and drug offences (13.3%) (Smallbone and Wortley 2004b). In other analyses involving the same sample, we found that more than 80% of recidivist offenders (those with at least one prior conviction for any offence) were first convicted of a nonsexual offence, and that this first conviction typically preceded their first self-reported sexual contact with a child (Smallbone and Wortley 2004a).

Miethe, Olson and Mitchell (2006) recently examined persistence and versatility in the criminal records of almost 10,000 sexual offenders and some 24,000 nonsexual offenders released from prisons in fifteen US states in 1994. Representing about 10% of all offenders released in the US in those states in that year, and drawing on complete criminal histories as well as recidivism records at three years post release, this study provides the most comprehensive test of the assumptions of persistence and specialisation among sexual offenders to date. Consistent with previous studies, Miethe *et al.* found low levels of persistence and specialisation in both absolute and relative terms (i.e. compared to nonsexual offenders). Low rates of sexual offence specialisation have also been observed in CSA offenders referred for civil commitment in the US (Harris *et al.* in press).

Recidivism and treatment outcome studies also clearly demonstrate criminal versatility among adult CSA offenders. For example, whereas in their meta-analysis of sexual offender recidivism studies Hanson and Bussiere (1998) reported average sexual recidivism rates for CSA offenders of 12.7% over five years at risk, average rates for 'any' recidivism (sexual or nonsexual) were 36.9% over the same average follow-up period. Similarly, results from a meta-analysis of sexual offender treatment outcome studies showed average baseline recidivism rates (i.e. for untreated offenders) of 16.8% for sexual recidivism and 39.2% for nonsexual recidivism (Hanson *et al.* 2002).

A key implication of these findings is that CSA offenders' motivation may be more similar to nonsexual offenders' motivation than has been traditionally assumed. Developmental risk factors for CSA offenders, as we will see in Chapter 4, are also similar to those for nonsexual offenders. This in turn suggests that established crime prevention methods designed for general offenders, such as developmental and situational prevention (Tonry and Farrington 1995), should be applicable to CSA offenders as well.

Modus operandi

It has been widely observed that both adult and adolescent CSA offenders typically have already established a nonsexual relationship with a child before the first sexual abuse incident occurs (Elliot, Brown and Kilcoyne 1995; Kauffman *et al*. 1998; Smallbone and Wortley 2000). For adult offenders, this relationship is often a parental, step-parental or acquaintance relationship (Simon and Zgoba 2006). For adolescent offenders, the relationship is often a sibling, step-sibling or foster-sibling relationship (Finkelhor 1980). Nonfamilial CSA offenders also very often have established a relationship with the child, and also often with the child's parent(s), before the first CSA incident occurs. Other common types of prior relationships established with CSA victims are quasi-parental relationships – teachers, sporting coaches, pastoral carers and others whose routine activities allow, and in many cases promote, close emotional and/or physical proximity to children. For adult (and to some extent adolescent) nonfamilial offenders, the pre-offence relationship with the victim typically is one where the offender's role involves a similar mix of care-taking and authority as is found in formal parental or guardianship roles.

A popular assumption is that adult CSA offenders consciously and actively join organisations or seek out relationships with single mothers in order to obtain sexual access to children. The evidence is mixed in this regard. For example, Sullivan and Beech (2004) examined clinical reports from forty-one CSA offenders who offended in the context of their professional work. These professionals included religious professionals (n = 27), teachers (n = 10), and childcare workers (n = 4). Only 15% said they chose their profession for the sole reason of obtaining sexual access to children. However, a further 42% reported that having the opportunity to access victims was part of their motivation in seeking the job. Only 25% stated unequivocally that having a chance to offend was not part of their job choice. By contrast, Smallbone and Wortley (2000) found that while 20% of the nonfamilial CSAs in their nonclinical sample reported that they had offended in a child-related organisation, only 2% said they had joined that organisation for the express purpose of obtaining sexual access to children. Similarly, while 45% of nonfamilial offenders said that they had formed close relationships with the parents of their victims, considerably fewer (29%) said they had ever befriended a parent in order to gain access to the child.

Abrupt sexual assault by strangers certainly occurs, but is atypical. Instead, in both familial and nonfamilial settings, the relationship between a CSA offender and a future child victim seems to involve an emotional attachment that has been established over time. Among Smallbone and Wortley's (2000) sample, 73% reported having known their victim(s) for more than one month prior to the first sexual contact, including 63% of the nonfamilial offenders. More than half of all offenders said they had known the child for more than a year. By contrast, only 5% said that their very first CSA offence involved a child who was a stranger at the time. The so-called 'grooming' process tends to involve a graduation from attention-giving and nonsexual touching, through low-level sexual talk and/or touching, to increasingly more explicit sexual behaviours (Conte, Wolf and Smith 1989; Smallbone and Wortley 2000). Overt aggression and physical violence may occur during, or as a means to obtain, sexual contact, but this too is atypical (Smallbone and Milne 2000; Smallbone and Wortley 2000).

A key challenge arising from these modus operandi data is how to distinguish early grooming behaviours from normal care-giving behaviours, and thus how to detect and intervene in CSA before the problem is fully established. Some prevention advocates argue that this is possible. For example, Stop It Now! (2006) publishes advice on its website about how to recognise CSA grooming behaviour, and encourages more vigilance in this regard. However, while this advice may indeed allow for some genuine grooming behaviour to be identified, it is likely that this would also produce a very high rate of false-positive identifications (i.e. identifying behaviour as CSA grooming when it in fact is not). Nevertheless, modus operandi studies suggest that a key focus of prevention efforts should be situations where adolescent and adult males are in unsupervised roles involving both authority and care-giving with respect to children.

CSA victim characteristics

Gender
Most victimisation prevalence estimates indicate that girls are much more at risk of sexual abuse than are boys. Based on victimisation

studies utilising various definitions and methodologies, lifetime CSA prevalence estimates generally range from 15% to 45% for girls (Finkelhor 1979; Russell 1983; Wyatt 1985), and from 4% to 16% for boys (Finkelhor *et al.* 1990; MacMillan 1997). Summarising from a number of US national data sources, Finkelhor and Dzuiba-Leatherman (2001) conclude that girls are approximately twice as likely as boys to experience sexual abuse, and that, unlike most other forms of childhood victimisation, this difference does not change substantially over the course of childhood and adolescence. These findings are very different from the picture that emerges from studies of CSA offenders, which indicate that offenders against male children often have many more victims than do offenders against female children (Abel and Rouleau 1990; Smallbone and Wortley 2001). This suggests that offences against boys are much more under-reported (both to authorities and to victimisation surveys) than are offences against girls, or that offenders against girls, and particularly familial offenders, are less likely to be arrested than are nonfamilial offenders against boys.

Differences have consistently been found in the sexual abuse experiences of girls and boys. The sexual abuse of girls predominantly involves sexual touching and fondling, whereas boys are more likely to experience masturbatory, oral and anal abuse (Ketring and Feinaur 1999). Boys also appear to be more likely than girls to experience threats and force as part of the sexual abuse (Kendall-Tackett and Simon 1992). Girls are more likely to be abused by family members, while boys are more likely to be abused by persons outside the family (Gold *et al.* 1998). More specifically, Kendall-Tackett and Simon (1992) found that girls were most likely to be abused by a stepfather, whereas boys were most likely to be abused by a family friend. Although the incidence of stranger abuse is low, in one study boys were three times more likely than girls to be abused by strangers (Tong, Oates and McDowell 1987). Finally, while girls tend to suffer a longer duration and greater frequency of abuse (Risin and Koss 1987), there is some evidence that boys are more likely to be abused by more than one perpetrator (Hunter 1991).

Age
The prevalence and type of CSA also vary according to the age of victims. Younger children appear to be at greater risk of familial abuse, whereas older children are generally more at risk of nonfamilial abuse. Fisher and McDonald (1998) examined more than 1,000 cases of substantiated CSA, of which 44% were familial and 56%

nonfamilial. The average age at abuse onset for familial victims was about seven years, while the average age for nonfamilial victims was almost ten years. Other victim studies have found similar abuse-onset age differences between familial and nonfamilial CSA (e.g. De Jong, Hervada and Emmett 1983; Goddard 1988). McKillop, Smallbone and Wortley (2007) constructed a victim database from the confidential self-reports of more than 200 adult CSA offenders. The offenders provided details on up to five separate victims, yielding 447 victims. The mean victim ages at abuse onset was eleven years for familial victims, 11.6 years for nonfamilial victims (whom the offender nevertheless knew) and 12.1 years for stranger victims. While neither victim age nor gender was associated with the duration or frequency of abuse, the closer the relationship between the victim and offender the longer the duration and frequency of abuse.

Outcomes for CSA victims

CSA victimisation has been empirically associated with a very broad range of negative short- and long-term outcomes for children. Compared to children who have not been sexually abused, CSA victims have been found to suffer increased anxiety and depression, somatic complaints, social withdrawal, anger and aggressive and sexual behaviour problems (Briere and Elliot 2001; Kendall-Tackett, Williams and Finkelhor 1993). However, as with other forms of maltreatment, negative outcomes are by no means universal among CSA victims. Some studies have shown that as many as 25% of maltreated children experience no detectable long-term symptoms (McGloin and Widom 2001). In a study that generated a great deal of controversy, Rind, Tromovitch and Bauserman (1998) reviewed nonclinical studies of the effects of CSA, concluding that the harm associated with CSA may be less pervasive, and on average less severe, than is typically reported in studies of clinical samples.

The heterogeneity in the outcomes of CSA has itself been the subject of empirical investigation. In general, more adverse outcomes have been associated with a longer duration of abuse, the use of force or violence and being abused by a father or father-figure (Hebert *et al.* 2006). Key protective factors seem to be support from non-offending parents (Spaccarelli 1994), and more generally a supportive family or school environment (Chandy, Blum and Resnick 1997; Elliot and Carnes 2001), particularly following disclosure.

Among the more troubling long-term outcomes for female CSA victims is that they are at a significantly increased risk to experience further sexual victimisation later in life, often in apparently unrelated circumstances. Estimates of sexual re-victimisation rates range from 15% to an alarming 72% (Van Bruggen, Runtz and Kadlec 2006). In a meta-analytic review, Roodman and Clum (2001) reported an effect size for sexual re-victimisation of .59. In one study, women who had experienced sexual abuse as a child were twice as likely as women who had not experienced CSA to be raped, even when controlling for the presence of childhood physical and emotional abuse (Messman-Moore and Brown 2004). Risk factors for sexual re-victimisation seem to be much the same as for other negative outcomes of CSA, with duration, severity and familial context of the original abuse experience all being empirically associated with re-victimisation (Van Bruggen *et al.* 2006). One explanation is that women who have been sexually abused as children are more likely to engage in risky sexual behaviour, such as engaging early in consensual sexual relationships, exercising less discrimination in their choice of sexual partners and having more casual sex partners (Van Bruggen *et al.* 2006).

Reporting of CSA

Victimisation surveys clearly show that most crime is not reported. For example, the 1995/96 US National Crime Victimisation Survey (NCVS), which includes offences against persons aged twelve and older, found that only 41% of violent offences are reported to police. For violent offences, the most likely to be reported are completed robberies involving injuries (66%), and the least likely are non-completed rapes (19%). As a rule, the seriousness of any type of offence increases the probability that it will be reported. For example, a report of the 1989 International Crime Survey (Van Dijk, Mayhew and Killias 1991) indicated that within the fourteen participating industrialised countries, while only 24% of the combined rapes, attempted rapes and indecent assaults were reported to police, completed rapes were twice as likely (48%) to be reported. Rape is also more likely to be reported if the offender is a stranger (Finkelhor, Wolak and Berliner 2001), if a physical injury is sustained (Bachman 1998) and if the victim is advised by family or friends to report (Greenberg and Ruback 1992).

In general, offences against children are even less likely to be reported than are comparable offences against adults. According to the NCVS, children are less likely than adults to have robbery (37% vs 59%), assault (27% vs 47%) and theft (10% vs 31%) offences reported to police. However, sexual assault involving both children (30%) and adults (29%) is under-reported to much the same extent. In an earlier national survey of ten to sixteen-year-olds, Finkelhor and Dziuba-

Leatherman (1994) found that only 6% of violent victimisations, including 3% of sexual abuse incidents, were reported to the police. Even when parents are aware of sexual abuse involving their children they appear to be reluctant to report the matter to police, with one survey finding that only 42% of parents who knew about sexual abuse reported it to the police (Finkelhor 1994).

Drawing on the limited available evidence, Finkelhor and his colleagues (Finkelhor and Ormrod 2001; Finkelhor, Wolak and Berliner 2001) have speculated on the reasons why offences against children may be so under-reported. With respect to CSA, because children are usually abused by people close to them they may be less likely to define the incident in terms of a criminal offence in the first place. In any case, younger children are unlikely to have direct access to police or other authorities, and so usually must disclose to an adult who in turn may or may not report the matter to authorities. In one study, about half of the parents who were aware of sexual abuse but did not report it said that they thought the incident was not serious enough, and as many as 90% wanted to deal with the situation without the involvement of police or other authorities (Finkelhor 1994). Older children may have more direct access to teachers and others, but at the same time may fear possible stigmatisation and ostracisation by peers, or blame and disbelief from non-offending adults. Particularly when the offender is close to the family, many children and non-offending parents are reluctant to see the offender facing a serious police investigation, and may fear the prospect of losing a valued relationship or seeing the offender convicted and imprisoned. Victims may also fear retribution from the offender.

While the reluctance to report CSA may be seen in the wider scheme of prevention efforts to be very undesirable, as Finkelhor *et al.* (2005) conclude, at an individual level it should not be presumed to be irrational. While concerns about disclosure are often associated with the desire to protect offenders, many other concerns may be more legitimately associated with the family's desire to protect children themselves. For example in one study, almost half of the families of sexually abused children felt that their experience with the justice system had been harmful, pointing to police insensitivity and the stress of the court process as major concerns (Sauzier 1989). Although there have been many recent improvements in police training and efforts to make the courts more 'child friendly', and while consumer satisfaction with official responses to CSA seem to have correspondingly increased (see e.g. Berliner and Conte 1995; Sas *et al.* 1993), many families are likely to continue to choose to keep

15

some CSA offences out of the hands of police and other authorities. Although one sensible policy direction would be to continue to make the disclosure of CSA offences a more positive experience for victims and their families, it is clearly more preferable to do what we can to prevent these offences from occurring in the first place.

CSA offence settings

Although little empirical attention has been given to the specific physical settings in which CSA occurs, both victim and offender studies indicate, unsurprisingly, that CSA is most likely to occur in places where adults or adolescents and children are most likely to spend time together. Wortley and Smallbone (2006a) identified three main types of locations in which CSA occurs: 1) domestic settings, usually the victim's or offender's home, which of course in familial offending is usually one and the same place; 2) institutional settings, such as residential homes, schools, recreational clubs, and so on; and 3) public settings, such as parks, play areas, public swimming pools, and so on. Most CSA seems to occur in domestic settings, and the least in public settings.

Offender modus operandi studies (e.g. Kaufman, Hilliker and Daleiden 1996; Kaufman *et al.* 1998; Smallbone and Wortley 2001) have been able to distinguish between the place where offenders first encounter their victims, and the place where abuse incidents themselves occur. Smallbone and Wortley (2001) asked adult CSA offenders whether they had *ever* first met their victim at certain places (total frequencies may therefore exceed 100%). Familial offenders, by definition, generally met their victims in the home in which both they and their victims lived. Exclusively nonfamilial offenders (i.e. those who said they had only ever abused children in nonfamilial settings) had most commonly first met their victims at a friend's home (37%), during an organised activity (19%), in a location in their own neighbourhood (17%) or while babysitting (17%). Similarly, for mixed-type offenders (i.e. those who said they had offended in both familial and nonfamilial settings), the most common location for first meeting their victims was a friend's place (48%), a neighbourhood location (30%) or while babysitting (30%).

The places where the abuse incidents themselves occurred were much the same for familial, nonfamilial and mixed-type offenders. Familial offenders were most likely to abuse their victims in their own homes (83%). However, a sizeable proportion of familial offenders (22%) said that, at least on one occasion, they had abused their victims while taking them for a car-ride. Seventeen per cent of familial offenders said that they had taken the child to an isolated place to abuse them. Similarly, the most common places for nonfamilial and mixed-type offenders to abuse their victims were in their (i.e. the offender's, not the victim's) home (46% and 77% respectively), while taking the child for a car-ride (22% and 47%) and in an isolated place (24% and 53%).

Hodson (2007) re-examined Smallbone and Wortley's data and identified those CSA offenders ($n = 13$, less than 6% of the total sample) who had first offended against children who were complete strangers to them. While CSA by strangers is relatively rare, these offenders generate a great deal of public anxiety. Their modus operandi is likely to be quite different to the great majority of CSA offenders who establish a relationship with the child before sexually abusing them, and may therefore present special challenges for prevention. Again, offenders were asked whether they had *ever* first met their victim at certain places, and total responses therefore exceed the number of offenders. Hodson found that ten of the thirteen stranger offenders had first met victims at a shopping mall, three at friends' homes, two in public parks, two in public toilets, one at a playground, and one at a public swimming pool. With respect to the locations where the abuse incidents themselves occurred, six stranger offenders took victims to an 'out of the way' place, three abused children in a public park, two in the offender's own home, two in a car, two in a public toilet, one in a playground, and one at a public swimming pool.

Even less research attention has been given to the more specific elements of CSA offence settings. Finkelhor and Baron (1986) found that children are more vulnerable to sexual abuse when parental supervision is compromised by absence, illness or alienation, and more generally when children have poor relationships with their parents. Finkelhor and Baron also found that children whose parents are undergoing divorce and children living in stepfamilies are at increased risk of CSA. Finally, Finkelhor (1984) has suggested that, in familial settings, unusual sleeping or other domestic arrangements may present increased risks for CSA.

Scope of the problem

The incidence and prevalence of CSA are very difficult to quantify in absolute terms. Certainly there is wide agreement that, due to under-reporting and difficulties associated with investigating CSA, official reports seriously under-estimate the scope of the problem. These problems no doubt attend to official reporting of other forms of child maltreatment as well, and it is not known whether CSA is more or less under-represented in official statistics than are other forms of maltreatment. Official statistics show that CSA represents only a small proportion of the officially reported victimisation experiences of children. For example, in the year 2004/05, Australian child protection authorities substantiated more than 44,000 incidents of child maltreatment. Of these, a little under 10% were cases of sexual abuse. The remainder were cases of emotional abuse (40%), neglect (30%) and physical abuse (20%) (Australian Institute of Health and Welfare 2006). Similarly, in the US approximately one million children were the subject of substantiated child protection reports during 1997, with 8% of these involving sexual abuse (McMahon and Puett 1999).

Official crime victimisation surveys, which might normally be expected to circumvent problems of under-reporting, unfortunately shed little light on the scope of CSA, since they typically do not enquire about offences involving young children. The US National Crime Victimisation Survey, for example, only gathers information concerning respondents aged twelve years or older. The International Crime Victimisation Survey gathers information concerning persons aged sixteen years or older, and does not ask specifically about sexual abuse.

Numerous other victimisation surveys that have focused specifically on CSA are available, although these are often beset by their own methodological problems. Prevalence estimates derived from these surveys vary widely, depending in large part on how broadly or narrowly CSA is defined. Using broad definitions, some authors have estimated that between 30% and 45% of adult women will have experienced CSA during their childhoods (Russell 1984; Wyatt 1985). Finkelhor *et al.* (1990) estimated that 27% of women will have experienced some form of sexual abuse prior to their nineteenth birthday. Lifetime prevalence of CSA victimisation for males is consistently found to be lower than for females, with estimates ranging from 13% to 16% (Berliner and Elliot 1996; Finkelhor *et al.* 1990).

In their national probability survey of two to seventeen-year-olds, Finkelhor *et al.* (2005) found that 8% of their sample had experienced some form of sexual victimisation during the one-year study period, including 3% who had been sexually assaulted and 2% who had experienced attempted or completed rape. Those who had experienced rape were reported to have experienced on average seven different kinds of victimisation during the study year. The majority of victimisation incidents involved peer victimisation. More than half (53%) had experienced physical assault, bullying or teasing, and 27% had experienced some kind of property victimisation (e.g. stolen or vandalised property). More than one-third (36%) had witnessed the victimisation of someone else or had in some other way been exposed indirectly to victimisation.

Finally, there is some evidence that the incidence of CSA may be declining, following a peak in the early 1990s. Jones, Finkelhor and Kopeic (2001) reported a steady 39% decline in substantiated CSA cases in the US, from 150,000 cases in 1992 to 92,000 cases in 1999. A similar decline in substantiated CSA cases was observed in Ontario, Canada, between 1993 and 1998 (Trocme *et al*. 2002). Although child protection authorities in Australia are continuing to report increases in substantiated CSA (Australian Institute of Health and Welfare 2006), one Australian age-cohort victimisation study has reported similar downward trends to those observed in Canada and the US (Dunne *et al*. 2003). In the US, the observed decline in CSA has coincided with a more general decline in crime rates, including violent crime. But despite these encouraging signs, CSA remains a serious and pervasive social problem, affecting hundreds of thousands of children across Western societies, and no doubt millions worldwide, each year.

Summary

CSA constitutes a relatively small proportion of the victimisation experiences of children, but is nevertheless a pervasive social problem that presents significant risks of physical and especially psychological and emotional harm to many children. Although definitional problems are likely to present some ambiguity in individual cases, this is not a significant problem for prevention efforts if they are to prioritise those forms of CSA that are known to present the greatest risk of harm. While sexual abuse occurs in a very wide range of circumstances, empirical research has identified systematic variations in offender characteristics, victim characteristics and the settings in which CSA occurs.

CSA offenders are almost always male, and adolescence and early middle-age seem to be the two main risk periods for the onset of CSA offending. While CSA offending is often persistent prior to being detected and arrested, sexual recidivism rates of convicted offenders are generally low. It is likely that a relatively small group of chronic, serial offenders is disproportionately responsible for a large number of victimisation incidents. While many offenders have little contact with the criminal justice system, more generally CSA offenders tend to be criminally versatile. Criminal history and recidivism studies consistently report that adult CSA offenders are about twice as likely to be convicted for nonsexual offences as they are for sexual offences. Adolescent CSA offenders have been observed to be up to eight times more likely to be re-arrested for a nonsexual offence than for a sexual offence. Offender modus operandi studies show that most CSA offenders have established a close nonsexual relationship with the child before the first abuse incident occurs.

Victimisation studies show that girls are about twice as likely as boys to experience CSA, although due to a relatively small number of chronic, serial offenders who abuse very large numbers of boys, offender studies often report more or less equal numbers of male and female victims. Girls are at greater risk of sustained abuse at a younger age and in familial settings, whereas boys are more likely to be abused for shorter periods, at an older age, and in nonfamilial settings. As many as one in four victims of child maltreatment, including CSA, evidence no long-term symptoms. More adverse outcomes have been associated with a longer duration of abuse, the use of force or violence, and being abused by a father or father-figure. The most important protective factors seem to be the availability of support from non-offending parents and others, including teachers. For reasons that are not yet well understood, sexually abused girls are at an increased risk of experiencing sexual re-victimisation as adults. For a variety of reasons, sexually abused children are reluctant to disclose the abuse to their family, and families are in turn often reluctant to report the abuse to police or other authorities.

Little research attention has been given to the specific locations and place characteristics associated with CSA. Most CSA offending occurs in domestic and institutional settings, with offenders and victims generally encountering one another as part of their day-to-day domestic and other routine activities. A proportionally very small group of stranger offenders seems to engage in a very different modus operandi, encountering victims and abusing them in public places.

Chapter 2

Explaining child sexual abuse: a new integrated theory

We set out in the previous chapter to describe patterns in the key empirical dimensions of CSA, namely when, where, how, to whom and by whom CSA occurs. We argued that to the extent these patterns can be reliably identified, the focus of prevention strategies can be narrowed and prevention resources accordingly prioritised. But developing effective prevention strategies requires more than a sound empirical base. Without good theory, evidence-based prevention strategies may inadvertently be directed towards managing its consequences, which are more readily observable, rather than targeting its causes. A clear theoretical framework is needed that organises and makes sense of the available evidence, and provides a firm basis for making empirically defensible inferences about causal mechanisms and processes. Our aim in the present chapter, then, is to articulate a comprehensive theory of CSA that is consistent with available evidence and that can serve as a conceptual foundation for CSA prevention policy and practice.

A comprehensive theory of CSA needs to account for CSA-related motivations, how these motivations interact with the specific situational elements that comprise the immediate pre-offence and offence settings and, for persistent offenders, how these motivations may change over time. These person–situation interactions need to be understood in the wider context of the social ecological systems within which the offender and victim are embedded. Accordingly, our integrated theory proposes that CSA occurs as a result of interactions between individual, ecosystemic and situational factors. Our theory has been developed as an extension and revision of Marshall and Barbaree's

(1990) integrated theory, which proposes that sexual offending occurs as a result of distal and proximal interactions between biological, developmental, sociocultural and situational factors. Since preventing CSA from occurring in the first place is clearly the most desirable prevention goal, our emphasis is given to explaining the onset of CSA offending. In summary, we argue that:

1　The evolutionary foundations of human social behaviour provide for remarkable flexibility, and thus diversity, in behavioural outcomes. This presents a universal biologically-based potential for both prosocial and antisocial behaviour. The biological foundations of male sexual behaviour in particular provide for sexual behaviour to be elicited in the context of both aggression and nurturance, and to be directed towards a wide range of potential sexual 'objects', including children. From a biological perspective, the potential to engage in CSA is more or less universal among adolescent and adult males, but so too is the potential to protect children from harm.

2　Whereas the biological foundations of human social behaviour pro-vide for diversity in behavioural outcomes, positive social cognitive development generally serves to restrain the potential for socially undesirable outcomes. Early attachment experiences provide the foundation for acquiring the capacity and motivation to exercise self-restraint, and for establishing a stake in social conformity. Early attachment experiences also shape later attachment (care-seeking), nurturing (care-giving) and sexual behaviour through what Bowlby (1969) called the 'internal working model of self and others'. From a developmental perspective, weak or insecure interpersonal and social attachments increase the risk for antisocial behaviour in general, and for CSA offending in particular.

3　The social ecosystems within which individuals are embedded a) convey the cultural and subcultural norms to which individuals are expected to conform; b) influence the availability of formal and informal resources for effective child protection; and c) delimit the routine activities of potential CSA victims and offenders, thereby presenting or restricting opportunity structures for CSA to occur. From an ecosystemic perspective, the potential for CSA to occur is dependent on the systemic risk and protective factors present in the social and physical environments of potential victims and offenders.

4   The situational factors comprising the immediate pre-offence and offence settings present the most proximal, and therefore exert the most direct, influence on CSA. Situations provide opportunities for CSA-related motivations to be enacted, and may also evoke CSA-related motivations by presenting cues, stressors, temptations and perceived provocations. From a situational perspective, CSA occurs as a result of proximal interactions between individual-level CSA-related vulnerabilities or dispositions and specific situational elements present in the immediate pre-offence and offence settings.

Biological foundations

Evolutionary theory contends that humans possess an evolved flexibility to respond to environmental variations, in the service of biological goals. Since the primary biological goal is to maximise reproductive fitness, humans are biologically organised particularly to deploy a wide range of social behaviour strategies in the service of individual survival, mating and parenting. Social behaviour strategies may involve empathy, trust, co-operation, nurturance and mutual concern, but they may also involve self-interest, deception, coercion, aggression and opportunism. In evolutionary terms, this flexibility allows for individual survival and reproductive success in both favourable (high resource) and adverse (low resource) environments. In social terms, it presents a universal potential for both prosocial and antisocial behaviour. Notwithstanding the possible effects of genetic or other biological variations, more or less stable individual tendencies towards prosocial or antisocial behaviour are shaped by social cognitive development. Positive social cognitive development generally constrains, but does not eliminate, the biological potential for antisocial conduct. Thus even when individual tendencies towards prosocial behaviour are firmly established, certain situations can nevertheless sometimes evoke antisocial conduct.

At one level we can conceive of CSA as one of many forms of antisocial conduct, and thus simply as the unrestrained expression of a general, biologically-endowed potential for self-interest, aggression, opportunism, and so on. Evidence of criminal versatility among CSA offenders suggests that in many cases CSA offending may indeed be part of a more general pattern of antisocial conduct. In particular, evidence that the onset of CSA offending is often preceded by a history of nonsexual offending suggests that opportunities to engage in CSA may be more readily recognised and exploited by individuals who have already established a pattern of self-serving, aggressive or rule-breaking behaviour. This formulation is consistent with Gottfredson and Hirschi's (1990) general theory of crime, which contends that crime is intrinsically rewarding and that all forms of criminal conduct can be explained as the failure to exercise self-control.

But while there are many similarities between CSA and other forms of criminal conduct, there are also some important differences that need to be theoretically accounted for. First, although many CSA offenders are criminally versatile, others apparently are not. Indeed, apart from their CSA offending many appear to be generally socially responsible – some perhaps even exceptionally so. Conversely most general offenders, even otherwise versatile and persistent offenders, apparently do not extend their antisocial behaviour to the sexual abuse of children. Second, although as with other forms of crime involvement in CSA offending peaks in adolescence, most adult CSA offenders apparently do not commit their first CSA offence until early middle-age or later. Whether or not it is preceded by a history of nonsexual offending, adult onset of CSA offending tends to occur at the time in their lives when offenders are most likely to have their own children or step-children, or are in some other parenting-like role. Third, although males are over-represented in almost all forms of crime, males are even more over-represented in CSA offending. Finally, CSA offending is not just a form of criminal behaviour, it is also by definition a form of sexual behaviour. In addition to recognising a general biological potential for antisocial behaviour, then, we also need to consider the biological foundations of male sexual behaviour and how these relate to the circumstances in which CSA is most likely to occur.

Sexuality, aggression and nurturance

In their original integrated theory, Marshall and Barbaree (1990) contended, as we do here, that human males are universally endowed with a biological propensity for self-interest and sexual aggression. Testosterone and other steroids have long been known to mediate both sexual and aggressive behaviour. Testosterone production increases rapidly following the onset of puberty, reaching adult levels after about two years (Sizonenko 1978) and coinciding with dramatic increases in both aggression and goal-directed sexual behaviour. As we have seen, adolescence is the first of two peak risk periods for the onset of CSA offending. In biologically mature males, a higher density of testosterone receptors is located in brain areas extending from the medial amygdala, through the preoptic, anterior hypothalamic area, down to the brain stem (Panksepp 1998). Sexuality and aggression are thus both structurally and chemically linked in various areas of the mature male brain. Males are also more generally aggressive than are females. Metabolism in the male brain is more active in the temporal lobe areas, where neural structures associated with aggression are concentrated, whereas in the female brain greater metabolic activity is found in the cingulate areas, which are thought to be associated with nurturance and other social motivation (Gur *et al.* 1995).

But while CSA offending can certainly involve overt aggression and sometimes even extreme violence, more typically it does not. Indeed, efforts to detect and prevent so-called 'grooming' behaviours associated with CSA are faced with the dilemma that these behaviours – spending time with children, showing a keen interest in their activities, and so on – often resemble the kinds of positive nurturing behaviours that in other circumstances we would be inclined to encourage. In some cases, particularly for persistent offenders whose modus operandi may be well rehearsed, these nurturing behaviours may conceal more nefarious intentions. But in many cases the first sexual abuse incident, especially for novice offenders, occurs after an apparently genuine guardianship or care-taking relationship has been established with the child. Studies of the modus operandi of adolescent and adult CSA offenders suggest that, while aggression features in some CSA incidents, nurturance (care-giving) and attachment (care-seeking) are also likely to play significant roles.

The search for the biological bases of human sexual behaviour has led to important discoveries that point to common neural structures and processes associated with sexual, attachment and nurturing behaviour (Insel 1997; Panksepp 1998). Particular attention has been given to the roles of the neuropeptides vasopressin and oxytocin. Vasopressin, which is more abundant in the male brain, mediates territorial marking, inter-male aggression and persistent courtship behaviour in non-human mammals, and is thought to also mediate some aspects of courtship and sexual behaviour in human males. Oxytocin, which is more prevalent in the female brain, inhibits aggression and promotes nurturance. Released in women particularly during sexual intercourse, parturition and breastfeeding, and in men during and after orgasm (but not during sexual arousal itself), oxytocin is directly implicated in social motivations involving trust, nurturance and bonding. In men, plasma vasopressin peaks during sexual arousal and declines quickly following ejaculation, whereas plasma oxytocin increases during sexual arousal, peaks during ejaculation, and gradually declines over the thirty minutes or so post-ejaculation (Murphy *et al.* 1987). While men can undoubtedly experience nurturing emotions and establish attachment bonds in the absence of sexual motivations, sexual interaction nevertheless tends to promote and perhaps reinforce nurturing and attachment motivations.

As Bowlby (1969) observed in his seminal work on attachment theory, the more or less simultaneous activation of attachment (care-seeking), nurturing (care-giving) and sexual behaviour is commonplace in adult pair bonds. Although distinctions can be drawn in terms of their maturational stages, social function and eliciting conditions, the attachment, nurturing and sexual behavioural systems share many behavioural components (e.g. proximity-seeking, kissing, embracing and prolonged eye-gazing), and the three systems commonly serve both complementary and reciprocal social functions within established adult pair bonds. For example, an upsetting or fearful experience for one partner may activate attachment behaviour, which cues the other's nurturing behaviour. This brings the care-seeker and care-giver into intimate physical and emotional contact, which may evoke sexual feelings in either partner. The sexual interaction would in turn serve to strengthen the couple's attachment bond. Both care-seeking and care-giving behaviour, which are most strongly elicited in circumstances of adversity, can therefore routinely elicit sexual feelings and behaviour. Indeed, research on reward mechanisms in the human brain shows that feelings of romantic or sexual attraction are intensified in times of adversity (Fisher *et al.* 2002; Schulz 2000). Thus attachment and nurturing behaviour can evoke sexual motivations, and sexual behaviour can in turn evoke attachment and nurturing motivations.

Attachment and nurturing behaviour are also characteristic of close adult–child relationships, and there is some evidence that the same biological mechanisms that underpin attachment behaviour in children also underpin attachment and nurturing behaviour in adults (Insel 1997). Just as adult sexual behaviour is often elicited in the context of attachment and nurturance, so too does CSA often occur in the context of close adult–child and adolescent–child relationships. Of course, strong social taboos attach to the expression of sexual behaviour between adults and children in any context, and particularly in circumstances where the adult has a familial or other guardianship relationship with the child. No doubt these social prohibitions serve as an almost universal deterrent to sexual engagement with children.

But for our present purposes, a key question is whether biological protections exist to inhibit the expression of overt sexual behaviour in the context of close adult–child or adolescent–child relationships.

One possibility, originally proposed by Westermarck (1889) as an evolutionary incest-avoidance mechanism, is that early and continued physical and emotional proximity to children inhibits later sexual interest in those children. Various data have been reported in support of the Westermarck theory. First, both siblings and nonsiblings who experience physical and emotional closeness in their early years have been observed to be less likely to later engage in sexual behaviour with each other than are children who experienced distance or separation in their early years (e.g. Bevc and Silverman 2000; Shepher 1971). Second, studies of arranged marriages have found higher levels of sexual dysfunction among couples who had lived together as children (McCabe 1983; Wolf 1995). Finally, early separation of fathers from daughters has been shown to increase the risk of later incestuous behaviour (Williams and Finkelhor 1995; Parker and Parker 1986). While the specific biological mechanisms of incest avoidance remain unknown, some evidence thus exists to support the proposition that establishing an early attachment bond with a child may in effect inoculate against later developing a sexual interest in that child.

No doubt the biological propensity to care for children and protect them from harm, underpinned by the nurturing behavioural system, also serves as a more general inhibitory mechanism against sexual engagement with children, at least in societies such as ours that prohibit such behaviour. However, biologically-based nurturing motivations are somewhat more tenuous for males than for females. Observed gender differences in brain organisation are thought to be responsible for women's tendency to experience stronger and more positive emotions in nurturing situations, and for women to 'exhibit a more natural persistence, warmth, and desire to communicate affectively' with children (Panksepp 1998: 249). Despite the human capacity to consciously appreciate the importance of childcare, and while there seems to be an increasing social trend for males to be involved in the care of children, biological evidence suggests that men's nurturing behaviour may be more instrumental, and thus more vulnerable to competing motivations, than is the case for women.

Sexual attraction

The biological basis of sexual attraction may be at least partly distinct from other aspects of the sexual, attachment and nurturing behavioural systems. Fisher *et al.* (2002) have proposed that the sexual drive and sexual attraction emotion-motivation systems have evolved separately to direct different aspects of reproductive behaviour. According to this formulation the sexual drive system, which is mediated chiefly by the estrogens and androgens (especially testosterone), serves to provide only the basic motivation to engage in sexual behaviour. The sexual attraction system (sometimes referred to as romantic passion) is thought to serve the separate but related purpose of directing sexual drive towards particular objects. In evolutionary terms, the sexual attraction system serves the purpose of concentrating mating effort on genetically appropriate partners. In social terms, it provides for sexual interest and courtship behaviour to be focused on specific kinds of individuals.

The primary neurochemical agents involved in the activation of the sexual attraction system are thought to be the catecholamines: specifically, increased central dopamine and norepinephrine, and decreased central serotonin. These neurochemical interactions, which are associated with the so-called reward systems in the brain, are thought to be responsible for the feelings of exhilaration and obsessive thoughts that characterise the subjective experience of sexual attraction. Just as many persistent CSA offenders have been clinically observed to experience problems with obsessive sexual fantasies about children, so too does normal sexual attraction involve intrusive, obsessive thinking that is typically reported as involuntary and uncontrollable (Fisher *et al.* 2002).

Although the sexual attraction system provides for sexual responsiveness to a very broad range of potential sexual stimuli, in evolutionary terms its central focus is on the kinds of sexual objects and circumstances that conferred a reproductive advantage in human evolutionary history. Both common and distinct patterns of sexual attraction have been observed in men and women. While both prefer sexual partners who are healthy, dependable and intelligent, men show a stronger preference for the physical qualities of prospective sexual partners, and particularly for physical indicators of youth and beauty (Buss 1994). Presumably this preference by males for youthful sexual partners was naturally selected because of the reproductive advantage it conferred in the ancient environment of evolutionary adaptedness. Of course, sexual involvement with pre-pubescent children cannot have conferred any reproductive advantage. We would therefore expect that CSA would disproportionately involve pubescent and post-pubescent children, and indeed this is the pattern that is consistently observed. By way of illustration, Finkelhor *et al.*'s

(2005) study of two to seventeen-year-olds, which examined a very broad spectrum of sexual victimisation incidents, found prevalence rates of 1.5% for two to five-year-olds, 5.3% for six to twelve-year-olds, and 16.8% for thirteen to seventeen-year-olds.

The biological potential for attraction to youthful sexual partners does not in itself present a social problem. Indeed as young people emerge into puberty their first goal-directed sexual interests are naturally directed towards their pubescent peers. In this respect virtually all human males (and females) will have experienced sexual attraction to pubescent youth. Rather, serious social problems can arise when sexual behaviour involves unrestrained self-interest, deception, coercion, aggression or opportunism, when sexual attraction is directed towards sexually and emotionally immature or otherwise vulnerable persons, and when sexual attraction is not redirected to older partners as the adolescent himself matures.

Developmental influences

Thus far, we have argued that the biological foundations of human social behaviour present a universal potential for both antisocial and prosocial behaviour, for male sexual behaviour to be elicited in the context of both aggression and nurturance, and for sexually mature males both to engage with youthful sexual partners and to protect children and others from harm. In evolutionary terms, this biological potential for diverse behavioural outcomes allows for reproductive success in both favourable and unfavourable social environments. In modern social terms, it presents seemingly contradictory behavioural tendencies that would be difficult to understand without considering both the biological foundations of human social behaviour and how behavioural outcomes are shaped over the course of individual social cognitive development.

In the present section we argue that the relationships between the biologically-based potential and behavioural outcomes concerning CSA offending are significantly mediated by social cognitive development. Consistent with control theories of crime, and with Marshall and Barbaree's (1990) original formulation concerning the etiology of sexual offending, our present theory focuses on the construct of individual vulnerabilities, rather than on the development of stable CSA-specific dispositions, to explain why some males recognise, succumb to, exploit or create opportunities to engage in CSA offending for the first time. Thus we contend that adolescent and adult males generally do not learn to engage in CSA offending; rather, in effect, they may fail to learn not to. More specifically, we contend that social cognitive development shapes the later expression of critical attachment-related behaviours, namely attachment, nurturing and sexual behaviour.

Attachment and self-restraint

The most important initial source of individual vulnerability or resilience regarding their involvement in antisocial conduct, including CSA offending, is a person's early childhood experiences, particularly with their parents or other care-givers. As any parent will observe, a great deal of parenting effort is directed towards constraining socially undesirable behaviour, such as aggression, coercion, self-centredness, deceptiveness, destructiveness and rule-breaking, in their developing child. A great deal of parenting effort is also required to encourage socially desirable behaviours such as co-operation, caring for others, truthfulness, and so on. This can be a very difficult task, requiring repeated and consistent effort. However, the task is generally made a good deal less difficult when it is undertaken in a climate of love, warmth, stability and emotional security, where desired behaviour is rewarded more than undesired behaviour is punished, and where the parents themselves consistently model the desired behaviours. Over time, with consistent, warm and positive parenting, a child will gradually acquire the capacity and motivation to exercise self-restraint. However, even in the best of circumstances self-serving motivations will not always be curtailed by self-restraint alone. At an individual level, certain situations may evoke socially irresponsible conduct even in those with a well-established capacity for self-restraint. At a social level, laws and other formal regulatory mechanisms, as well as informal social control mechanisms, are needed to constrain undesirable social behaviour.

Empirical research suggests that secure early attachment relationships provide the developmental foundation for acquiring key mechanisms of self-restraint, namely: 1) the capacity to autonomously regulate emotions, especially intense negative emotions (Ainsworth *et al.* 1978); 2) empathy and perspective taking (Sroufe 1988); 3) the adoption of a co-operative, rather than a coercive, orientation to influencing others (Main and Solomon 1986); and 4) the translation of moral reasoning to moral action (Van Ijzendoorn 1997). Secure attachment has also been noted as the foundation upon which the confidence to expose oneself to the risks of physical and emotional intimacy first emerges (DeLamater and Friedrich 2002). The acquisition of both the capacity and motivation to exercise self-restraint, and the skills and confidence required to engage in physical and emotional intimacy, are likely to be compromised by insecure attachment, which in turn is likely to arise in circumstances where care-givers are unavailable, emotionally distant, inconsistent, overly intrusive or rejecting, and particularly where care-givers are abusive or violent. Insecure childhood attachment has been empirically associated with hostility, aggression, impulsivity, difficulties in regulating negative emotion, poor empathy and perspective taking, increased risks of sexual and physical victimisation, coercive interpersonal styles, substance dependence and anxious, fearful, dismissive or disorganised adult attachment. Early childhood experiences with primary care-givers thus have far-reaching potential effects on individual functioning, and especially on interpersonal functioning, into adolescence and adulthood.

With the arrival of puberty, goal-directed sexual behaviour will generally involve attempts to engage sexually with others. If a proclivity towards under-restrained social behaviour has already been established, it is likely that this will be further generalised to include goal-directed sexual behaviour. Thus, insecure early attachment experiences are linked to later aggressive and opportunistic sexual behaviour through weak self-restraint and through the incorporation of sexual behaviour into a broader orientation towards social and interpersonal behaviour. The developmental links between attachment and CSA offending may also be considered in terms of the biological and developmental links between the attachment, nurturing and sexual behavioural systems.

Attachment, nurturing and sexual behaviour

Bowlby (1969) proposed that primary attachment experiences lead to the construction of an 'internal working model of self and other' – essentially a mental representation involving: 1) perceptions of oneself as the kind of person that others will respond to in certain ways; and 2) expectations of others in terms of their availability and reliability. These internal working models are proposed as the mechanism by which dispositions towards close relationships are carried forward into subsequent stages of development. While by no means immutable, primary attachment relationships tend to lead to relatively stable expectations about close relationships in general, and about intimate and sexual relationships in particular (Hazan and Shaver 1987).

Secure orientations to close relationships are characterised by trust, friendship and positive emotions. For securely attached adolescents and adults, sexual behaviour is more likely to be guided by mutual interests and to involve emotional commitment (Hazan, Zeifman and Middleton 1994; Shaver 1994). Insecure orientations to close relationships may be characterised by avoidance, which involves fear of emotional closeness and lack of trust, or by pre-occupation, which involves anxiety, emotional neediness and unclear interpersonal boundaries. Avoidant attachment has been empirically associated with sexual behaviour involving less emotional intimacy and less enjoyment of physical contact. Pre-occupied attachment has been associated with enjoyment of holding and caressing, but not of explicitly sexual behaviour (Hazan *et al*. 1994). When early attachment experiences have involved abuse or violence, orientations to close relationships may become disorganised, potentially involving aggressive and coercive strategies for achieving intimate contact with others.

Chronic attachment disorganisation is likely to lead to persistent problems with maintaining the functional independence of the attachment, nurturing and sexual behavioural systems. Thus, subjective distress, which would normally cue attachment (care-seeking) behaviour, or proximity to vulnerable others (especially children), which would normally cue nurturing behaviour, may instead cue sexual feelings and behaviour. However, since even in ordinary circumstances attachment, nurturing and sexual cues may subjectively be difficult to differentiate, the functional independence of these three behavioural systems may from time to time also be compromised in individuals whose attachment orientation is not chronically disorganised. Acute disorganisation of the attachment, nurturing and sexual behavioural systems can occur in individuals with lower levels of attachment insecurity, and indeed even in individuals with no discernible attachment problems. In general, however, we would expect more serious early attachment problems to be associated with an earlier onset, persistence and generalisation of attachment-related vulnerabilities, and for these vulnerabilities to be more resistant to remediation.

The developmental transmission of early attachment problems to later attachment, nurturing and sexual behaviour is neither direct nor inexorable. Indeed, more generally, continuity of attachment styles from childhood through adolescence to adulthood seems to be considerably less stable than had originally been assumed (Pietromonaco and Feldman Barrett 2000). Some resilient children may emerge from insecure early attachment relationships effectively unscathed, and conversely profound vulnerabilities can emerge in some children who have experienced secure early attachment relationships. Secure early attachment nevertheless tends to serve as a critical buffer against the vicissitudes of individual social experience. For insecure children, new interpersonal experiences may provide alternative opportunities to develop a more secure attachment orientation and to acquire a robust capacity for self-restraint. Insecure adolescents and adults may similarly alter their attachment orientation fortuitously, for example by becoming involved in an enduring, secure intimate relationship. Finally, although an individual's attachment orientation may in general predict relatively stable patterns of attachment-related behaviour, this behaviour may well vary according to certain features of a given interpersonal context. Thus while attachment, nurturing and sexual behaviour are all partly biologically determined and are all shaped by social cognitive development, they are also all highly situation-dependent.

In summary, we contend that insecure childhood and adult attachment tend to create general vulnerabilities in terms of individuals' capacity to exercise self-restraint, particularly in interpersonal settings. Further, we contend that insecure interpersonal attachment presents difficulties in establishing wider attachments to social institutions and to the community in general, thereby weakening individuals' stake in social conformity. Insecure attachment also tends to produce more specific vulnerabilities for engaging in emotionally detached, personally risky or socially irresponsible sexual behaviour. Finally, because of the biological, developmental and situational links between attachment, nurturing and sexual behaviour, early attachment problems will tend to increase the risk of acute, and sometimes chronic, disorganisation of attachment-related behaviours.

Ecosystemic factors

According to social ecological theory (Bronfenbrenner 1979), indi-vidual behaviour is influenced by the multiple ecological systems within which the person is socially embedded. An individual's social ecosystem comprises themselves (i.e. their own internal biological and psychological systems), their family, peer, neighbourhood and community systems, and the broader sociocultural environment. In general, the degrees of influence exerted by these multiple systems vary along a continuum ranging from the most proximal to the most distal, in terms of both time and place. Thus for example early developmental experiences will exert less direct influence on a given behavioural event than will the circumstances immediately preceding that event, and cultural or community systems will exert a less direct influence than will family or peer systems. Ecological theory asserts that individuals actively interact with their environment, and thus both influence and are influenced by it, again to varying degrees according to the proximal–distal continuum. Applied to CSA, the CSA incident itself represents a temporal and spatial convergence of the offender's and the victim's social ecologies, and the situational elements comprising the abuse incident will therefore exert the most direct and powerful effects. We will consider the role of immediate situations in the next section. In the present section we consider the influences of the wider social ecosystems on CSA. We argue that the social ecosystems in which potential CSA offenders and victims are embedded: 1) convey the social and cultural norms to which individuals are expected to conform; 2) influence the availability of formal and informal resources for effective child protection; and 3) delimit the routine activities of potential CSA victims and offenders, thereby presenting or restricting opportunity structures for CSA to occur.

Cultural values and norms

Cultural norms exert their influence on individual attitudes, beliefs and behaviour through the social ecosystem in which the individual is embedded, according to the proximal–distal continuum. Thus the influence of the values and norms conveyed by immediate family or friends will be more direct, and therefore stronger, than the influence of those conveyed by the broader sociocultural environment. Since family members and friends are likely to share aspects of their social ecosystems, the values conveyed by the more proximal elements of an individual's social ecosystem will often reflect those conveyed by its more distal elements. Individuals nevertheless occupy a unique position within their social ecology. Ultimately, the extent to which individuals adhere to prevailing social norms depends on the strength of their connection to mainstream social institutions, and more generally to their stake in social conformity. As we have already noted, individuals' stake in social conformity is in turn partly dependent on the security of their interpersonal attachment bonds.

For our present purposes, we are concerned with the cultural and subcultural norms that affect the meaning individuals attach to laws and other social rules, to interpersonal and social attachments, and to sexual behaviour. More specifically, we are concerned with the meaning attached to CSA, particularly to what constitutes CSA, what it means to be a CSA offender and what it means to be a CSA victim. In modern Western societies, these definitions, values and expectations are conveyed at a broad cultural level predominantly by mass media, notably news, entertainment and advertising media. At a community level, they are conveyed through routine social contact with neighbours, schools, workmates, acquaintances, and so on.

Subcultural norms, which may deviate substantially from mainstream cultural norms, may effectively disconnect individuals and groups of individuals from the influence of prevailing social norms. Membership of criminal subcultures, for example, is likely to expose individuals to very different norms and values than those conveyed through the broader social ecosystem. However, even within otherwise antisocial subcultures certain limits may be imposed on the permissibility of sexual engagement with children. Prisoner subcultures, for example, are notorious for positioning CSA offenders at the bottom of the prisoner status hierarchy. In many correctional jurisdictions CSA offenders need to be accommodated separately from mainstream prisoners because of the risks of violence and harassment to which they would otherwise be exposed. This state of affairs suggests that, while the mainstream criminal subculture permits and even encourages other forms of violence, abuse and exploitation, it conveys very strong (if not always clear or coherent) messages that the sexual and other abuse of children is not permissible. Given that the general criminal population may otherwise be a high-risk population for involvement in CSA offending, these prohibitions against child-related offences may play an important, albeit perhaps limited, role in constraining otherwise persistent and versatile offenders from involvement in CSA offending.

Just as otherwise antisocial subcultures may promote norms that prohibit CSA offending, so too may otherwise prosocial subcultures promote norms that weaken prohibitions against CSA offending. Recent problems with sexual abuse in the Catholic Church and other religious institutions illustrate how, for groups of individuals who might otherwise aspire to the highest moral standards, values attached to the protection of institutional and personal reputations, for example, can be given more weight than values attached to the protection of children. It seems clear that in these circumstances the effects of CSA can be institutionally construed in terms that minimise or overlook the personal harm that may be caused. Attachments to mainstream social institutions, and particularly to religious institutions, have long been thought to serve an important protective function with respect to delinquency and crime (Hirschi and Stark 1969). On the other hand the capacity for institutions, particularly closed or 'total' institutions, to engender all kinds of abuses has been well documented (Goffman 1959; Haney, Banks and Zimbardo 1973).

There has been some empirical attention to the different cultural standards affecting sexual abuse, although this has tended to concentrate more on rape and sexual assault than on the sexual abuse of children. Cross-cultural studies suggest that the prevalence of rape is positively related to values associated with negative attitudes to women and the permissibility of other forms of violence (Otterbein 1979; Sanday 1981). In modern Western societies, negative attitudes to women and acceptance of 'rape myths' have been shown to be associated with both self-reported inclinations to rape and actually engaging in rape (Burt 1980; Malamuth 1981). Presumably the prevalence of CSA is affected to some extent by prevailing values concerning sexuality, the social and sexual status of children and the degree of importance afforded to child protection.

Cultural definitions and expectations concerning CSA undoubtedly also affect the meaning attached by victims to their own victimisation. Anthropological studies show that in some cultures adults have routinely engaged in genital stimulation of infants and children for the purposes of pacifying them, a practice regarded in those cultures as nonsexual (Whiting and Child 1953). In some South West Pacific islands (Davenport 1965), and in Papua New Guinea (Herdt 1982), young boys being initiated into the male cult were required to fellate older males in order to ingest the ejaculate, which was thought to be necessary for them to acquire fertility. In modern Western societies these behaviours would of course be widely regarded as socially and sexually deviant, and as potentially harmful. While it would be glib and unhelpful to conclude from this that CSA is merely a social construction, it is undoubtedly the case that some of the harmful consequences for victims follow from their perceptions of the social meaning attached to their sexual victimisation. This presents important challenges for social discourse about CSA, and particularly for how social messages about the harm caused by CSA are conveyed to children and others.

Child protection resources

For children, the social ecological systems in which they are embedded will influence the extent to which they are protected from all manner of environmental hazards. Although families are usually the first line of defence, certain features of local communities and neighbourhoods mediate risk factors for child maltreatment, including CSA. Neighbourhood poverty, housing stress, unemployment, increased childcare burden and alcohol availability have all been found to be associated with the incidence of child maltreatment (see Freisthler *et al.* 2006, for a recent review), presumably because they weaken the capacity of parents and other adults to care for and protect children. Two studies have examined the effects of neighbourhood characteristics specifically on rates of CSA. Drake and Pandley (1996) examined associations between different kinds of reported child maltreatment in 185 US neighbourhoods and the proportion of owner-occupied properties, median residential property value, the rate of school drop-outs, the proportion of two-parent families, race and poverty. Of these variables, both physical abuse and sexual abuse were negatively related to property values, and positively related with poverty. Ernst (2000) similarly examined associations between rates of reported maltreatment in 159 US neighbourhoods and a range of social and economic indices. Sexual abuse was again negatively related to property values, but in this study was unrelated to poverty. Other findings with respect to sexual abuse were negative associations with the proportion of women in the workforce and the proportion of new residents, and a positive association with the proportion of single-parent households.

Particularly for older children, peer influences can serve both to protect and endanger. Schools no doubt usually serve a protective role, but may also bring children into contact with an adolescent or adult offender. Children who are either socially isolated or have strong attachments to antisocial peer groups may be at particular risk. Most of the empirical and theoretical attention given to the role of school and peer systems in child maltreatment has focused on the effects of maltreatment on school and peer interactions, rather than on the effects of these systems on the incidence of maltreatment itself. For obvious demographic reasons, school and peer systems may generally be of more direct relevance to adolescent CSA offenders and victims than they are to adult offenders. However, some adult familial offenders may actively interfere with a victim's peer associations in an effort to isolate the victim, cultivate their dependence on them and to reduce the risk of the victim's disclosure to their peers. Moreover, it is not uncommon for nonfamilial CSA to occur in school settings themselves, as well as in church, sporting and other institutional settings.

Adolescent CSA offenders have been observed to be more socially isolated than other adolescents (Righthand and Welch 2001), although it is sometimes not clear whether this relates to the causes or consequences of their offending. Certainly victims of child maltreatment, including CSA, have been observed to experience problems with school and peer relationships. In general, maltreated children tend to achieve lower school grades, are more likely to repeat grades, are more likely to receive special education, and are less likely to be popular with their peers (Dodge-Reyome 1994; Eckenrode, Laird and Doris 1993). But school systems can also attenuate the negative effects of child maltreatment. Chandy, Blum and Resnick (1997) found that for sexually abused male adolescents, resilience was best predicted by their belief that adults at school cared about them. For sexually abused girls, involvement in extracurricular school activities is positively associated with self-esteem, the ability to make friends and exposure to positive adult role models (Valentine and Feinaur 1993).

According to social ecology theory, the most proximal component of the ecological system within which CSA occurs, and thus the one that exerts the most direct effects, is the family. In general, the same kinds of family characteristics are associated with both the risk of maltreatment and its effects, and thus family factors tend to serve more or less simultaneously as mediating and moderating influences. Family poverty, parental psychopathology, parental alcohol problems, high residential mobility, few or weak social supports and authoritarian parenting practices, have all been found to be associated with child maltreatment (Zielinski and Bradshaw 2006). For maltreated children, including sexually abused children, the response of their non-offending parent(s) is one of the strongest predictors of outcomes for the child (Finkelhor and Kendall-Tackett 1997; Toth and Cicchetti 1993). In one study, one of the strongest predictors of resilience among sexually abused adolescents was the perception that their parents cared about them (Chandy, Blum and Resnick 1997). In the same study, one of the strongest predictors of negative outcomes for sexually abused girls was maternal alcoholism.

Like other family risk factors, insecure parent–child attachments may both increase the risk of sexual abuse and exacerbate its negative effects (Alexander 1992). Where the abuse occurs in the family, insecure attachments may both weaken the deterrents that otherwise prevent a father or stepfather from seeing the child in sexual terms, and weaken the protections the non-offending parent may otherwise provide. Where the abuse occurs outside the family, insecure parental attachments are associated with both a lack of parental monitoring and supervision, and emotional neediness in the child that may render them more susceptible to emotional and sexual overtures by nonfamilial CSA offenders.

Routine activities

As for any other crime (Cohen and Felson 1979), any CSA incident requires the presence of a potential offender and a potential victim, together with the absence of a capable guardian. This combination of circumstances occurs when the social ecosystems of the potential offender and victim converge in time and space. For most CSA incidents, this occurs within the one family or extended family system, but there are obviously many routine activities that bring children and adolescents or adults into contact with one another. Generally, the older person in these circumstances is likely to provide a formal or informal guardianship role, and does not abuse the child simply because they have the opportunity to do so. But in some circumstances abuse-related motivations in the potential offender coincide with the presence of a vulnerable child at a time when there is no other person present who would otherwise protect the child.

In an examination of the effects of neighbourhood factors on nonfamilial abuse of adolescent males, Tremblay (2006) showed that some subcultural enclaves can provide 'convergence settings' where both offenders and victims interact with other offenders and victims. In Tremblay's study, adult male 'boy lovers' reported that they were able to utilise both actual (physical neighbourhood) and virtual (Internet) convergence settings for mutual support and in some cases for active offence-related networking. Tremblay contended that, similarly, adolescent male 'hustlers' make use of known neighbourhood enclaves to find customers for prostitution. This active use of convergence settings by both offenders and victims is no doubt the exception rather than the rule for CSA. More often, the places where potential CSA offenders and potential victims meet will be places used for ordinary routine activities, such as homes, schools, recreational venues, and so on.

Situational factors

According to situational crime prevention theory, situations influence criminal behaviour in two broad ways. First, situations can provide the opportunities – for example, a lapse in supervision – that allow a criminal response to be realised (Clarke 1997). In this case, mere opportunity is likely to evoke criminal behaviour only in those with a suitable disposition at the time the opportunity presents itself. This might be a well-established criminal predisposition, or it might arise impulsively. A highly predisposed offender may actively scan his environment in search of criminal opportunities, and may even go to significant lengths to manipulate the environment to create suitable opportunities, whereas an impulsive offender may simply recognise an opportunity when it arises. All else being equal, opportunities that present a low risk of detection, that require little effort and that promise a highly desired reward, are more likely to result in a criminal response.

Both the risk of detection and the effort required are increased by the proximity of three kinds of 'controllers' – capable guardians, place managers and handlers (Clarke and Eck 2003). Applied to CSA, a capable guardian is a person who is both committed to and capable of protecting the child, such as a parent or other care-giver. A place manager is a person responsible for controlling behaviour in a specific location where children are likely to be, such as a teacher, a sporting coach or a security guard at a shopping mall. A handler is a person who knows the potential offender and who can exert some positive control over their behaviour, such as a parent, teacher, spouse or friend. Ordinarily, of course, people either do not recognise the situation as a criminal opportunity in the first place, or recognise the opportunity and simply resist any temptation that might arise because they possess a well-established capacity for self-restraint and a strong stake in social conformity.

The second, additional way in which situations influence criminal behaviour is by presenting behavioural cues, social pressures and environmental stressors that precipitate a criminal response (Wortley 2001). According to this formulation, situations contain dynamic properties that act directly on offenders' motivations.

Cornish and Clarke (2003) have proposed a typological model to explain the interactions of situations and criminal dispositions, which Wortley and Smallbone (2006a) have adapted to explain offender-situation interactions in CSA. Cornish and Clarke describe three types of offenders or potential offenders. The first type, which Cornish and Clarke call the 'antisocial predator', possesses strong criminal dispositions and is highly invested in criminal behaviour. These offenders actively search for criminal opportunities and manipulate environments to create suitable criminal opportunities, but they may also succumb easily to temptations and provocations, and exploit opportunities as they fortuitously present themselves. In the context of sexual abuse, we think a more suitable term for this type of offender is the 'committed' offender. Applied to CSA, then, committed offenders are most likely to be persistent offenders who may have begun offending in adolescence or early adulthood and are now highly disposed to engage with children for sexual purposes. Alternatively, they may be persistent general offenders who include CSA as part of a broader criminal orientation. Their sexual offending (and their nonsexual offending if applicable) is likely to persist despite from time to time being arrested and sanctioned. They are likely to create opportunities to engage sexually with children, and may also succumb easily to temptations and exploit opportunities as they arise. But through experience they will learn how to minimise risks of detection, and so may overlook opportunities that present too great a risk. They are likely to commit nonfamilial offences, which may require some sustained effort, but may also become stepfathers or have their own children whom they may also abuse. Committed offenders constitute proportionally the smallest group of the three types.

Cornish and Clarke (2003) called the second type of offender the 'mundane offender'. In adapting the model to CSA, Wortley and Smallbone used the term 'opportunistic', which we will continue with here. With respect to CSA, the opportunistic offender abuses children in the context of a broader pattern of opportunistic and occasionally criminal behaviour. These offenders are likely to have a criminal record before committing their first sexual offence, even if this includes only occasional, low-level offences. They may have been caught for stealing from their employer, driving without a licence or perhaps a provoked assault. In other aspects of their lives they may generally adhere to ordinary social mores, including marriage, having children, taking up gainful employment, and so on, although their relationships may be difficult and unstable. Opportunistic offenders will tend not to actively create opportunities to abuse children, particularly if doing so would require any sustained effort. In simple terms, where the committed offender is the opportunity-*maker*, the opportunistic offender is the opportunity-*taker*. They engage in CSA not because of stable predispositions but because they are quick to recognise the opportunities as they fortuitously present themselves. Because they have neither a strong capacity for self-restraint nor a strong stake in conformity, they succumb easily to temptations and perceived provocations. Opportunistic CSA offenders are likely to abuse children in families, perhaps as a step-parent, or may offend after becoming involved with a vulnerable and (in their estimation) attractive child outside their family. They are probably the most numerous of the three groups, at least within convicted sexual offender populations.

Cornish and Clarke referred to their third type of offender as the 'provoked offender' in the original scheme. Again, Wortley and Smallbone (2006a) changed this term for the purposes of adapting the typology to CSA offenders, using the term 'situational offender' instead. The situational offender is in most respects a law abiding citizen. His CSA offending occurs later in life, perhaps in middle-age or later, and is unlikely to persist after being detected, even informally. He may even desist spontaneously, for example if the child is able to protest. These offenders are unlikely to actively create opportunities to sexually abuse children, and may even in general not recognise the opportunities that arise. Rather, their CSA offending behaviour arises directly from behavioural cues and environmental stressors. While they are generally able to exercise self-restraint, a momentary lapse may be enough to turn what is probably at first a sense of emotional congruence with a child into a sexual incident. At this point, many situational offenders may experience a strong guilt reaction and desist. However, while they may otherwise have a strong stake in conformity, they may be able to rationalise their offending behaviour so long as it remains undetected. After the first one or two offences, and unable to disclose the abuse for fear of the very serious consequences they know would follow, they may feel trapped by the situation, and over time perhaps increasingly justify it to themselves. Situational offenders may abuse children in family settings as a stepfather or even as a biological father. Alternatively, they may offend against a nonfamilial child with whom they have developed a close emotional relationship. They may for example be a school teacher who abuses a 'special' girl or boy in their class, or a priest or youth leader who abuses a child they have become fond of.

Situational influences on the onset offence

While this offender-situation typology may help us to understand patterns of CSA offending among active offenders, it does not explain how these different patterns first emerge and then perhaps change over time. More specifically, it does not explain how offenders come to commit their first CSA offence. For this, we need to return once again to attachment theory to consider how biological, developmental, ecosystemic and situational factors interact to produce CSA offending, and in particular how situational factors may influence attachment, nurturing and sexual behaviour. As we saw earlier in this chapter, male sexuality is biologically linked to both aggression and nurturance, and it is therefore likely that CSA offending behaviour too may involve either or both of these elements. Some CSA offending may be motivated by sexual aggression, and the offender may not experience any feelings of nurturance towards or emotional concern for their victim. But in other cases overt aggression may play much less of a role, and instead sexual feelings about a child may arise in the context of nurturing feelings and behaviour. CSA offending, like other forms of male sexual behaviour, may involve all three of these components.

Bowlby (1969) himself noted the close associations between attachment, nurturing and sexual behaviour, commenting that 'although [they are] distinct behavioural systems, attachment behaviour and sexual behaviour … have unusually close linkages' (Bowlby 1969: 230), and that in humans, 'overlaps between attachment behaviour, parental behaviour, and sexual behaviour are commonplace' (Bowlby 1969: 233). Of course, it is usually exclusively within parent–child attachment relationships and within adult–adult attachment and sexual relationships that we see such intimate behaviours as kissing, caressing, holding, prolonged mutual eye-gazing and intimate body-contact. This should not be surprising since, once again, attachment behaviour, nurturing behaviour and sexual behaviour are mediated in part by the same neurobiological structures and processes. In the primary attachment relationship, attachment and nurturing behaviour are usually complementary and unidirectional – the child's attachment needs are responded to by the attachment figure's nurturing behaviour. In later intimate relationships, attachment and care-giving are more typically reciprocal, such that by turns 'each partner … looks to the other as stronger, wiser, or more competent, and the other reciprocates by providing care, comfort, reassurance, and thus feelings of security' (Ainsworth 1991: 42). To recall the example used earlier in this chapter, a distressed partner may seek to be comforted by the other (attachment behaviour), while the other responds by providing comfort and reassurance (nurturing behaviour), and this brings the two into close emotional and physical proximity, which in turn may arouse strong sexual feelings in either the care-seeker or the care-giver.

In the absence of effective cognitive and behavioural self-restraint, significant risks therefore exist for insecure adolescent or adult males to experience sexual feelings in the presence of children, especially in the context where attachment or nurturing behaviour has been situationally activated, and especially in the absence of a secure attachment bond with the child, which may otherwise deter sexual motivations and behaviour. Thus, situational cues that might otherwise precipitate attachment (care-seeking) or nurturing (care-giving) behaviour, instead precipitate sexual feelings and behaviour.

Summary

We have sought in this chapter to draw on several established theoretical models to articulate a new comprehensive, integrated theory of CSA. In summary, we propose that the biological foundations of human social behaviour provide a universal potential for both prosocial and antisocial behaviour, for male sexuality to involve both aggressive and nurturing motivations, and for males both to be attracted to youthful sexual partners and to protect children from harm. These seemingly contradictory tendencies are located partly in the distinct but functionally related emotion-motivation systems that have evolved to direct human reproduction, namely the attachment (care-seeking), nurturing (care-giving) and sexual behaviour systems.

Developmental experiences, and particularly early attachment relationships, shape later attachment, care-giving and sexual behaviour in two main ways. First, secure early attachment relationships provide the social cognitive foundation from which a stable capacity for self-restraint is originally acquired. More broadly, secure interpersonal attachments provide a foundation for establishing secure social attachments and ultimately for establishing a strong stake in social conformity. Conversely, insecure early attachment experiences are likely to result in a reduced capacity for self-restraint and weaker social attachments. Second, insecure early attachment experiences serve more directly to compromise the functional independence of the attachment, care-giving and sexual behaviour systems. Thus situational cues that would otherwise cue attachment or nurturing motivations may instead cue sexual motivations.

CSA occurs within a broader social ecosystem comprising individual victims and offenders themselves, and the family, peer, neighbourhood, community and sociocultural systems in which they are embedded. The influence of these systems on individual behaviour varies according to their position on a distal–proximal continuum, with more proximal systems (e.g. families) exerting a more direct effect than more distal systems (e.g. neighbourhoods). Distal effects are thought to influence individual behaviour via their effects on more proximal systems. Family systems in particular tend to serve as both mediating and moderating influences on CSA; that is, family factors can both increase (or decrease) the risk for CSA to occur and exacerbate (or attenuate) its effects on the child.

As the most proximal elements of the social ecosystem of CSA (in terms of both time and place), immediate situations are likely to exert the most direct and therefore the strongest effects. We drew on situational crime prevention theory to explain how situations influence criminal behaviour generally and CSA offending in particular, and how the presence of capable guardians and others may deter CSA offending. We presented a typology to describe person–situation interactions for different types of CSA offenders. Finally, we returned once again to attachment theory to explain how insecure adolescent or adult males may experience sexual feelings in the presence of children, especially when attachment (care-seeking) or nurturing (care-giving) motivations have been situationally activated.

Chapter 3

Identifying prevention targets

In Chapter 1 we reviewed empirical evidence concerning when, where, how, to whom and by whom CSA occurs, and in Chapter 2 we presented a new integrated theory that aims to organise and make sense of the available evidence and to provide a firm basis for making empirically defensible inferences about causal mechanisms and processes. The next step towardss a comprehensive, evidence-based approach to preventing CSA is to identify key prevention targets. Our aims in the present chapter are: 1) to review current approaches to prevention in CSA and related fields; 2) to consider the implications of the integrated theory for preventing CSA; and 3) to draw on these analyses to suggest key CSA prevention targets.

Current approaches to prevention

Current approaches to preventing CSA are dominated by formal interventions designed to take effect only after offenders have already begun offending, and after children have already been sexually abused. In particular, current CSA prevention policies rely almost wholly on the traditional criminal justice goals of detection and investigation, specific and general deterrence, general and selective incapacitation, and offender rehabilitation. Some significant non-criminal-justice responses have also emerged, notably child-focused prevention programmes and community education campaigns, but these have generally concentrated on encouraging victims and others to report abuse incidents rather than on preventing the abuse from occurring in the first place. Comparatively little attention has been given to alternative prevention strategies, particularly those that systematically aim to prevent CSA incidents before they might otherwise occur.

There are a number of alternative prevention models that could be drawn upon to guide the development of a broader and more carefully targeted CSA prevention policy. In the present section we consider how prevention approaches employed in the areas of public health, crime and child maltreatment may inform a more comprehensive and effective CSA prevention policy. Later in this chapter, we draw on key elements of these approaches, and on the theoretical framework outlined in the previous chapter, to devise a rational model involving four distinct sets of prevention targets: 1) offenders and potential offenders; 2) victims and potential victims; 3) the situations in which sexual abuse occurs; and 4) communities. Strategies associated with these key prevention targets are worked through in more detail in the following chapters.

The public health model

Although some commentators have urged for CSA to be recognised as a serious public health problem (e.g. McMahon and Puett 1999), public policy has failed to exploit the full range of preventive opportunities suggested by the public health model. The public health model provides a conceptual framework for distinguishing interventions aimed at: 1) preventing CSA before it would otherwise occur (primary prevention); 2) reducing risks for CSA in circumstances where known risk factors are already present (secondary prevention); and 3) preventing further CSA offences by known CSA offenders, as well as preventing further victimisation among known CSA victims (tertiary prevention).

While the public health model has broad conceptual appeal, public health researchers and practitioners have themselves questioned the extent to which the model provides clear practical guidance. For example while there have been some attempts to apply the model to crime prevention, there has been no widely shared understanding of what primary, secondary and tertiary prevention might mean when applied to crime (Tonry and Farrington 1995). This has been a problem for many other public health areas as well. In recent years the terms *primary*, *secondary* and *tertiary* have generally been replaced with the terms *universal*, *selected* and *indicated*, respectively, because these latter terms are thought to more clearly differentiate preventive interventions according to how targeted groups can be defined (Holden and Black

1999). However, these terms are not always clearly interchangeable, and to preserve their important conceptual distinctions we will use the original terms *primary*, *secondary* and *tertiary* here.

Primary prevention, which targets whole populations, relies on the discovery of risk and protective factors associated with a specific problem. Targeted populations may be large (e.g. whole communities), medium (e.g. residents of particular neighbourhoods) or small (e.g. employees of a particular organisation). Unlike secondary and tertiary prevention, primary prevention aims to intervene before the problem first emerges. A significant reduction in the incidence of heart disease, achieved through large-scale health promotion programmes, is often used as an example of successful primary prevention (Greenland and Hayman 1997). Positive results have been attributed largely to reductions in associated risk behaviours (e.g. smoking, poor diet, lack of exercise, stressful lifestyle activities) in the general population. Primary prevention may target distal (e.g. chronic smoking) or proximal risk factors (e.g. acute stress).

The application of primary prevention strategies to the problem of CSA would require knowledge of the distal and proximal risk and protective factors associated with CSA. While there is an emerging evidence base that could be used to develop such strategies, more carefully targeted research is needed, particularly on the developmental, ecosystemic and situational risk and protective factors associated specifically with CSA. Since primary prevention aims to prevent CSA from occurring in the first place, particular attention needs to be given to factors associated with the onset of the problem. Primary prevention of CSA would thus involve two distinct points of focus: 1) to prevent children from being sexually abused for the first time; and 2) to prevent potential offenders from committing a first CSA offence.

Secondary prevention targets selected groups within larger populations, usually on the basis that the selected group has been identified either as being at risk with respect to a given problem, or as having already shown some manifest features. In the example of heart disease, secondary interventions are those that specifically target smokers, over-eaters or infrequent exercisers, or those showing early signs of heart disease (e.g. high blood pressure, circulation problems). The aim is to interrupt the transition from risk to manifest problem, or, once the problem has begun to emerge, to slow or halt its progression. With respect to preventing CSA, individual-, family-, school- and community-level interventions and support for youth at risk of either CSA victimisation or CSA offending would be an example of the former, while the treatment of high-risk adolescence onset CSA offenders and early intervention with adult onset CSA offenders would be examples of the latter.

Tertiary prevention targets individuals, or groups of individuals, for whom symptomatology is clearly present. Continuing for the moment with the example of heart disease, tertiary prevention encompasses medical and allied health interventions for persons in advanced stages of heart disease, including emergency procedures for those suffering heart attacks. Tertiary prevention of CSA encompasses strategies designed to: 1) reduce recidivism among known CSA offenders, particularly specific deterrence, selective incapacitation, and offender rehabilitation strategies; and 2) reduce continued or repeat victimisation of persons who have already experienced CSA.

From a public health perspective, a comprehensive CSA prevention policy would involve a mix of primary, secondary and tertiary prevention strategies, with a clear priority given to primary prevention. Instead, current policy and practice gives its highest priority to tertiary prevention, and gives little attention to opportunities for primary or secondary prevention. One reason for the current imbalance of prevention efforts may be a policy preoccupation with detecting and punishing CSA offenders, apparently underpinned by the pessimistic (and, we would argue, erroneous) assumption that nothing useful can be done until potential offenders have begun offending and until children are sexually abused.

Victim-focused sexual abuse research has produced an extensive knowledge base that could contribute to a more effective prevention policy, but lacks both a clear prevention theory and a systematic prevention framework. General offender- and offence-focused research has produced strong prevention theories (e.g. developmental and situational crime prevention theories) and sound applied prevention frameworks (e.g. Tonry and Farrington's [1995] crime prevention model), but this work has been concerned with preventing delinquency and crime in general, and has ignored the specific problem of CSA. Sexual offender-focused research has produced its own rich and extensive empirical literature, but this has been dominated by a clinical research agenda focused on risk prediction and treatment with convicted sexual offenders. The emphasis here has generally been on discovering factors associated with recidivism, rather than on understanding the origins of the problem. A shift in policy focus towards primary and secondary prevention would require new research priorities directed towards understanding how and under what circumstances CSA first occurs, for both victims and offenders.

A more fundamental problem with transposing the public health model to the prevention of CSA is that, unlike many public health applications such as heart disease, preventing CSA requires simultaneous attention to multiple potential targets (e.g. potential or actual offenders, potential or actual victims, families, child-related institutions and other high risk places). Thus while the public health model is conceptually important, particularly in drawing attention to alternatives to the current policy preoccupation with formal tertiary-level responses, applied prevention must be guided by models that distinguish specific types of interventions, and that identify specific prevention targets.

Crime prevention

Arguably the most influential model employed by crime prevention researchers and practitioners is that proposed by Tonry and Farrington (1995). This model distinguishes four types of intervention: 1) developmental crime prevention (e.g. Tremblay and Craig 1995); 2) situational crime prevention (e.g. Clarke 1997); 3) community development approaches (e.g. Hawkins *et al*. 1992); and 4) criminal justice interventions (policing, the courts and corrections). An important strength of this model is that it identifies these four distinct conceptual and applied domains, each of which is associated with its own body of theoretical and empirical knowledge and practice experience. Like the public health model, Tonry and Farrington's crime prevention model draws attention to alternatives to criminal justice and other tertiary-level interventions. These alternative approaches are intended to supplement, not necessarily to replace, traditional criminal justice approaches. Tonry and Farrington's model is thus broadly consistent with the public health approach in so far as both suggest a combination of primary, secondary and tertiary prevention strategies.

Developmental crime prevention is based on the understanding that individuals vary in their propensity to engage in delinquent and criminal conduct, and that criminal dispositions or vulnerabilities themselves often emerge from earlier developmental problems. Drawing on extensive knowledge about risk and protective factors associated with violence and antisocial behaviour, and on theoretical conceptions of developmental pathways leading to involvement in delinquency and crime, developmental crime prevention aims to reduce the emergence of individual criminal dispositions or vulnerabilities by reducing known risk factors and strengthening known protective factors. In the main, applied developmental crime prevention projects have concentrated on secondary-level interventions; that is, on developmental interventions directed towards individuals or families identified as at-risk. However, developmental prevention can also be applied as a primary prevention strategy by targeting risk and protective factors in whole populations. There are many examples of successful developmental crime prevention projects (e.g. Farrington 1994; Olds 2002; Weikhart and Schweinhart 1992), but none of these has specifically targeted reductions in CSA, nor indeed in sexual offences more generally.

Situational crime prevention shifts attention from the criminal dispositions or vulnerabilities of offenders to the features of the potential crime scene that might facilitate criminal behaviour. Situational prevention techniques involve the systematic manipulation of aspects of the immediate environments of potential offenders and potential victims in an attempt to block or inhibit criminal behaviour. This approach is based on a dynamic view of human action that stresses the variability of behaviour in response to immediate circumstances. It is the identification of the immediate physical and interpersonal context in which CSA occurs that would form the basis of situational prevention of CSA, and that distinguishes this approach from the more popular offender-centred approaches. While there are many examples of successful situational crime prevention projects (see e.g. Clarke 1997), as with developmental prevention, this approach has not yet been systematically applied to the problem of CSA (Wortley and Smallbone 2006a).

Community development approaches to crime prevention involve establishing community partnerships to systematically identify local crime-related problems and devise local solutions to these problems (Hawkins *et al.* 1992). Typically, a local committee is established to undertake a crime audit and to oversee the implementation and evaluation of local crime prevention activities, with funding and other resources generally provided by a central government agency. Community development projects may draw from a wide range of proven or promising prevention strategies, including developmental, situational and criminal justice strategies. While community development approaches are thus pragmatic and eclectic, key features of these approaches are the active participation of local communities, and employing a systematic, evidence-based approach to identifying and responding to specific, local crime problems. Once again, we are not aware of any examples of community development crime prevention approaches being applied specifically to preventing CSA.

The fourth element of Tonry and Farrington's (1995) crime prevention model is criminal justice interventions. These include the day-to-day activities of police and other statutory authorities, the courts and various diversionary programmes, and adult corrections and youth justice agencies. Criminal justice interventions thus encompass the detection and investigation of CSA, specific and general deterrence strategies, the general and selective incapacitation of CSA offenders and the treatment of adolescent and adult CSA offenders.

Child maltreatment prevention

Prevention efforts focused on sexual abuse have taken a very different historical course to those focused on other kinds of child maltreatment. Considerable attention was already being given to the prevention of child maltreatment when, in the 1980s, sexual abuse began to be widely conceived of as a distinct form of maltreatment that required its own unique explanations and responses (Finkelhor and Daro 1997). Efforts to prevent other kinds of maltreatment have tended to concentrate on identifying the circumstances that put families at risk of child abuse and neglect (e.g. young, poor, isolated or stressed parents), and providing those at risk of maltreating children with the education and resources required to facilitate effective parenting. In some cases high-risk families are provided with the support of a home visitor, or respite in times of acute stress. Parental education, family support and home visitation services – the mainstays of child maltreatment prevention – have in recent decades been given much less attention in the prevention of sexual abuse. Since the 1980s, efforts to prevent sexual abuse have instead focused on children themselves as potential victims. Typically, these programmes are delivered universally in an educational format, usually in schools, and aim to teach children how to identify abusers, how to resist their advances and to disclose abusive incidents to a responsible adult.

It is not at all clear why children should be expected to be taught to protect themselves from sexual abuse. There certainly seems to be no similar expectation that children should be taught to protect themselves from physical or emotional abuse or neglect. Finkelhor and Daro (1997) have suggested four reasons why sexual abuse prevention has taken such a different course from that taken in the prevention of physical and emotional abuse and neglect. First, the work of doctors, nurses and social workers in preventing child maltreatment was already well established by the late 1970s and early 1980s when the women's movement began to have success in having sexual abuse recognised as a major, distinct social problem. Feminist-oriented sexual abuse advocates had a broader community focus and favoured educational, rather than ecological or therapeutic, approaches. Current victim-focused sexual abuse prevention programmes continue to be influenced by this educational, advocacy model. Second, along with increased community awareness about sexual abuse came an increasing level of community condemnation and stigma attached to sexual offenders. Engaging potential offenders voluntarily, as in other maltreatment prevention approaches, seemed to be much more difficult because potential sexual abusers would be very unlikely to identify themselves as being in need of assistance for fear of being stigmatised and punished, rather than helped. Third, it has been more difficult to identify high-risk populations for sexual abuse than for other forms of maltreatment because no clear profile of potential sexual abusers has been available. This may be partly because research on sexual abuse has tended to concentrate on individual-level, rather than on family- or community-level explanations, and partly because the identified perpetrators of sexual abuse are usually men rather than women (who are more likely to be the identified perpetrators in other forms of maltreatment). In any event, even if potential sexual abusers could be identified, it has been assumed that they would be harder to engage than, say, young mothers in a maternity ward.

Finally, parents generally were quick to support school-based educational approaches for their children because they believed the risks of sexual abuse originated from outside their family, and were thus more worried about their ability to protect their children from sexual abuse than from other forms of child maltreatment. This perspective was initially supported by the early community education focus on 'stranger danger'. By the time it became widely recognised that the most significant risks for sexual abuse, as with other forms of maltreatment, are presented by persons whom children already know and often live with, school-based educational approaches were already widely established. This recognition of the 'close to home' context of sexual abuse has led to some changes in the content, but generally not in the focus or format, of child-focused sexual abuse prevention programmes.

Another notable approach to sexual abuse prevention has been large-scale community education programmes that have aimed to increase community awareness and to disseminate information and advice about sexual abuse and how it might be prevented. Some of this work has emerged from government initiatives, but the most sustained effort seems to have come from sexual abuse prevention advocacy groups. In recent years some of these advocacy groups, such as Stop it Now!, have become increasingly well organised and more socially and politically engaged, and have become more sophisticated in their use of mass media technologies, particularly television and the Internet. These activities can be seen as an extension of the feminist-influenced, educational, advocacy model of sexual abuse prevention that emerged in the late 1970s and early 1980s.

Implications of the integrated theory for preventing sexual abuse

The integrated theory presented in Chapter 2 proposes that CSA occurs as a result of distal and proximal interactions between biological, developmental, ecosystemic and situational factors. On one hand the theory suggests that the scope of current sexual abuse prevention efforts needs to be widened; on the other hand, it suggests that the focus of preventive interventions themselves needs to be narrowed.

By situating sexual abuse within the wider problem of crime, child maltreatment and other socially irresponsible conduct, the integrated theory suggests that much may be gained by drawing on prevention concepts and strategies applied in these related fields. With its emphasis on distinguishing motivational and situational factors associated with offence onset from those associated with persistent offending, the integrated theory is consistent with the public health approach of developing separate strategies for primary, secondary and tertiary prevention. The particular emphasis in the theory on explaining the onset of CSA offending is also consistent with the emphasis of the public health model on giving priority to primary prevention strategies.

The different levels of explanation proposed in the integrated theory map directly onto the prevention approaches suggested by Tonry and Farrington's (1995) crime prevention model. The proposed interactions between biological and developmental factors suggest the importance of drawing on developmental crime prevention concepts and strategies. The significance attached to the offender's and victim's social ecosystems suggests that there would be value in drawing on both community development approaches to crime prevention and on community-focused maltreatment prevention approaches. The critical role of situational factors proposed in the integrated theory, especially in evoking CSA offence-related motivations, opens the possibility of applying situational crime prevention concepts and methods. The ongoing risk presented by persistent CSA offenders suggests that criminal justice interventions, including policing, specific deterrence, selective incapacitation and offender rehabilitation strategies, are likely to remain important components of a comprehensive prevention approach.

The integrated theory also provides guidance for narrowing the focus of prevention strategies. In the remainder of this section we consider how each level of explanation proposed in the integrated theory allows us to identify more specific prevention targets. We also consider the practical implications of distinguishing offence-related motivations associated with the onset and progression of CSA offending.

Biological foundations

Understanding the biological foundations of CSA offending allows us to reconsider where and under what circumstances the risk for sexual abuse is likely to present itself. The conclusion that the biological potential for CSA offending is more or less universal among adolescent and adult males may at first appear very disconcerting, and to make the task of prevention all the more difficult. However it is important to keep in mind that for the vast majority of males this potential is never realised, due to opposing biologically-based nurturing motivations that serve to protect children and to the very powerful restraining effects of social cognitive development, social norms, informal child protection systems and natural situational barriers. Further strengthening these restraints through developmental, community and situational prevention techniques would therefore be expected to further reduce the incidence of sexual abuse.

Perhaps the most important insight arising from our biological analysis is that the risks for CSA are likely to be concentrated in circumstances where older males have developed close emotional relationships with children, but have not established a protective early secure attachment bond with the child. We would therefore expect the risks for sexual abuse to be concentrated among step-fathers, temporary care-givers, step- or foster-siblings, teachers, pastoral carers, sporting coaches and others whose routine activities bring them into regular close contact with children. Considering the interactions between biological, developmental, ecosystemic and situational factors, our analysis indicates that the risks for sexual abuse are further increased in circumstances where the older male has already established a propensity for aggressive, self-serving or rule-breaking behaviour, when they possess an insecure and especially a disorganised attachment orientation, when the child is particularly emotionally vulnerable or needy, when formal and informal child protection systems are inadequate, and when the risk of detection for the potential offender is low. A key insight of the integrated theory is that many sexual abuse incidents may be understood as an acute disorganisation of attachment-related behaviours in the offender. The focus of educational strategies should therefore be concentrated on adolescent and adult males with insecure interpersonal attachments and weak social attachments, and who are likely to have contact with vulnerable children. The focus of situational strategies should be concentrated on settings where older males are likely to come into routine unsupervised contact with vulnerable children.

Developmental influences

The observation that individuals' exposure to adverse developmental circumstances increases risks for a very broad range of negative developmental outcomes is by no means new. This simple insight points immediately to the possibility that negative outcomes might be prevented by reducing individuals' exposure to, or limiting the negative impact of, adverse developmental events. Our integrated theory highlights several ways in which early developmental experiences may increase later risks specifically for CSA offending, all of which originally spring from problems in the forging of early attachment bonds. Secure early attachment relationships, we contend, provide the foundation for acquiring a stable and effective capacity for self-restraint, and thus for socially responsible conduct. Early attachment experiences also provide the psychosocial foundation for establishing broader social attachments, which in turn influences the extent to which individuals are likely to establish a strong stake in social conformity. More specifically, early attachment experiences provide the cognitive, affective and behavioural foundation for attachment-related behaviours – attachment (care-seeking), nurturing (care-giving) and sexual behaviour – in adolescence and adulthood.

The integrated theory therefore suggests a number of points at which developmental interventions may be most effectively targeted. Clearly the first of these is the primary (infant care-giver) attachment relationship itself. Taking a life-course developmental perspective, the integrated theory also points to adolescence and early middle-age as the key risk periods for the onset of CSA offending, and to the transition to parenthood as a key time to assist with establishing protective attachment bonds. Middle childhood may also be an important point of focus for inculcating positive values concerning intimate relationships, and for responding to emerging antisocial and sexual behaviour problems. At a tertiary prevention level, psychological treatment for adolescent and adult CSA offenders may need to target current manifestations of earlier developmental problems, especially those related to self-restraint (e.g. empathy, emotional self-regulation), orientation to interpersonal relationships, managing emotional intimacy, and the offender's social attachments.

Ecosystemic influences

Our social ecological analysis situates the problem of sexual abuse in the context of the ecosystems in which the potential victim and potential offender are socially embedded. This perspective locates potential causal mechanisms and processes, as well as potential preventive factors, in individual, family, peer, institutional, neighbourhood and service agency systems, as well as in the broader sociocultural environment. Social ecological models underpin much of the theoretical and applied work in the fields of child maltreatment prevention, developmental crime prevention and clinical developmental psychology, but perhaps surprisingly have had much less influence in the specialised field of sexual abuse prevention, which has instead concentrated more or less exclusively on individual-level explanations and interventions. Ecosystemic concepts and methods may open new possibilities for preventing CSA by focusing on specific systemic risk and protective factors.

The integrated theory highlights three (of many) ways in which ecosystemic factors influence potential offenders and potential victims. The first is that social ecosystems convey the social and cultural norms to which individuals are expected to conform. Understanding how the influence of mainstream social norms and values is filtered through, and sometimes blocked by, the various levels of individuals' social ecosystems suggests the need to reconsider the targeting and content of current community awareness strategies. Social ecology theory asserts that the influence of more proximal systems, such as family, peer and institutional systems, is generally stronger than the influence of more distal social systems. This suggests that targeting the more proximal elements of individuals' social ecosystems would be more effective and more efficient than universal community awareness and education strategies. For example, ensuring that church or school institutions maintain a strong culture of ethics and accountability is likely to have more powerful and immediate protective effects than relying on community-wide awareness campaigns to influence the behaviour of individuals within these high-risk settings. The purpose and content of broader community education and awareness campaigns may also need to be reconsidered. In particular, universal education strategies that draw attention to the harmful effects of CSA need to control for the risks of exacerbating the psychological harm for CSA victims, who of course will be exposed to the same information as that intended to educate and deter potential offenders.

A second way in which social ecosystems influence CSA is through their effects on the availability of formal and informal resources for effective child protection. This basic insight has guided child maltreatment prevention practices for decades. Applying the same rationale to CSA prevention re-opens the possibility that ecological interventions commonly used in the prevention of other forms of child maltreatment, such as parental education, family support and home visitation services, could also play an important role in the prevention of sexual abuse. Finally, the integrated theory proposes that social ecosystems delimit the routine activities of potential CSA victims and offenders, and thereby present or restrict opportunity structures and processes for CSA to occur. Once again the main focus here is on the proximal systemic influences of family, peers, schools, and so on. Interventions designed to improve the capacity of families to monitor the whereabouts and activities of their children, to promote secure family attachments, to minimise children's exposure to antisocial or high-risk-taking peer groups, to facilitate children's exposure to supportive prosocial peer groups and to actively safeguard children in schools, recreational and other institutions, would all be sensible additions to a comprehensive CSA prevention policy.

Situational influences

Alongside developmental, community and criminal justice approaches, situational prevention is one of the four key approaches to crime prevention included in Tonry and Farrington's crime prevention model. Situational prevention has not been applied in the field of sexual abuse prevention, nor indeed in the broader field of child maltreatment prevention. Like social ecology theory, situational prevention theory shifts attention from an exclusively individual-level focus to the context in which the potential offender and potential victim interact. Situational prevention concentrates particularly on the immediate physical and interpersonal context of potential abuse incidents. Because applied situational prevention involves a micro-level analysis of the situational features of potential crime settings, it offers a much greater potential than other prevention approaches to narrow the focus of prevention targets.

The application of situational prevention techniques requires two basic conditions: a specific, circumscribed location; and the capacity to exercise significant control over the location. The first condition is satisfied in domestic settings, where most CSA occurs, but exercising control in domestic settings presents significant (although, we would argue, not necessarily insurmountable) challenges for primary pre-vention. Applying situational prevention in domestic settings is readily applicable at a secondary or tertiary prevention level, for example to prevent re-offending by a known familial offender. Both conditions are satisfied in child-related institutional and organisational settings, where a significant proportion of CSA cases is known to occur, and it is in these settings that situational prevention may be most suited to primary and secondary prevention. Because of its high degree of specificity, situational analyses would need to be conducted on a case-by-case basis, and situational interventions will almost certainly vary from one application to another. At the same time, the principles of situational prevention can be readily applied to a very broad range of organisational and other circumscribed settings.

Our integrated theory does not point directly to the need to teach children to protect themselves from sexual abuse, and indeed we have some ethical reservations about placing the responsibility for CSA prevention onto children themselves. Leaving these reservations aside for the moment, child-focused prevention may nevertheless be thought of as a special case of situational prevention. In particular, teaching children self-protection skills would constitute what is referred to by situational prevention practitioners as 'target hardening', perhaps an unfortunate term in the present context. But while situation prevention principles may be usefully applied to child-focused prevention, the role of children themselves in CSA incidents needs to be understood in a much wider context. To the extent that child-focused prevention can be ethically and empirically justified, our integrated theory would suggest that child-focused strategies should be considered in terms of biological, developmental and ecosystemic, as well as situational, influences on CSA. As others (e.g. Kaufman *et al.* 2006) have also pointed out, child-focused prevention strategies should be informed empirically by research on CSA offenders' modus operandi; that is, on the systematic study of CSA offenders' pre-offence, offence and post-offence behaviour.

Onset and progression of CSA offending

The emphasis in our integrated theory is on explaining the onset of CSA offending; that is, on explaining why a potential offender commits a CSA offence for the very first time. We have argued that, since the most desirable goal of prevention is to prevent potential offenders from committing these offences in the first place, particular attention needs to be given to understanding the onset offence. Of course, much is also to be gained by preventing already active offenders from committing further offences. However, different prevention strategies are likely to be required to deter potential, novice and persistent offenders.

Outcomes of the onset offence are likely to be critical in determining whether and under what circumstances novice offenders progress to, or desist from, further offending. Important outcomes of the onset offence are likely to be the offender's emotional, cognitive and behavioural responses to the first incident, whether the victim is able to prevent further abuse incidents, whether anyone else becomes aware of the offence, and if so whether a third party possesses the capacity and willingness to intervene. Presumably progression to further offending is more likely if the offender experiences the first incident as rewarding, and if their offence-related thinking and behaviour remain inadequately restrained. Over time, offence-related emotions, cognition and behaviour may be positively and negatively reinforced, and in the absence of effective early intervention this may lead to chronic offending. Our integrated theory suggests that both the offender's CSA-related motivations, and the role of CSA-related situations, are likely to change following the onset offence. For example, committed offenders are more likely to recognise and perhaps actively create opportunities to abuse children, and may become very skilled in identifying and engaging with vulnerable children and in avoiding detection. Thus whereas routine, unobtrusive situational interventions may deter many potential offenders from committing a first sexual offence, in some cases 'harder' situational interventions may be required to deter committed, persistent offenders. Additionally, criminal justice interventions, including high-quality psychological treatment and risk management strategies, would be critical components of prevention targeting persistent offenders.

Offenders, victims, situations and communities

Our empirical and theoretical analysis of CSA, together with our review of current prevention approaches in CSA and related fields, points to a broad array of potential prevention targets. Our remaining task in the present chapter is to organise these targets into a coherent conceptual framework that will allow us to proceed in subsequent chapters to consider in more detail a variety of prevention approaches. Our dual aim here is to achieve conceptual and practical parsimony, while not losing sight of the complexity of the problem and of the multifaceted approach to prevention that is clearly required.

The array of potential prevention targets suggested by our analysis can be reduced to four elements that, to borrow from Cohen and Felson (1979), constitute the basic 'chemistry' of CSA: 1) offenders (or potential offenders); 2) victims (or potential victims); 3) situations (the specific places and circumstances in which CSA occurs); and 4) communities (the social ecosystems in which CSA occurs). As we will see in later chapters, prevention activities associated with each of these four elements involve quite different intervention techniques, and require different kinds of knowledge and expertise. In the remainder of the present chapter we outline our rationale for organising prevention targets in terms of these four basic elements. In subsequent chapters we expand on this by addressing in more detail the knowledge base underpinning the various prevention approaches and considering issues concerning implementation and evaluation.

Offender-focused approaches

Clearly the most desirable prevention goal is to prevent potential offenders from sexually abusing a child in the first place. When CSA has occurred, it is important to prevent the offender from pro-ceeding to commit further offences. There are five main ways in which potential, unidentified or known offenders can be targeted with preventive interventions: 1) developmental prevention; 2) detection and investigation of CSA offences; 3) general and specific deterrence; 4) incapacitation of known offenders; and 5) treatment of adolescent and adult CSA offenders. We can further reduce these to three offender-focused prevention approaches: 1) developmental prevention; 2) criminal justice interventions (incorporating detection and investigation, deterrence and incapacitation strategies); and 3) treatment approaches. Developmental prevention is considered in more detail in Chapter 4, criminal justice interventions are considered in Chapter 5, and the treatment of adolescent and adult offenders is taken up in Chapter 6.

Victim-focused approaches

As with offender-focused prevention, the first priority for victim-focused prevention is to prevent potential victims from experiencing a first CSA incident. It is also important from a victim-focused perspective to quickly and effectively respond when children have experienced CSA. Once CSA has occurred, the priorities are to limit the harm caused to the child and to prevent further sexual (and other) victimisation.

Victim-focused prevention programmes may include counselling and support services for known victims, programmes designed to encourage as-yet-unidentified victims to report sexual abuse, and programmes that engage with potential victims in an effort to avoid or deter abuse. Services for known victims are principally tertiary-level interventions, as are programmes designed to encourage victims to report sexual abuse. However, since it is known that a longer duration of sexual abuse is associated with more negative outcomes (Kendall-Tackett, Williams and Finkelhor 1993), early reporting may reduce the potential impact and thus constitute secondary prevention. Victim-focused programmes (or, more accurately, programmes targeting *potential* victims) that prevent sexual abuse from occurring in the first place would constitute primary prevention. We examine victim-focused prevention approaches in more detail in Chapter 7.

Situation-focused approaches

Even when a motivated potential offender and a vulnerable potential victim encounter one another, a CSA offence is unlikely to occur unless the circumstances are 'right' for the offence to occur. Routine Activities theory (Cohen and Felson 1979) contends that, together with the presence of a motivated offender and a suitable target, the absence of a capable guardian is one of three essential elements for any crime to occur. Rational Choice theory (Cornish and Clarke 1986) contends that, all other things being equal, an offence of any kind is more likely to occur when the commission of the offence requires the offender to expend little effort, when the risk of detection is low and when the offence promises a highly desired reward for the offender. Finkelhor (1984) argues more specifically that for an incident of sexual abuse to occur, a motivated offender must overcome his own internal inhibitions (e.g. empathy for the potential victim), overcome external inhibitions (e.g. waiting until an otherwise capable guardian is absent) and overcome the resistance of the victim (e.g. by enticing or threatening the child). Our own integrated theory contends that potential CSA offence situations represent much more than simply obstacles that an already-motivated offender must recognise and overcome. Particularly for potential and novice offenders, situations may also evoke CSA-related motivations by presenting cues, stressors, temptations and perceived provocations. In Chapter 8 we consider more fully the implications of these situational explanations for preventing CSA.

Community-focused approaches

Our integrated theory situates sexual abuse in the context of the social ecosystems in which the potential offender and potential victim are embedded. Recall that the integrated theory highlights three main ways in which social ecosystems influence the occurrence of CSA: 1) by conveying social norms and values; 2) by affecting the availability of effective child protection resources; and 3) by delimiting the routine activities of potential offenders and potential victims. Our ecosystemic level of analysis provides a conceptual bridge between CSA prevention activities and both community development approaches to crime prevention and community-focused approaches to preventing child maltreatment. In Chapter 9 we examine current community-focused approaches to CSA prevention, and consider how CSA prevention could draw on the knowledge base and practice experience of the related fields of crime prevention and child maltreatment prevention.

Summary

Current approaches to preventing CSA are dominated by formal interventions designed to take effect only after offenders have begun offending and after children have already been sexually abused. In this chapter we reviewed prevention approaches in the fields of public health, crime, child maltreatment and sexual abuse, concluding that the current scope of sexual abuse prevention needs to be widened, and that prevention targets need to be narrowed.

A public health approach identifies three main points of focus for preventing CSA: 1) preventing potential offenders from committing a first CSA offence, and preventing children from being abused for a first time (primary prevention); 2) early intervention with CSA offenders and victims, or with those at risk of becoming offenders or victims (secondary prevention); and 3) preventing recidivism among known CSA offenders, and limiting harm and preventing continued or repeat victimisation of persons who have already experienced CSA (tertiary prevention). A key strength of the public health model is that it draws attention to the need for prevention policy to encompass primary, secondary and tertiary prevention strategies, and to give particular priority to primary prevention. A limitation for our present purposes is that the public health model does not identify specific prevention targets or interventions.

Tonry and Farrington's (1995) crime prevention model identifies four prevention domains: 1) developmental prevention; 2) situational prevention; 3) community development approaches; and 4) criminal justice interventions. With its emphasis on developmental, situational and ecosystemic influences, our integrated theory provides a conceptual basis for applying developmental, situational and community crime prevention methods to the prevention of sexual abuse.

Our integrated theory suggests a broad array of potential targets for preventing CSA. One way to organise these targets is in terms of the four elements that constitute the basic chemistry of sexual abuse: 1) offenders and potential offenders; 2) victims and potential victims; 3) potential offence situations; and 4) communities. In the following chapters we consider in more detail how prevention strategies associated with each of these elements can contribute to a comprehensive approach to CSA prevention.

Chapter 4

Developmental prevention

We have argued that the most desirable goal for preventing CSA is to prevent potential offenders from sexually abusing children in the first place; in other words, to prevent those who might otherwise sexually abuse a child from first doing so. One way to achieve this goal would be to prevent the emergence, over the course of individual social cognitive development, of dispositions or vulnerabilities associated with the onset of CSA offending. This approach, known as developmental prevention, involves systematic efforts to reduce the number of individuals exposed to adverse developmental circumstances, to reduce the negative impact for those who have been exposed to adverse circumstances, and to strengthen protective factors associated with responsible social and sexual conduct.

In the present chapter we outline the conceptual and empirical foundations of developmental prevention in general, and developmental crime prevention in particular. Then, drawing on evidence and theory concerning CSA offending, we consider a range of targets and methods for the developmental prevention of CSA offending. Although developmental prevention concepts may also be applicable to psychological interventions with known offenders, our emphasis in the present chapter is on interventions designed to prevent CSA offending before it might otherwise occur.

Conceptual and empirical foundations

Developmental crime prevention comprises a range of activities that form part of a much broader effort directed at improving the health and well-being of children by providing resources and services to (usually socially disadvantaged) individuals, families, schools or communities. In recent years, governments of many English-speaking countries have made major investments in developmental prevention programmes. In the US, Head Start programmes designed to enhance intellectual development and subsequent school achievement in disadvantaged three and four-year-olds attracted increased public funding during the 1990s, at a time when spending on social programmes was generally in decline (Kamerman 2000). In the UK, major public investments have been made in Sure Start programmes which, like their US counterparts, focus on families with children under four years of age, especially in socially disadvantaged communities (Tunstill *et al*. 2002). The Canadian Institute for Advanced Research has highlighted the importance of investing public resources in improving child development outcomes (McCain and Mustard 1999), and the Australian Federal Government has made major new investments in its *National Agenda for Early Childhood* (Australian Government Taskforce on Child Development 2003). Internationally, reports by the World Bank, OECD and UNICEF have all called attention to the importance of investing resources in early childhood development to improve later life chances (McCain and Mustard 1999).

Underpinning developmental prevention is an extensive empirical base that identifies reliable associations between a broad range of developmental risk and protective factors and a broad range of negative or positive developmental outcomes. Adverse early developmental circumstances have been linked for example to physical and mental health problems, conduct problems, school problems (e.g. truancy, suspension, early drop-out, poor academic achievement), drug and alcohol problems, early sexual activity, having multiple sexual partners, teenage pregnancy, unstable relationships, personal victimisation, low income, unemployment and involvement in delinquency and crime. Indeed, the recent growth in the application of developmental prevention models specifically to preventing delinquency and crime arose in part from unanticipated findings from some of the early US Head Start programmes, namely that improved preschool education produced marked reductions in later participation in delinquency and crime. Undoubtedly the best-known example is the High/Scope Perry Pre-School Project (Schweinhart, Barnes and Weikhart 1993), a randomised control experiment implemented from 1962 to 1967 which aimed to test whether later educational achievement would be improved for three to four-year-old children from disadvantaged neighbourhoods through a daily preschool programme and weekly home visits by teachers. Children in the experimental condition were more likely than the controls to complete high school and to be involved in further education, and by age forty were more likely to be employed, had higher incomes, and were more likely to be home-owners. But it was the outcomes relating to participation in delinquency and crime that especially caught the attention of crime prevention theorists and practitioners. At age fifteen, the children from the experimental group had lower self-reported offending, at nineteen they were less likely to have been arrested, and at twenty-seven they had half the number of arrests, than the control group. At age forty, 55% of the control group had been arrested five or more times, compared to 36% of the experimental group (Schweinhart 2004).

The major empirical sources for the identification of developmental risk and protective factors associated specifically with delinquency and crime have been numerous large-scale prospective longitudinal studies. Some of these have included delinquency as one of numerous outcomes of interest (e.g. *Dunedin Multidisciplinary Health and Development Study*, Moffit 1990; *Mater University of Queensland Longitudinal Study of Pregnancy*, Najman *et al*. 2001), and others have concentrated more directly on delinquency and crime outcomes (e.g. *Cambridge Study in Delinquent Development*, Farrington 1995; *Pittsburgh Youth Study*, Loeber *et al*. 1996). Despite sampling and other methodological differences, there has been considerable agreement about the kinds of developmental risk factors associated with serious delinquency and crime. Lipsey and Derzon (1998) conducted a meta-analytic review of studies that had examined predictor variables observable prior to adolescence that were empirically related to participation in violent or serious antisocial conduct between fifteen and twenty-five years of age. For six to eleven-year-olds, the strongest predictors were early delinquent conduct and substance use. For twelve to fourteen-years-olds, the strongest predictors were involvement with antisocial peers and weak social ties. Although a range of individual, family, peer, school and neighbourhood risk factors have been identified in these studies, developmental prevention practitioners have been especially interested in those factors that are most amenable to early intervention. Family-level risk and protective factors are thought to be particularly important in this regard. Lipsey and Derzon found that, for both six to eleven-year-olds and twelve to fourteen-year-olds, the strongest family-level predictors were antisocial parents, low family socioeconomic status, and poor parent–child relations (low parental involvement, low supervision, low warmth, and so on). In a separate meta-analytic review, Hawkins *et al.* (1998) found that living with a criminal parent, harsh discipline, physical abuse and neglect, poor family management practices, low levels of parental involvement with the child, high levels of family conflict, parental attitudes favourable to violence, and separation from family, were all reliable family-level predictors of later violent offending.

While there is broad agreement about the empirical foundations for developmental crime prevention, individual prevention programmes differ in their theoretical approach, and thus in their key intervention targets and methods. Some programmes concentrate on improving childcare and strengthening parent–child attachments (e.g. Elmira Prenatal/Early Infancy Project, Olds 2002), others on improving children's cognitive abilities (e.g. High/Scope Perry Pre-School Project), and others more directly on reducing antisocial behaviour (e.g. Montreal Prevention Project, Tremblay *et al.* 1995). The Elmira Project is especially noteworthy for its positive long-term outcomes for both teenage first-time mothers and their children. Drawing explicitly on attachment and social ecological theories, the project involved home visits to pregnant young mothers by nurses trained to target birth outcomes, early parenting and social engagement. An early evaluation showed a reduced incidence of physical abuse and neglect by the mothers in the experimental group (i.e. those who received the home visits) compared to mothers in a randomised control group (those who did not), after two years. After fifteen years, the mothers from the experimental group had fewer arrests than the mothers who did not receive the home visits. Remarkably, the children from the experimental group, unborn at the beginning of the intervention, had less than half the number of arrests, smoked and drank less, and had had fewer sexual partners, compared to the control group children.

This demonstration that the earliest possible developmental intervention (in effect, with unborn children) can have positive effects on later antisocial conduct and related problems is consistent with attachment and other developmental theories that suggest substantial stability in the effects of early childhood experiences. It is also consistent with Gottfredson and Hischi's (1990) control theory of crime, which argues that criminal propensities are typically established before the age of five. However, developmental pathways models leave a great deal of unexplained variance in delinquency and crime outcomes. Although developmental risk factors generally have an additive effect (i.e. the more risk factors, the higher the risk), many children with multiple risk factors manage to avoid any long-term involvement in delinquency and crime, and many children with no identifiable developmental risk factors nevertheless later engage in serious antisocial conduct. As Sampson and Laub (2006) have pointed out, early developmental risk factors typically possess at best modest predictive validity over the longer term, and developmental outcomes are influenced at least as much by individual choices, chance events and situational factors as they are by early developmental experiences.

In their review of the developmental crime prevention literature, the Australian Developmental Crime Prevention Consortium (1999), led by Ross Homel, proposed a developmental prevention model that emphasises the importance of developmental phases and transitions. Developmental phases are periods in life during which individuals are typically presented with certain critical social and psychological challenges. The successful transition from one life phase to the next is partly dependent on having successfully negotiated the challenges presented in previous life phases. The significance of developmental phases '... lies in the way society expects that people ... will be engaged in some types of activities rather than others, will spend their time in the company of some people rather than others, or will be subject to particular sources of authority' (Australian Developmental Crime Prevention Consotrium 1999: 131). While early childhood experiences are likely to affect the success or otherwise of this transition, so too will new risks and opportunities be presented that will in turn affect the developmental pathway through the new life phase. Thus the experience of preschool is likely to affect the next major transition to elementary school, the experience of elementary school will affect the transition to high school, and so on. Key developmental phases and their associated transitions identified by Homel and his colleagues include the perinatal period, infancy, preschool, school and adolescence. Later in the life course, other critical developmental transitions are likely to include the transitions to employment, committed relationships, having children, having grandchildren, retirement and old age. On one hand, a range of more or less unpredictable events, such as accidents, ill health, relationship breakdowns, problems with children, retrenchment, and so on, are likely to exert profound effects on an individual's developmental life course. On the other hand, earlier developmental successes and failures are likely to influence the way both the more predictable transitions and the less predictable life events are negotiated.

Although the usual focus for developmental prevention is children aged from birth to five years (Shonkoff and Meisels 2000), by taking a life-course perspective of human development the concept of developmental prevention can be extended to include preventive interventions implemented at virtually any point in a person's life, so long as the intervention is focused on identified developmental risk or protective factors and is aimed at forestalling the emergence of problems later in life. The most effective interventions are likely to be those closest to the points of transition, since these transition points represent times of both acute risk and opportunity. As Homel (2005) remarks, 'these points of transition are when interventions can often occur most effectively, since at times of change individuals are both vulnerable to taking false steps and open to external support or advice' (Homel 2005: 81). Thus, the concept of early intervention has two distinct meanings in developmental prevention – early in life and early in a developmental phase. In terms of social ecological theory, which identifies proximal factors as more direct and powerful influences on individual behaviour than distal factors, developmental interventions directed at the earliest point in any given developmental phase (chronologically proximal) and at the social factors nearest to the individual, such as the person's immediate environment or their family or peers (ecologically proximal), are likely to be the most effective.

While the weight of evidence shows that developmental crime prevention is generally both effective and cost efficient, not all the programmes that have been carefully evaluated have demonstrated positive outcomes. For example, although the Seattle Social Development Project (Hawkins *et al.* 1999) produced positive outcomes for its combined child, parent and teacher interventions with grade one children, similar interventions with grade five and six children did not produce the same positive outcomes. For the earlier intervention (grade one) group, stronger school attachments, better school achievement, less violent behaviour, less heavy drinking, fewer sexual partners and fewer pregnancies, were reported at age eighteen. However, these outcomes were not evident for the later intervention (grades five and six) group.

A project that has caused particular consternation among developmental crime prevention theorists and practitioners was the Cambridge-Somerville Youth Study (Powers and Witmer 1951), which seems to have produced negative long-term outcomes for its experimental group. This early experiment in developmental crime prevention used a matched-pairs randomised design and included both 'normal' and 'difficult' boys aged from ten to sixteen years. The intervention itself was complex and multifaceted, involving school assistance, medical and psychiatric support and general mentoring. Thirty years after the intervention, negative effects for the experimental group were found for criminal recidivism, serious mental illness, alcohol problems and even early death. While it has been difficult to tease out the active iatrogenic elements of the intervention, Dishion, McCord and Poulin (1999) highlighted the possibility that group-based components may have contributed to the negative outcomes. Many of the boys had been advised to participate in group-based social activities such as Scouts, YMCA activities and summer camps. In Dishion *et al.*'s analysis, most of the negative effects of the intervention appeared among the boys who had been sent to summer camp more than once. Dishion *et al.* also present other examples where, consistent with wider observations about the importance of peer influences on youth antisocial behaviour, group-based interventions with high-risk youth appear to have produced a 'peer deviancy training' effect, presumably through reinforcement of antisocial attitudes and behaviour.

These examples illustrate the importance of both the timing of particular kinds of interventions, and the focus and methods of the interventions themselves. On the whole, however, the evidence suggests that developmental crime prevention 'works'. But for our present purposes, we need to address the question of whether developmental prevention can 'work' to prevent CSA as well.

Developmental prevention of child sexual abuse offending

CSA offending is by definition both a form of antisocial or criminal conduct, and a form of irresponsible sexual conduct. Prospective delinquency studies have shown that similar developmental risk factors are associated with both antisocial and problematic sexual behaviour, and developmental crime prevention programmes targeting these risk factors have shown positive long-term effects on both antisocial and sexual behaviour. We would therefore expect that current approaches to developmental crime prevention would reduce the incidence of CSA offending as part of their more generic effects on reducing the incidence of socially irresponsible behaviour.

In Chapter 2 we set out a new integrated theory of CSA offending. Key themes of particular relevance to developmental prevention are: 1) that human males are biologically disposed both to sexual aggression and to being sexually interested in young sexual partners, and are less likely than females to establish strong attachment bonds to children; 2) that CSA offending, like other criminal conduct, can be understood in general terms as a failure to exercise self-restraint; 3) that early attachment experiences provide the original social cognitive foundation for establishing mechanisms of self-restraint and for establishing an internal (cognitive and affective) model of close relationships; and 4) that given the biological, developmental and situational links between attachment (care-seeking), nurturing (care-giving) and sexual behaviour, early attachment-related problems are likely to be associated with more specific vulnerabilities with respect to attachment, nurturing and sexual behaviour in adolescence and adulthood. Our integrated theory is consistent with life-course approaches to developmental crime prevention (Homel 2005; Sampson and Laub 2006), insofar as it considers the combined effects of more or less stable individual dispositions or vulnerabilities, the social ecosystems in which potential offenders and potential victims are embedded and immediate situational factors.

Developmental prevention of CSA offending also needs to be considered in the context of human sexual development. DeLamater and Friedrich (2002) have outlined a model of sexual development that is very helpful for our present purposes. Like life-course developmental theories of crime, DeLamater and Friedrich's model construes sexual development as a life-long process that is shaped socially by individuals' relationships with their family, peers and intimate partners. According to this model, key developmental challenges for achieving healthy sexual maturity are: 1) establishing a stable gender identity and an associated gender-role identity; 2) establishing a stable sexual identity; 3) managing physical and emotional intimacy; 4) establishing a healthy sexual lifestyle; and 5) achieving sexual satisfaction.

Underscoring a recurrent theme in this book, DeLamater and Friedrich point to the primary attachment relationship as the social cognitive foundation of human sexual development, arguing that attachment bonds are facilitated by positive early physical contact for infants, and that secure early attachment in turn provides a developmental foundation for stable, secure and satisfying emotional attachments in adulthood. Early childhood is also the period when children form a gender identity (the sense that one is male or female) and are simultaneously socialised according to gender-role norms, which involves learning how males and females are expected to behave. Sexual interest and activity increase between the ages of three and seven, when children will typically form conceptions of marriage and long-term relationships, practice adult roles and engage in heterosexual play. To the extent that parents react awkwardly or negatively to children's growing sexual curiosity, children are likely to instead turn to their peers for information about sex. This encouragement to keep sex and sexuality hidden from adults during middle and late childhood may, incidentally, allow any emerging sexual problems to proceed unobserved. In particular, the effects of sexual abuse, or emerging patterns of sexual anxiety, pre-occupation or coercion, may be difficult to detect for parents and other guardians in part because of the general taboos imposed on sex and sexuality.

Children usually experience their first feelings of sexual attraction in pre-adolescence, at around ten to twelve years of age, but a stable sexual identity – the sense that one is sexually attracted to particular types of people, and one's sense of being sexually attractive to others – tends to emerge in adolescence itself. Major biological changes occur around this time, underpinning strong motivations for adolescents to engage with others for sexual purposes in a much more goal-directed way than is the case in earlier developmental periods. This requires a capacity for managing physical and emotional intimacy, which is no doubt influenced by earlier attachment experiences but is also now influenced strongly by cultural and subcultural norms. While some adolescents name parents, peers and sex education courses as influential sources of information about intimacy and sexuality, the majority say they acquire most of this information from mass media sources (movies, television, magazines and music) (DeLamater and Friedrich 2002).

Sexual lifestyles are many and varied. The norm is heterosexual marriage, although there has been an increasing trend towards cohabitation as an alternative or prelude to marriage. Three main factors appear to contribute to sexual satisfaction: 1) accepting one's own sexuality; 2) listening to one's partner and being aware of their likes and dislikes; and 3) talking openly and honestly (Maurer 1994). Over time, the frequency of sexual intercourse tends to decline, either for a range of biological reasons, through habituation or through unhappiness in the relationship, although sexual interests and activities can continue well into the seventies and beyond.

By drawing on knowledge of the developmental risk factors for crime and related problems, retrospective studies of convicted CSA offenders, models of sexual development and our own integrated theory, we are able to identify a range of more or less specific targets for the developmental prevention of CSA offending. Utilising Homel and his colleagues' model of developmental phases and transitions, we think the key life phases and transition points for interventions that would be most likely to reduce CSA offending are: 1) early attachment relationships; 2) the transition to school; 3) the transition to high school; and 4) the transition to parenthood (and where relevant the transition to child-related employment and related formal activities). Within each of these socially distinct life phases can be located a range of developmental risk and protective factors associated with CSA offending. In the remainder of this chapter we first present a rationale, and then consider a range of opportunities and potential obstacles, for intervening at each of these developmental phases and transitions.

Early attachment relationships

There is little disagreement that secure early attachment relationships provide a critical developmental foundation for both prosocial behaviour and healthy sexual development. In terms of our integrated theory (see Chapter 2), early attachment experiences provide the social cognitive foundation for the acquisition of capacities for behavioural self-restraint, namely emotional self-regulation, empathy and perspective taking, and a co-operative orientation to close relationships. As children's experiences broaden and they interact more widely with peers and the community at large, these early attachment experiences also set the scene for wider social attachments to be established, which for many establishes a strong stake in social conformity. These self-restraint mechanisms are important for moderating social and interpersonal behaviour generally, and for engaging in later intimate and sexual relationships in particular. Our theory also suggests that a secure attachment orientation protects against the later disorganisation of attachment, nurturing and sexual behaviour, which we argue is often implicated in CSA offending, and especially in its onset.

Early attachment problems do not lead directly or immutably to later antisocial and sexual behaviour problems. Rather, as Sampson and Laub (2006) point out, early developmental factors possess only modest predictive validity with respect to individual behaviour, especially over the longer term. Nevertheless, empirical evidence from a variety of research paradigms indicates that early attachment experiences set the scene for individuals' general orientation to social and sexual relationships. Longitudinal attachment studies have shown that attachment in infancy predicts social behaviour in school settings. For example, Sroufe (1988) observed differences among children whose infant attachment had been classified as secure, anxious or avoidant. At school, the secure children were more empathic, more popular, more resourceful and more resilient. Children previously classified with anxious attachment were more impulsive, more easily frustrated in social settings and more likely to engage in attention-seeking behaviours, and avoidant children were observed to be more hostile, unempathic and antisocial.

The links between attachment status and antisocial behaviour have been found to be stronger in socially disadvantaged children, and avoidant attachment in particular has been shown to be more strongly related to aggressive antisocial behaviour in boys than in girls (Lyons-Ruth 1996). Severe attachment problems have been implicated in serious adolescent and adult psychopathology, including personality disorders, substance dependence problems and persistent aggression (Lyons-Ruth 1996). Early attachment-focused interventions have been shown to ameliorate many of these potential negative outcomes. For example, the Elmira Prenatal/Early Infancy Project (Olds 2002), which focused in part on assisting disadvantaged young mothers to establish secure attachments with their newborn children, resulted in reductions in the incidence of physical abuse and neglect by the mothers, and in the long term with significant reductions in the incidence of both antisocial and indiscriminate sexual behaviour among the children themselves.

As the Elmira Project demonstrates, efforts to improve infant–caregiver attachments in disadvantaged families are likely to lead to a broad range of positive short- and long-term outcomes, probably including a reduced prevalence of CSA offending. Widening the reach of attachment-focused interventions beyond small-scale prevention experiments is of course a matter of social policy. Attachment theory is sufficiently well-developed, sufficiently supported by empirical evidence and perhaps generally well enough understood by education, psychology, medical, social work and nursing professionals to provide a coherent, practical basis for identifying and intervening in early attachment problems. Much of this work could be incorporated into routine service delivery across a very broad range of existing social services agencies, and strengthened by professional training in attachment concepts and intervention methods. A key challenge with such an approach would be to improve co-ordination and coherency across a wide variety of service organisations that currently tend to operate in an independent and compartmentalised way. Improvements are also needed in the accessibility of services to more disadvantaged groups. As is the case in clinical developmental psychology generally, the people who are most in need of services are often the people who are least likely to receive it. A shift from traditional clinic-centred services towards field-based outreach approaches is therefore clearly needed.

Even bigger challenges exist for universal early childhood prevention approaches. As Hertzman (2002) has pointed out:

> … improving child development is a question of improving the environments in which children grow up, live and learn; it is not a question of fulfilling specific service mandates to narrowly-defined client populations. The challenge is one of adopting an environmental perspective when agencies have traditionally understood their role to be the provision of one-on-one client services (Hertzman 2002: 5).

Again a key problem lies in the co-ordination of policy and service areas, not just across the traditional education, health and welfare sectors, which is important in itself, but extending to economic and related policy areas as well. Policy areas such as industrial relations, for example, which might not normally be thought of in terms of child development, nevertheless can have a major impact on families' capacities to provide high quality childcare (Hertzman 2002).

Transition to school

The transition from the family-centred developmental phase of early childhood to school or preschool involves exposure to new learning and play activities, lengthy periods of absence from parents, negotiating new relationships with peers, being subject to new social rules and developing relationships with new authority figures (e.g. teachers). Children do not enter this period as blank slates; rather, their earlier developmental successes and failures are likely to influence the way in which they respond to new opportunities and threats. Their earlier attachment experiences, in particular, are likely to influence the extent to which they are able to effectively manage their day-to-day frustrations, co-operate with and care for others, be cared for by others, resist temptations for rule-breaking, and feel connected to the school community. This transition also represents the first opportunity for children to be closely and systematically observed outside the home environment by education and other professionals (e.g. school nurses or counsellors), and thus for the early identification and remediation of learning, health and behavioural problems.

Longitudinal delinquency studies show that the strongest predictors among six to eleven-year-olds of later serious or violent delinquency are having already become involved in delinquent conduct, substance use, male gender, low family socioeconomic status and having antisocial parents. Other significant predictors include aggression and other problem behaviour, psychological problems (e.g. hyperactivity, high daring, impulsivity), weak social ties and poor school attitude and performance (Lipsey and Derzon 1998). There are likely to be many ad hoc efforts to ameliorate these problems in early educational settings, many of which would no doubt be beneficial, however two preventive interventions that were systematically planned and carefully evaluated are of particular note here: the High/Scope Perry Preschool Project (Schweinhart *et al.* 1993), whose aims, methods and general findings we summarised earlier in this chapter; and the Seattle Social Development Project (Hawkins *et al.* 2003).

The Seattle Project aimed to improve educational and behavioural outcomes by targeting three key risk factors: aggressive behaviour, academic failure and poor family management practices. With an overarching aim of strengthening children's bonds to school, the intervention involved a co-ordinated programme of teacher training, parent training and social skills training for the children themselves. The full intervention, which was sustained over the entire elementary school years (grades one to six), was compared to a late intervention condition (grades five and six only) and a third no-intervention group, which was included as a control condition. A six year follow-up (when participants were seventeen or eighteen-years-old) showed that, compared to the no-intervention controls, the full intervention group had stronger school bonding and better school achievement, were less likely to repeat a grade, and were subjected to fewer formal disciplinary actions. Youth from the full intervention group were also less likely to have been involved in violent incidents, had become sexually active later, had had fewer sexual partners, and were less likely to have either become pregnant or caused a pregnancy. Other than having fewer school disciplinary problems, the late intervention (grades five and six only) group showed no significantly better outcomes than the control (no intervention) group.

The Seattle Project intervention was explicitly based on Hawkins and Weis' (1985) social development model (see also Catalano and Hawkins 1995), which hypothesises that strong bonds to school protect against the emergence of socially irresponsible behaviour. These social bonds comprise two components: attachment, defined as a positive emotional link to the school; and commitment, defined as having a personal investment in the school community. Note that the concept of 'attachment' in this context is merely analogous to, and not a direct extension of, human attachment as it is defined in attachment theory. While early attachment bonds with primary care-givers influence social behaviour in a broad range of settings, no doubt including school environments, beyond the family of origin attachment bonds themselves are typically established with only a few people, notably with long-term sexual partners and with one's own children. Most people of course form a broad range of other affiliative relationships, and may well feel very strongly about them, but attachment relationships are highly selective. Thus while children may establish important and meaningful affiliative relationships with people within the school community, and while their primary attachment experiences are likely to influence their expectations of these relationships and even the sense of 'attachment' to the school as a social institution, even the strongest sense of connection to school should not be confused with the deeper, more exclusive human attachment bonds.

Leaving these nuances aside, the Seattle Social Development Project demonstrates that sustained attention to teachers', parents' and children's behaviour in the elementary school years is likely to produce positive long-term benefits in terms of both antisocial and sexual behaviour. In terms of our integrated theory, such interventions are likely to strengthen children's capacity and motivation to exercise self-restraint, and should therefore also reduce the incidence of later CSA offending. The inclusion of parent training may also ameliorate attachment-related problems and reduce exposure to related family risk factors such as high conflict, low parental involvement and harsh discipline. But less is known about the risk factors specifically for CSA offending, and especially about those risk factors that may be evident in the elementary school years.

Even in normal circumstances sexual behaviour is by this stage likely to be covert, so it may be difficult to detect early problems with sexual anxiety, preoccupation or coercion. Indeed, perhaps ironically, it is when children's sexual behaviours *are* observed that adults are more likely to become concerned. In any case, popular assumptions that unusual sexual behaviour among children foreshadows later sexual offending behaviour have generally proved to be unhelpful. Most statistically unusual sexual behaviours in children are not 'abusive' in the sense of being harmful to others (Johnson and Doonan 2005). Even for the proportionally small group of children who seem sexually preoccupied and under-restrained, their behaviour is often not intended to harm others. Rather, their sexual behaviour may be instrumental in seeking comfort from other children, perhaps because they cannot obtain these feelings of comfort at home due to emotional or physical abuse or neglect. These children's sexual behaviour is more likely to be directed towards other, similarly vulnerable children, often with some semblance of mutual consent. However, a small number of elementary school children do engage in sexual behaviours that may be considered abusive and harmful. According to Johnson and Doonan, these children's sexual behaviour is less situation-limited (i.e. occurs across time and different settings), they are persistently undeterred by others' refusal to participate, they tend to employ manipulation, bribery, trickery, intimidation or force, and they are unresponsive to consistent adult supervision and intervention.

Popular assumptions that abusive and other unusual sexual behaviours in the elementary school years must be a product specifically of sexual abuse are not supported by empirical evidence. Rather, particularly for the most serious cases, children who engage in abusive sexual behaviours are likely to have been exposed more generally to chaotic home environments and to multiple forms of abuse, neglect and violence (Johnson and Doonan 2005). Since more serious, persistent sexual aggression among school children may, even in a small proportion of cases, foreshadow later sexual (and probably nonsexual) aggression, detection of these behaviours should lead to concerted efforts to arrest the problem as early as possible.

Retrospective studies of adolescent CSA offenders have produced mixed results with respect to the prevalence of earlier academic and other school problems. Some studies have found that these young people are likely to have experienced academic difficulties (e.g. Fehrenbach *et al.* 1986); others have found that up to one-third of adolescent sex offenders had above average academic performance (Ferrara and McDonald 1996), although Ferrara and McDonald also found that as many as one-third of these young people evidence some form of neurological impairment. Studies of adolescent CSA offenders indicate that these young people are more likely to experience internalising problems (e.g. anxiety, social withdrawal) than they are to demonstrate externalising problems (e.g. overt aggression) (Righthand and Welch 2001). This is likely to make the identification of behavioural risk factors more specific to CSA offending much more difficult. Teachers and other school personnel are probably more likely to be alerted to externalising problems, and children with internalising problems may simply be overlooked, or misconstrued as compliant and untroublesome. There is therefore a need to alert school staff to be sensitive to both externalising and internalising problems among children. Once again, interventions like those in the Seattle Social Development Project, which seek to improve children's social engagement at school, may be very helpful in this regard.

Transition to high school

Entry to high school for most children involves an important transition from the now familiar environment of the elementary school to a new and often much larger and more diverse school environment, with different expectations and rules, and new opportunities and risks. At the same time many things may remain largely unchanged at home or in the broader community environment, except of course for the changes in these environments that occur as a result of the change in the young person's social status (e.g. less parental monitoring and supervision). Youth with an accumulation of earlier developmental successes, particularly those with a stable, warm and supportive family environment, are more likely to be robust to the new risks and to thrive on the new opportunities. But even the most well-adjusted youth will vie for independence from adult control and be exposed to new peer influences and temptations for rule-breaking. As a result, many (if not almost all, see Moffit 1997) will themselves become involved at least transiently in antisocial conduct, no doubt for some including irresponsible sexual conduct. Youth with prior developmental problems, especially those whose family environment remains or has become unstable or conflicted, will be more vulnerable to these new influences and temptations for rule-breaking. A small minority of youth, whom Moffit (1997) called 'life-course persistent' offenders, will already have a history of serious conduct problems and these are at the greatest risk of proceeding to a serious and persistent pattern of antisocial conduct, perhaps including CSA offending.

Although for many youth the onset of puberty (generally ranging between age ten and fourteen, DeLamater and Friedrich 2002) will have preceded their entry to high school, the transition to high school is a social marker for achieving the social and sexual status of adolescence. As biological and psychological sexual development proceeds, secondary sex characteristics signal sexual maturity to the youth and to others, sexual drive intensifies, patterns of sexual attraction emerge and a sexual identity begins to take shape. According to our integrated theory, male youth will need at this time to draw on an established capacity for behavioural self-restraint to ensure that the urgency of their sexual drive and the direction of their sexual attraction do not lead them to sexual aggression or other sexual misconduct. For many, shyness and reserve will present difficulties even in ordinary circumstances. For others, a momentary or chronic lack of self-restraint may well lead to some form of sexual misconduct. Sexual harassment among adolescents and young adults in fact seems to be very common (Koss, Gidycz and Wisniewski 1987; Russell 1984), with the incidence of peer sexual assaults increasing in adolescence along with other antisocial conduct. Absolute rates of CSA offending among adolescents are unknown, although estimates indicate that as many as 30% to 50% of all CSA offences may be committed by adolescents and young adults (Bourke and Donohue 1996; Finkelhor and Dziuba-Leatherman 1994). At the same time, many youth are establishing their first mutual intimate and sexual peer relationships.

Lipsey and Derzon's (1998) meta-analysis of longitudinal delinquency studies indicates that the strongest predictors among twelve to fourteen-year-olds of later serious or violent delinquency are, in descending order of magnitude, weak social ties, association with antisocial peers, psychological problems (e.g. concentration and impulsivity problems, psychopathology), school attitude and performance problems, aggression and general delinquent conduct, having antisocial parents, and poor relationships with parents. Once again, because of the aggregation of offence-types in these studies (sexual offences, presumably including CSA offences, are generally aggregated with violent offences), we do not know which of these may be specific risk factors for CSA offending. However, given the similar developmental themes in retrospective accounts by CSA offenders themselves, and that CSA offending fits conceptually within the cluster of negative outcomes predicted by similar developmental risk factors, we would expect substantial concordance.

According to our integrated theory, we would expect CSA offending in both adolescence and adulthood to first arise in the context of either aggressive or (paradoxically) nurturing behaviour, and to involve a failure of self-restraint related to emotional regulation, empathy or a coercive orientation to social relationships. Sexual aggression in this context is likely at first to be an extension of a more general pattern of nonsexual aggression, and may arise as a chronic or acute disorganisation of attachment and sexual behaviour (e.g. distress cuing sexual behaviour instead of attachment [nonsexual care-seeking] behaviour). CSA offences that arise in the context of nurturance are likely to involve both a failure of restraint and an acute disorganisation of the emotion-motivation systems underlying attachment, nurturing and sexual behaviour. In this case, attachment motivations (e.g. the need to be comforted by someone) or nurturing motivations (e.g. the motivation to comfort a child perceived to be in need) may be over-ridden by sexual motivations cued by the intimate physical contact brought about by what is now this simultaneous mix of distinct but functionally related emotion-motivation systems. Offences themselves may be preceded by fantasy and covert behavioural rehearsal, but these too are likely to have originally been cued in much the same way as we have described. Self-restraint problems may be acute or chronic, with chronic problems arising from prior learning dating from as early as the primary attachment relationship in infancy. Although the overtly aggressive pattern is certainly seen in clinical settings, the nurturant pattern is more often observed in some clinical samples. In an Australian clinical sample of more than 200 court-referred adolescent males (Smallbone, Rayment and Shumack unpublished data), the majority of those who had committed sexual offences against children aged twelve or younger had committed their first sexual offence in the context of nurturing (e.g. babysitting) or play activities (e.g. wrestling), often in an intimate setting (e.g. bedroom). While the level of coercion varied, only 8% were found to have used excessive force. More than 50% of the offender sample had substantiated child protection histories, predominantly involving physical and emotional abuse, with one-third of the sample subject to a current child protection order at the time of their first sexual offence.

Very little is known about specific risk factors evident in adolescence for late (adult) onset CSA offenders. While retrospective accounts produce consistent themes as previously described, there is too little specificity in these studies to know the effects of both offender types (e.g. early or late onset) and the timing of adverse developmental events (e.g. early childhood or adolescence). Our integrated theory suggests that in adolescence, many late onset CSA offenders will experience the same kinds of family, peer and school problems evident in many other vulnerable youth, and indeed many will engage in nonsexual antisocial conduct during adolescence and perhaps into adulthood. Most will nevertheless manage, even if sometimes tenuously, to go on to achieve gainful employment, get married and have a family of their own. Crime-related risk factors evident in adolescence may not be present at all in some other adult onset CSA offenders.

Fewer resources have been directed to planned developmental crime prevention interventions targeting adolescents than to interventions targeting younger children, probably in part because by adolescence antisocial dispositions or vulnerabilities arising from earlier developmental phases are usually now manifest as frank delinquent conduct. By this stage, preventive efforts have largely been subsumed within the ambit of youth justice and criminal justice systems, or are closely aligned with them, and many offender-focused prevention resources are redirected to reducing risks for recidivism (see Chapters 5 and 6). Nor have those prevention programmes that have targeted adolescents met with as much success. Improved academic outcomes, and in some cases reduced drug use and delinquency, have been reported for some universal high-school-based prevention programmes (Gabriel 1996; Gottfredson 1986; Gottfredson and Gottfredson 1992), and pre-high school (US middle school) programmes seem to have had only marginal success (e.g. Orpinas, McAlister and Frankowski 1995).

We therefore have a rather limited basis for suggesting specific targets for developmental prevention of CSA offending aimed at the transition to high school, beyond those associated with the more general delinquency-related risk factors. Our integrated theory nevertheless suggests several possibilities. Although school curriculum-based programmes have met with limited success in preventing general delinquency (Wasserman and Miller 1998), standard educational curricula focusing on intimacy and sexuality may nevertheless be helpful. There is probably much less need for our present purposes to concentrate on reproductive issues, although there may be other good reasons to do this; rather, as Finkelhor and Daro (1997) have suggested, educational approaches should

> work toward acceptance rather than stigmatisation of sexual diversity, reduce feelings of shame and inadequacy, enhance communication between people and the ability to empathize with another's sexual reality, and model sexual activities in the context of mutual respect and affection (Finkelhor and Daro 1997: 623).

A co-ordinated curriculum could include as part of science courses attention to the links between biological and psychological aspects of attachment and sexuality, while social education could include exposure to thinking about gender roles. Perhaps more controversially, male youth might profit from being taught that noticing sexuality in children, or even having sexual feelings about children, is not of itself a biological or psychological abnormality, and does not of itself lead to abusive behaviour. Anecdotally, many CSA offenders report

83

that the prelude to their first sexual offence took them by surprise, and that once they realised they were experiencing sexual feelings about their victim they were either mystified or concluded that they must be mentally disturbed – an understandable conclusion in the current sociocultural climate where CSA offenders are condemned and stigmatised. But of course it is the *exploitation*, rather than the *recognition*, of children's sexuality that defines CSA offending. Helping young men to understand this difference, and to establish a firm boundary between the two, may have a preventive effect for those whose CSA offending first arises in the context of attachment or nurturing behaviour.

Transition to parenthood

Developmental phases beyond adolescence have been given virtually no attention by developmental crime prevention practitioners, whose work has historically been guided by 'early in life' conceptions of the development influences on delinquency and crime. Sampson and Laub's (1993) life-course approach to developmental criminology proposes that adult development continues to present many new risks for criminal behaviour, and that offending in adulthood is generally constrained by informal social controls, particularly by social bonds such as marriage and employment. Weak social attachments to marriage and employment are thought to remove important constraints on antisocial behaviour, particularly for those with stronger antisocial dispositions. This model may be more applicable to understanding differences in criminal career trajectories following earlier participation in delinquency and crime than it is to understanding late onset offending, and does not in any case deal specifically with CSA offending. Nevertheless, the model may be applicable to the many late onset CSA offenders who have already been convicted for nonsexual offences before they commit their first sexual offence (Smallbone and Wortley 2004a). But it seems unlikely that social bonds alone are sufficient to constrain CSA offending. Many late onset CSA offenders are married or in de facto relationships, and indeed many offend within the context of these relationships. Many are also actively involved in social institutions, even holding trusted positions such as teaching and priesthood, where they may also offend. On the other hand, while strong social bonds may be insufficient to deter CSA offending, an absence of social bonds is nevertheless likely to increase the risk for CSA offending, as it probably does for other offending in adulthood.

Our integrated theory proposes that informal social controls (having a strong stake in conformity) are a key aspect of self-restraint, but that a range of psychological resources are also required for effective self-restraint, particularly for restraining strong biologically-based sexual urges and related motivations. In the absence of empathy and perspective taking, emotional self-regulation and a co-operative interpersonal orientation, informal social controls may apply only to the possibility of being caught by someone, rather than to the offending behaviour itself. Secure personal attachments are likely to exert a more direct and more powerful restraining influence than the ecologically more distal social attachments.

Our integrated theory suggests that a key risk factor for CSA offending in adulthood is physical and emotional proximity to (especially emotionally vulnerable) children in circumstances where the potential offender is in an unsupervised care-giving and authority role, and especially in circumstances where a secure attachment bond has not been established with the child. Men with a history of insecure attachment relationships themselves are likely to find it more difficult in turn to establish a secure attachment with their own children, and especially with step-children. This suggests two related points of focus for developmental interventions in adulthood. First, assisting adult males to establish secure attachment relationships with their adult partners may lead to general improvements in their attachment orientation, and thereby improve their general capacities for self-restraint and at the same time reduce risks for the disorganisation of attachment, nurturing and sexual behaviour. In Sampson and Laub's terms, this would also enhance the influence of informal social controls through strengthening the social bond of marriage. Developmental interventions with these aims could be delivered through the many relationships counselling services that are already available. Some governments have recently made renewed commitments to funding relationships counselling services for those contemplating marriage, and indeed there is even debate from time to time about whether such services should be made compulsory for newly-weds. The Australian government, for example, provides funding for relationships counselling through its Family Relationships Services Program (FRSP), which has operated since the 1960s. Although the FRSP initially focused on marriage guidance services, its current aims are: 1) to enable children, young people and adults to develop and sustain safe, supportive and nurturing family relationships; and 2) to minimise the emotional, social and economic costs associated with disruption to family relationships (Department of Families, Community Services and Indigenous Affairs 2007).

Second, assisting adult males to establish secure attachment relationships with their own children may, as Finkelhor and Daro (1997) have noted, reduce the risks that they may later see the child in sexual terms. Notwithstanding observations that young fathers are more difficult than young mothers to engage voluntarily in primary prevention initiatives (Finkelhor and Daro 1997), efforts to improve attachments between vulnerable mothers and their children (e.g. Olds 2002) should nevertheless clearly be extended to include vulnerable fathers as well. More thought is needed about how traditional prevention approaches focused on vulnerable young mothers (e.g. by identifying high-risk mothers in hospital maternity wards) could be modified to target and engage high-risk fathers as well, an issue we consider more fully in Chapter 9.

There are two other general circumstances that present significant risks for CSA offending: families in which stepfathers and others who perhaps have less emotional investment in children are given guardianship roles; and child-related employment and other settings where men are given guardianship and intimate care-giving roles, particularly with vulnerable children. In the former case, prevention efforts may need to target single mothers themselves, perhaps by assisting them to make better judgements about on whom they rely to assist with independent and unsupervised childcare responsibilities, and more broadly by providing sufficient resources that reduce single mothers' economic and emotional dependence on men with whom they may not be engaged in healthy, stable relationships. In the latter case, educational and organisational interventions with men taking up child-related employment are needed. The current focus on employment screening, which relies on detecting known offenders, will of course do very little to prevent CSA offending by men who have not yet done so or who have not been caught. Instead, universal workplace-based programmes aimed at alerting men to the risks, providing good supervision, articulating clear codes of conduct, and so on are needed. We take this issue up further in Chapter 8.

Summary

Developmental crime prevention forms part of a larger developmental prevention effort aimed at improving life-course outcomes for children by reducing empirically identified developmental risk factors and strengthening protective factors. Developmental crime prevention has not yet been applied specifically to the prevention of CSA.

Much less is known about developmental risk factors for CSA offending than for delinquency and crime in general. Neither prospective longitudinal studies nor developmental prevention programmes have reported outcomes separately for CSA offending. However, there are two reasons to expect that much the same developmental factors that predict delinquency and crime will also predict CSA offending: 1) retrospect self-reports by both adolescent and adult CSA offenders suggest very similar developmental themes to those identified in prospective delinquency studies; and 2) CSA offending conceptually fits within the cluster of negative development outcomes (which include both antisocial and sexual behaviour problems) that are predicted by these risk factors.

Most developmental crime prevention programmes have been guided by 'early in life' conceptions of the developmental pathways to delinquency, and have therefore given little attention to developmental interventions beyond adolescence. The age–crime curve for CSA offending is bimodal, with one peak in adolescence and early adulthood (like for most other crime), and a second peak in early middle-age (unlike for most other crime). More recent life-course developmental criminology models, which propose that risks for engaging in crime continue to be presented across the lifespan, may therefore be particularly applicable to CSA offending. These models concentrate on life-phase transitions as both key points of acute risk and as key points of opportunity for developmental interventions.

In this chapter we identified four general points of focus for developmental prevention of CSA offending: early attachment experiences, the transition to school, the transition to high school and the transition to parenthood. We have argued that early attachment relationships provide the social cognitive foundation for the development of capacities for behavioural self-restraint, and for the emergence of an internal (cognitive and affective) model for interpersonal and especially intimate relationships with both adult partners and children. Developmental prevention programmes that have targeted early attachment relationships (e.g. Olds 2002) have shown positive outcomes in terms of both antisocial and irresponsible sexual behaviour. Developmental interventions targeting preschool and school children should focus on the wider manifestations of earlier attachment problems, including peer relationships and social attachments to the school community itself. While statistically unusual sexual behaviour among elementary school children does not generally foreshadow later sexual offending, more serious cases (e.g. overt sexual aggression) should be given priority for remedial action.

By the time children reach high school, developmental prevention efforts tend to be replaced with criminal justice programmes. Non-criminal justice interventions with adolescents have been less successful than those targeting earlier developmental phases. Nevertheless, we have argued that standard educational curricular are needed to assist adolescents with the transition to establishing sexual partnerships. Finally, we have argued that developmental approaches in adulthood should focus on the transition to parenting by aiming to improve both adult attachment relationships and attachment relationships between fathers and their children. Prevention efforts in adulthood should also focus on assisting single mothers to be able to make good decisions about whom to involve in their children's care, and on adult males entering child-related employment and similar activities.

Chapter 5

Criminal justice interventions

Our focus in the previous chapter was on developmental interventions that aim to prevent potential offenders from first engaging in CSA. Of course, once sexual abuse has occurred, it is also very important to prevent the offender from proceeding to commit further CSA offences. We now turn our attention to the role of criminal justice systems in preventing and responding to sexual abuse.

Criminal justice systems are comprised of three core elements: police, the courts and corrections. Policing activities are generally oriented towards crime detection and investigation, although there is an expectation that policing will also prevent some crimes from occurring in the first place. The courts and corrections are generally oriented towards four main goals: retribution, deterrence, incapacitation and rehabilitation. Retribution is a non-utilitarian goal based on an 'eye-for-an-eye' philosophy. Even though retributive sentiments no doubt drive much of the current policy on CSA prevention (e.g. policies designed to increase penalties and sentences), because retribution is not of itself concerned with prevention we will not deal with it further here. We will discuss offender rehabilitation separately in the next chapter. Our present focus will therefore be on various forms of consequences to crime that are thought to serve as deterrents, and on procedures that aim to prevent crime by incapacitating the offender.

In the present chapter we examine criminal justice responses to crime in general, and to CSA in particular. We begin by examining the evidence concerning the role of policing in preventing crime, and consider the implications of this more specifically for preventing

CSA. We then consider the traditional correctional goals of deterrence and incapacitation, with a particular focus on how these goals might contribute to preventing CSA.

Detection, investigation and prevention

The formal activities of the criminal justice system begin with the detection and investigation of crimes that have already occurred, a role generally performed by police and other investigatory and law enforcement agencies. There continues to be a great deal of debate about the extent to which policing and other law enforcement activities contribute to crime prevention, and particularly about the extent to which policing can prevent potential offenders from first committing an offence. In their review of the effectiveness of policing in crime prevention, Sherman and Eck (2002) examined evidence relating to eight separate hypotheses. In short, these hypotheses are that reductions in crime can be achieved by: 1) increasing police numbers; 2) reducing police response times; 3) increasing random police patrols; 4) concentrating police attention on crime 'hot spots'; 5) increasing the number of arrests in response to reported or observed offences (reactive arrests); 6) concentrating police attention on high-risk offenders and offences (proactive arrests); 7) increasing the frequency and improving the quality of police–citizen contacts (community policing); and 8) identifying and minimising proximate causes of crime (problem-solving policing). We will deal briefly with each of these in turn, and consider their implications for preventing CSA.

Before proceeding, it is important to note that while police play a central role in the investigation of CSA allegations, in many jurisdictions it is child protection authorities, often working closely with police, who will make the initial response. We therefore need to consider the evidence concerning policing in terms of its implications for how statutory child protection authorities are organised to respond to (and indeed to prevent) CSA. Of course, there are limits to the extent that evidence concerning policing can be generalised to the work of child protection authorities. Police occupy a special social status, they are much more visible and their activities extend far beyond child protection. Nevertheless, we think at least some lessons about child protection policy and practice can be learned from an examination of policing research.

Research on the effects of police strikes, while methodologically limited, shows clearly that the absence of police is likely to produce immediate and substantial increases in crime and disorder (Sherman and Eck 2002). This research does not deal specifically with the effects of police presence and absence on CSA offending, but rather has focused on changes in the incidence of violent and property crime. Nevertheless, to the extent that CSA can be understood as a form of crime we may conclude that the general presence of police also serves to constrain the prevalence of CSA to some (unknown) extent. Transposing these general findings to the field of child protection is, however, problematic. As we saw in Chapter 1, most CSA occurs in homes, it tends to be even more under-reported than many other types of crime and when it is reported there is often a substantial delay between the alleged incident and the report. Nevertheless while a temporary absence of police or child protection authorities may have little or no immediate effect, we can still conclude that the permanent and 'visible' presence of both police and child protection authorities serves to constrain the prevalence of CSA. From an ecosystemic perspective, the existence of child protection laws and the general presence of police and child protection authorities may serve an important declarative function by conveying community norms and expectations about child protection.

Evidence concerning the marginal effect of *increasing* police numbers is much more equivocal. In short, this evidence suggests that it is not so much the absolute numbers of police, but the ways in which police resources are organised, that can produce a crime prevention effect. This is likely to be the case for child protection services as well. Clearly increasing the numbers of child protection workers is desirable in terms of establishing an adequate capacity to respond quickly and effectively to CSA allegations, but arguably it is the way in which these increased resources are organised that is the key issue for prevention. As Gittler (2002) has noted, reforms are needed that shift the focus of child protection agencies away from an ad hoc, reactive, punitive approach, towards providing services that are comprehensive, co-ordinated, flexible, family-centred, culturally competent and prevention-oriented.

Although early studies supported the hypothesis that reducing police response times would increase the number of arrests police are able to make, more recent and more careful analyses have cast serious doubt on the effectiveness of this policing strategy (Sherman and Eck 2002). A rapid response by police requires a very short period of time between the commission of a crime and its being reported to police (reporting time), quick action by police to organise their response (dispatch time) and having the police travel quickly to the crime scene (travel time). Evidence suggests that if this whole process takes more than a few minutes, the offender is likely to have already fled the scene. Since the question of response times is relevant only to emergency calls to police, it will in any case have very limited application to increasing the arrests of CSA offenders, and even less application to preventing CSA in the first place. One important exception is cases of sexually motivated child abduction or other unusual CSA offences that may be observed by someone who immediately contacts police. Thus in rare cases a rapid response by police may lead to the arrest of a CSA offender, and may even prevent the completion of an offence or the escalation of an offence to abduction or serious violence.

Research on the use of random patrols by police is again limited to examining effects on property and violent offences, especially 'street' offences. Even before considering these limitations for our present purposes, there is little evidence for the effectiveness of random patrols. Nor can we see any relevance of random patrols for preventing CSA offences, and so we will not deal further with this here. Evidence is stronger for the use of directed police patrols concentrating on crime 'hot spots' (Sherman and Eck 2002), but again this seems to have little general relevance for preventing CSA. However, it may be possible for directed patrols to target CSA 'hot spots' if these can be identified. Video game parlours, public swimming pools, places where young people may be engaged in prostitution, specific Internet sites and other places where it may become known that CSA offenders are operating, would be possible targets. Intelligence-driven responses would need to consider both the specific places and times of 'hot spot' activity. Police intelligence may suggest the need for example to visit a particular game parlour, on weekdays, in the hour or so after school.

The specific deterrence effects of reactive arrests seem to vary in complex ways according to offender age (youth or adult), crime type and whether or not the offender is employed. Arresting young offenders in particular has been associated with *increased* offending, a finding that Sherman (1993) has suggested may be due in large part to defiance. Among the implications of this for our present purposes may be that less formal justice mechanisms, such as diversion or restorative justice programmes, may need to be more widely considered for some adolescent CSA offenders (see e.g. Daly 2006). Arresting employed domestic violence perpetrators has been shown to reduce recidivism, while arresting unemployed domestic violence perpetrators appears to *increase* repeat offending (Sherman *et al.* 1992), presumably because the former have a greater stake in conformity. There is some evidence that reactive arrests increase general deterrence in small towns and cities, but in larger towns these effects seem to be negligible or nonexistent (Sherman and Eck 2002). Once again none of these studies has investigated the effects of arresting CSA offenders. The observation that many CSA offenders offend repeatedly before being caught, but have low recidivism rates following conviction, suggests that being caught plays a critical role in desistence. However, it is not known whether a formal arrest is required or whether less formal responses to the disclosure or detection of CSA would have the same effect.

The evidence for police adopting proactive arrest policies is stronger than it is for the less focused use of reactive arrests. As Sherman and Eck (2002) have noted, 'with the exception of arrests targeted on drug problems, there appear to be substantial results from focusing scarce arrest resources on high-risk people, places, offenses, and times' (Sherman and Eck 2002: 312). Evidence for the positive effects of proactive arrests on violent offending is weak, and, once again, there is no research examining the effects of proactive arrests on CSA offending. Nevertheless, as we pointed out in Chapter 1, as with other crime a small number of CSA offenders seem to be disproportionately responsible for a large number of CSA victims, so there is at least a good hypothetical reason to direct proactive arrest policies towards repeat CSA offenders.

Numerous tests of community policing initiatives, where police seek to engage more directly and informally with community members, have failed to show crime reduction effects. However, one aspect of community policing – increasing police legitimacy – has been shown to have considerable promise, especially for youth offenders (Sherman and Eck 2002). Police simply being seen to be fair and polite to citizens and crime suspects alike seems to produce a crime reduction effect. These general findings are consistent with emerging evidence that humane and empathic police interviewing of suspected CSA offenders is more likely to result in a confession (Kebbell, Hurren and Mazerolle 2006), and with established evidence that therapeutic engagement with, and outcomes for, convicted CSA offenders are enhanced by empathic, warm and rewarding therapist behaviour (Marshall and Serran 2004). The lesson here seems to be that both police and child protection authorities should strive to be fair and humane in their investigations of CSA allegations and to avoid confrontational and punitive behaviour, including with those suspected of having committed CSA offences.

The final aspect of policing reviewed by Sherman and Eck (2002) is problem-oriented policing, which is defined as the utilisation by police of scientific knowledge to identify and minimise the proximate causes of specific kinds of crime. Tests of this method of policing have generally been positive, although again there has been no test for its effects specifically on CSA offending. However, Sherman and Eck conclude that the principles of problem-oriented policing are conceptually sound and that this approach may have wide application. In one demonstration of how problem-oriented policing may be applied to CSA offending, Wortley and Smallbone (2006b) recently produced a problem-oriented policing guide to Internet child pornography. This guide provided a comprehensive review of scientific knowledge on the topic with a special focus on how this knowledge might be used to inform practical policing strategies. Among the specific recommendations were for local police departments to: 1) acquire technical knowledge and expertise in Internet pornography; 2) establish links with Internet Service Providers; and 3) prioritise policing efforts, for example by targeting offenders who may be abusing children or producing pornography. This is only one example of how problem-oriented policing may be directed towards the prevention of CSA.

The psychology of punishment

The allocation and administration of punishment is a cornerstone of criminal justice policy. As we have noted, punishment is often applied for retributive purposes, but while retributive punishment may serve a range of needs for crime victims and other affected parties, retribution does not of itself serve a crime prevention purpose. Our interests here are instead concerned with the utilitarian purposes of punishment, namely the presumed deterrent effects of punishment as it is applied in criminal justice settings.

Punishment has been extensively studied in laboratory settings with both humans and infrahuman animals (see Axelrod and Apsche 1983; Dinsmoor 1998). These studies show that for punishment to be maximally effective in suppressing a target behaviour it must be certain to occur, it must occur immediately upon enactment of the target behaviour, it must have sufficient severity and the punisher must be seen as relevant by the person being punished. The first three of these features are referred to in the criminological literature as certainty, celerity and severity.

The final principle of effective punishment (i.e. relevance) is rarely if ever discussed in publications dealing with criminal justice. This is perhaps surprising, since it has long been observed that some persistent offenders view incarceration as a badge of honour or as an expected cost of operating, thereby reducing its relevance and therefore its impact as a punisher. Attempts at restorative justice (Koss, Bochar and Hopkins 2006; Strang and Braithwaite 2002) in fact seem to get closer to employing relevant punishers than do any other responses of the justice system. Restorative justice programmes have been implemented in many countries and in several states of the US (see Koss *et al.* 2006). In fact, more that 50% of countries have such programmes (Schiff and Bazemore 2002) and in some jurisdictions restorative justice procedures have been used specifically with sexual offenders (Daly 2002). Restorative justice often aims to bring together offenders, victims and their communities, and may involve sentencing circles as well as family and community conferences (McCold and Wachtel 2002). Unfortunately most high-risk sexual offenders (including high-risk CSA offenders) would not be suitable for such programmes until they are released from prison which, in most cases, would be long after the offences themselves. In these circumstances restorative programmes would not meet the principle of immediacy of punishment. Another problem for restorative justice programmes is that some victims do not wish to participate in such a programme (Strang 2002). When restorative justice methods have been evaluated the focus of the appraisal has not been on subsequent re-offending by the perpetrator but rather on the satisfaction of the victim or on the victim's experience of fairness (McCold and Wachtel 1998; Strang *et al.* 1999). However, there are reasons to expect that these programmes may have more relevance than imprisonment for some offenders and should, as a consequence, deter re-offending.

This issue of the relevance of a punisher has not been as fully explored in the experimental literature as we might hope. It is clear that the suppression of eating specific foods occurs when nausea is the consequence of ingesting the food (Garcia and Koelling 1966); other punishers, such as electric shocks, are far less effective for eating problems (Baker 2001; Domjan 1998). The same appears to be true concerning conditioned aversions to smell (Rolls 2005). Some early experiments with psychopathic offenders indicated two very interesting points concerning the effects of punishment. Schmauk (1970) compared the responses of psychopaths (or sociopaths as he called them) and nonpsychopaths to various punishers. While the nonpsychopaths responded rapidly and strongly to both electric aversive shocks and to verbal condemnation, neither of these punishers had any effect on the psychopaths. However when both groups had money or cigarettes taken away from them as punishment, the psychopaths responded more rapidly and more strongly than did the nonpsychopaths; the latter were also responsive to these punishers but not to the same degree as the psychopaths. In a later study by Stewart (1972) it was shown that psychopaths respond oppositionally (i.e. by increasing the rate of the supposedly punished response) to punishments they perceive to be harsh. This oppositional response to punishments that are perceived as unjust is well documented in children and particularly in those children who engage in antisocial conduct (Campbell 1990). Similar principles are likely to be involved in the findings reported above concerning the positive effects of police legitimacy. If some offenders are likely to respond to punishment with oppositional behaviour, we can expect that increasing the severity of punishment beyond what is proportional to the crime will have the unintended effect of increasing crime. As we will see there is evidence that some attempts to implement increased sanctions for crime has had that exact effect, as revealed by increases (albeit slight) rather than decreases in recidivism (Gendreau *et al.* 2001).

Returning to the first three principles of effective punishment, it is clear from laboratory studies that punishment must occur with certainty if it is to have the desired effect. If a punishing response is perceived to be uncertain, the human or animal subject may, depending also upon the perceived severity of the punisher, simply ignore the consequence and persist in the behaviour. Of course punishment administered by the courts may be reasonably certain if the crime is reported and if the perpetrator is caught and successfully prosecuted, but the ratio of convictions to identified crimes is very low, making the actual administration of punishment very uncertain. Data from the Home Office (1993) concerning the drop-outs from reported offences to convictions and prison sentences in the UK gloomily reflect on the application of the certainty principle of effective punishment. Estimating the rates of crime from official records and victim surveys, the Home Office reported that only 2% of offences result in a conviction and only one in seven of these results in a custodial sentence. This produces a probability of punishment (in so far as a prison sentence functions as a punisher, which is another question altogether) for a crime of one in 300. Punishment for crime is, therefore, very uncertain.

The experimental literature also indicates that for punishment to work it must occur in close temporal proximity to, if not immediately contingent upon, the target behaviour. This is the principle of celerity. Celerity is easy to manage under laboratory-controlled conditions, but impossible to achieve within the criminal justice system. For justice to prevail there has to be a delay between a suspect's arrest (which, of course, already involves a temporal gap from the crime) and their trial so that they can pursue legal assistance, and so that their lawyers can access the prosecutor's evidence and prepare the defence. Thus the celerity principle of punishment is rarely, if ever, met.

Essentially these observations leave us with just the severity of punishment as the only feature of consequences that the justice system can readily manipulate. The severity principle is that punishment must be sufficiently strong if it is to suppress a target behaviour. But what constitutes sufficiently strong? In the laboratory an experimenter can precisely manipulate the intensity of a punishment to determine its optimal level in controlling a particular behaviour. No such flexibility is available to the justice system, although there have been enough practical attempts to increase the severity of punishment to allow for reasonable conclusions. Studies of these manipulations of the consequences of crime, at least on convicted offenders, have been discussed under the general term 'deterrence'; we will follow that practice.

Deterrence stategies

Cullen and Gendreau (2000) note that imprisonment and other sanctions have long been considered effective deterrents for crime, a view that is often considered by policy-makers to be self-evident (De Jong 1997; Doob *et al*. 1998; Spellman 1995). Indeed both the Italian jurist and philosopher Cesare Beccaria (1738–94), and the English philosopher and social reformer Jeremy Bentham (1748–1832), considered the application of punishment for crimes to be the foundation of criminal justice. Deterrence in the form of punishment is thought to reduce crime both by sending a message to a particular offender (specific deterrence) and by alerting others, who may be contemplating offending, that they can expect to be punished (general deterrence). Some advocates of deterrence strategies have claimed that only severe sanctions will reduce future offending (Andenaes 1968).

These points of view notwithstanding, a sensible basis for punishing criminal behaviour should be based on the utilitarian principle that any particular response to crime should be implemented only if it is demonstrably effective in reducing the future offending of those so sanctioned, as well as reducing the crime rate in the general population. Evidence of either of these effects would justify, from a utilitarian viewpoint, the use of punitive consequences. There are, of course, ethical considerations that must also be considered. For example, much of the debate about the use of capital punishment revolves around ethical objections to such a final and irreversible response but, these concerns aside, the evidence indicates that capital punishment has no general deterrent effect (Bohm 1991). As we will see, the evidence on the use of other severe forms of punishment does not support the idea that this leads to reduced crime in terms of either general or specific deterrence effects.

General deterrence

As noted earlier, for punishment to be effective the consequences need to be certain, reasonably immediate and sufficiently severe. From the available evidence indicating a very low ratio of crimes to convictions (Home Office 1993), we can conclude that neither the certainty principle nor the celerity principle (immediacy of punishment) are achieved by the judicial response to crime.

For general deterrence to be effective, the certainty of the consequences must be at the forefront of the thinking processes of those contemplating offending. If such people do weigh up the possible consequences, and believe them to be certain, then perhaps they will be dissuaded from offending. But do potential offenders actually consider the possibility of being caught and punished? In fact studies of the self-reported thinking processes of people contemplating crime suggest that, while they may be sensitive to the immediate prospects of detection, they do not weigh at all heavily the potential of being punished; other factors are clearly given more weight.

Carroll (1982), for example, interviewed groups of offenders and non-offenders, asking them to consider opportunities to commit crimes that varied in the likely gains as well as in the probability and severity of the potential punishment. The responses of the subjects in both groups revealed that they paid far more attention to the possible gains they might derive from committing the crime, with little consideration being given to the likelihood or severity of punishment. In other similar studies (Carroll and Weaver 1986; Light, Nee and Ingham 1993; Morrison and O'Donnell 1994) much the same results were obtained. Identified offenders in these studies reported that prior to offending they were focused on making sure they achieved the goals of their crime with little or no reflection on the consequences of being caught. These studies included offenders who engaged in shoplifting, vehicle theft and armed robbery. The focus of each of these types of offenders was primarily on the execution of the crime.

In addition to these results, which rather dismally reflect on the possible influence of punishments on those considering crime, studies have also looked at general deterrence effects on other specific crimes. In a representative national sample of citizens in the US, Meier and Johnson (1979) found that those who reported using marijuana perceived the punishment for its use as disproportionately severe and yet there was no relationship between perceived severity of this punishment and use of marijuana. Grasmick and Bryjak (1980) asked subjects to indicate their involvement in eight different types of crime. These subjects were also asked to estimate the probability they would be caught if they committed the crime, their likelihood of being imprisoned if they were to be arrested, and the possible severity of problems they would endure if they were punished. Grasmick and Bryjak found that the perception of more severe punishment was associated with an increased probability of committing a crime; quite the opposite of what would be expected if severity was to act as a deterrent. However, when the severity of personal problems resulting from punishment was taken into account, those who perceived punishment to be highly likely were less likely to offend. Thus, those citizens who have the most to lose by being imprisoned (loss of job, reputation, family, friends, etc.) appear to be the most influenced by possible punishment in considering whether or not to commit a crime.

This demonstration of a general deterrent effect, however, is precisely on those citizens who are, in the first place, less likely to commit offences. Persistent criminals, on the other hand, appear less likely to be deterred from crime on the basis of considering the possibility of detection and punishment. Indeed, for some criminals being imprisoned may be seen as enhancing their reputation rather than diminishing it (Katz 1988). Consistent with the findings of Grasmick and Bryjak (1980) are the results of two other studies. While Borack (1998) found that random drug testing on US Navy personnel had a large suppressant effect on drug use, criminal sanctions had little or no effect on the drug use of homeless street youths (Baron and Kennedy 1998). Obviously, the naval personnel had a lot to lose but the street youngsters did not. Baron and Kennedy concluded that the 'perceptions of sanctions differ depending upon one's position in the social structure' (Baron and Kennedy 1998: 30). These general findings are consistent with our integrated theory presented in Chapter 2, in which we argue that a strong stake in social conformity is an important constraint on CSA offending, as it is with other offending.

Overall the evidence of increasing sanctions for crime is not at all encouraging for those who support the idea that such sanctions have a general deterrent effect. Antunes and Hunt (1973) claimed, on the basis of their consideration of the evidence available at that time, that as severity increased so did crime. Doob and Webster (2003), on the other hand, concluded from their review of the recent literature that varying the severity of sentences had no effect on crime rates. Consistent with Doob and Webster's view, Gendreau *et al.* (1993), in their comprehensive review, found no effect of more severe punishment on either the numbers of people imprisoned, the costs of crime or, importantly, on crime rates. Numerous reviewers (Andrews *et al.* 1990; Gendreau *et al.* 1993; McCord 2006; McGuire 2002; Ross 1992) have concluded that on the basis of the available evidence, severe punishments have, on the whole, had little or no general deterrent effects.

Specific deterrence

Even though the evidence indicates that increased severity does not effectively deter most people from committing crimes, it may be that severity has effects on those who receive the punishments: that is, do the certainty, celerity, severity and relevance of punishment produce specific deterrent effects? As we saw earlier, if people disposed to commit crimes perceive the risk of detection and punishment to be unlikely, we would not expect sanctions to reduce future crimes. However, experiencing punishment directly may change the perceptions and thought processes of convicted offenders when they subsequently consider offending. Such experiences may heighten their attention to potential sanctions as they consider offending, and thereby reduce re-offending. Indeed, it has been argued by advocates of the use of specific deterrence (van Hirsch *et al.* 1999) that incarceration produces such significant costs to offenders (Nagin 1998; Orsagh and Chen 1988) that a rational person would not engage in further crime.

Several authors have reported no relationship between increased severity of penalties and recidivism (Kershaw, Goodman and White 1999; Lloyd, Mair and Hough 1994). One of the problems with many studies of specific deterrence effects is that they have failed to control for differences among the comparison groups in terms of their likelihood of committing further crimes. As a result, apparent differences in the effects of sanctions may simply reflect differences in pre-existing risks of re-offending. Lloyd *et al.* (1994) conducted a study that controlled for differing risk levels of offenders who committed serious crimes. These offenders were given one of four types of sanctions: incarceration, community service orders, probation orders or probation with additional sanctions. What they observed was that the actual rates of re-offending matched the rates expected from a consideration of the offenders' prior offence records among all four groups. Lloyd *et al.* concluded that when account was taken of prior histories 'most of the differences between the disposal groups disappeared' (Lloyd *et al.* 1994: 43). Thus there was no evidence of a specific deterrent effect for these various levels of sanctions.

The lengths of prison sentences also bear either no relationship to recidivism rates or have a contrary effect; that is, recidivism rates increase with increasing severity of the sanctions. In their systematic and comprehensive meta-analytic review, Gendreau, Goggin and Cullen (1999) examined the post-release records of 68,248 offenders grouped into samples that were matched on five risk factors. They compared the rates of subsequent crimes for offenders given a prison sentence of an average of thirty months with those given sentences averaging seventeen months. Offenders who served longer sentences, contrary to the expectations of deterrence advocates, showed an increase, albeit small, in subsequent re-offending. Even in studies where convicted offenders were randomly allocated to different levels of sanctions, most report no effects on recidivism. Weisburd, Sherman and Petrosino (1990) examined sixty-eight such studies and found that forty-three reported no differences in re-offending across different severities of punishment; in only two studies were there better outcomes for more punitive sanctions. Most offenders, McGuire (2002) concluded, seem little affected by the sanctions imposed on them.

In terms of the evaluation of severer forms of sanctions, similar findings have been obtained. Studies of 'boot camps' conducted under the auspices of the US National Institute of Justice (see MacKenzie *et al.* 1995; MacKenzie and Souryal 1994) found no support for deterrence theory. These researchers compared boot camp inmates with other prisoners and with probationers at several sites. The impact, MacKenzie and Souryal (1994) observed, was negligible. They concluded that 'boot camp programmes did not reduce offender recidivism' (MacKenzie and Souryal 1994: 41). Quite similar findings were produced by evaluations of special prisons in the UK that were specifically designed to give offenders a 'short, sharp shock'. Thornton *et al*. (1984) found no discernible effect on reconviction rates of those who served time in these centres.

Some states in the US became concerned with costs of incarceration but at the same time viewed probationary sentences as too soft. As a result more severe and restrictive forms of community sentences were imposed and it was even asserted that these types of probation sanctions could be more punishing than prison (Petersilia 1990). The most common form of these responses was described as Intensive Supervision Programming (ISP) (Erwin 1986). These ISPs quickly spread throughout the US and were presumed to have not only retributive effects and to limit overcrowding in prisons, but also they were expected to reduce re-offending. ISPs involve marked increases in contact with supervisors, confining offenders to their homes, enforcing curfews, random drug testing, restitution by offenders to their victims, electronic monitoring and having the offender pay for their own supervision. An examination of their effects, however, involving over 19,000 offenders, revealed no impact at all on recidivism (Gendreau, Goggin and Fulton 2001). Other forms of community-based sanctions, such as electronic monitoring, have been shown to produce an increase in recidivism (Gendreau *et al*. 2001).

Overall, deterrence-based programmes have had either no impact or have led to an increase in recidivism rates (Andrews *et al*. 1990; Lipsey 1992, 1995). This is true of programmes that increase the length of prison sentences (Kershaw, Goodman and White 1999; McGuire 2002) as well as those that increase the severity of community sanctions (Gendreau *et al*. 2001). In fact, as Kershaw, Goodman and White (1999) concluded 'there is no discernible difference between the effect of immediate custody and community penalties on reconviction rates'.

Deterrence effects on youth offenders

Responses of the criminal justice systems in the US towards youth sexual offenders have changed in recent years. Previously such responses were guided by the idea that because they were so young these youth would be readily rehabilitated (Becker and Hicks 2003). Recently however the emphasis has shifted to a more punitive response. Registration and notification laws in the US have been applied to juvenile sexual offenders in at least twenty-seven states (Trivits and Repucci 2002). Pending US federal legislation will require all youth sexual offenders to have their names and other information on a national register for life (Reitzel and Carbonell 2006). There has also been an increase in the harshness of sentencing guidelines in the US with an increased rate of referrals from juvenile to adult courts for these young offenders (Becker and Hicks 2003). Matching this tendency, more youth sexual offenders are being committed to long-term, intensive treatment facilities (Veneziano and Veneziano 2002). The question is 'do these punitive responses to youth sexual offenders achieve their goals?' This is not an easy question to answer as most of these approaches are of quite recent vintage and there has not been as yet sufficient time to evaluate their effects as either specific or general deterrents. However, there are two pieces of evidence that do not encourage optimism about punitive effects with young offenders.

First, Dowden and Andrews (1999) report the results of two large-scale meta-analyses they conducted. In these meta-analyses 229 studies were evaluated including a significant number of studies of deterrence effects on youth offenders. The most relevant report for our present purposes was the observation of a negative effect of enhancing the fear of official punishment. That is, procedures that were meant to enhance the sensitivity of these youngsters to future punishment had the effect of increasing rather than decreasing subsequent crime. One procedure, in particular, that has been used in an effort to dissuade young offenders from continuing to offend was to have them speak with adult offenders imprisoned for life. It was thought that having these lifers explain their experiences in prison would scare the juveniles into giving up crime. These 'Scared Straight' programmes, as they were called, became quite popular for while in the US (Heerin and Shichor 1984), but appraisals of the effects revealed quite disappointing results. Studies reported either no effects on subsequent recidivism among participating youth (Buchner and Chesney-Lind 1983; Lewis 1983) or an increase in re-offending (Petrosino *et al.* 2003).

Conclusions regarding deterrence

The evidence appears to contradict assumptions that increasing the severity of punishment for crimes will result in either general or specific deterrent effects. This may be the result of the justice system having limited control over the certainty or immediacy of punishment such that the effects of severity become largely irrelevant. Also as we have seen the salience of punishment does not appear to be a significant part of the consideration offenders give to the planning of their crimes, although this appears to differ across potential offenders dependent upon the magnitude of their perception of the losses they will suffer by being convicted. Consistent with this idea is the observation that in those rare cases when sanctions are effective, it is the lowest risk offenders who are most influenced to give up crime (McCord 2006). Most importantly, Paternoster *et al.* (1983) point out that research indicates that formal deterrence strategies have weak, if any, effects on reducing crime as compared with developing positive attachments to social norms. The development of such positive social norms typically results from offenders being engaged in treatment, the effects of which consistently show that appropriate treatment reduces recidivism across a broad range of offending behaviours (Andrews and Bonta 2003; Gendreau *et al.* 2006; Lipton *et al.* 2002), both with adult (Redondo, Sanchez-Meca and Garrido 2002) and with youth offenders (Lipsey 1992). In the next chapter we will consider treatment programmes for offenders in detail, but before that we consider the evidence for the effectiveness of incapacitation approaches.

Incapacitation strategies

Alongside deterrence and rehabilitation, incapacitation is the third utilitarian goal of criminal justice interventions. Incapacitation aims to reduce crime by removing criminal opportunities for individual offenders, or perhaps more accurately by removing offenders themselves from the opportunity to commit crimes. Historically, banishment, exile, transportation, mutilation and death have been used for the purposes of incapacitation. Nowadays imprisonment is perhaps the most readily recognised method. In the present section we consider two approaches that have been used specifically for sexual offenders, and particularly for CSA offenders: chemical castration and 'dangerous offender' laws that aim to imprison persistent sexual offenders for indefinite periods.

Chemical castration

One incapacitation strategy that has been suggested particularly for CSA offenders, usually in the context of sentencing, is so-called 'chemical castration'. Physical castration refers to the removal of the testes, which are the bodies that produce testosterone in males. As we explained in Chapter 2, it has long been known that testosterone mediates sex and aggression, so it has been thought that eliminating testosterone would eliminate sexual drive and thereby eliminate sexual offending. Evidence of the effectiveness of physical castration strongly suggests that it does reduce, but does not eliminate, sexual recidivism (Bradford 1990). Unfortunately physical castration and its pharmacological analogue, chemical castration, have a variety of problematic side-effects and have associated ethical problems (Glaser 2003; Mellela, Travin and Cullen 1989). In any event most Western countries no longer permit physical castration except as a life-saving intervention (e.g. as a treatment for testicular cancer).

Chemical castration involves the administration of an anti-androgen or hormonal agent that is known to affect the production of testosterone. The administration of these agents may have the goal of eliminating the production of testosterone, or reducing it to levels sufficiently low (usually near the bottom end of the normal range) that the person can readily exercise control over their sexual urges, which are typically less frequent and of lower intensity than before the intervention (see Bradford 2000).

The appropriate treatment use of pharmacological agents with sexual offenders is to use these agents to lower, not eliminate, sexual drive and then only with those sexual offenders who clearly have problems of control over the expression of their sexual interests. There are, however, a very small number of sexual offenders who may require chemical castration. Those sexual offenders who are at the top of the highest risk group and whose offences involve deliberate and serious physical harm to the victim (e.g. sexual sadists), are the only ones for whom chemical castration seems possibly appropriate. Bradford (2000) has described an algorithm for the administration of pharmacological agents in the treatment of sexual offenders, in which the most dangerous offenders (i.e. those with maximum likelihood to both offend again and to cause serious harm) are said to require such high doses of an anti-androgen or hormonal agent, as to produce chemical castration.

All too often, in the discussions in courts, these facts and suggestions are not heard, and as a result decisions are made that are not empirically based. The implementation of chemical castration is too frequently driven by either a desire to placate the public or in ignorance of the issues surrounding the use of pharmacological agents with sexual offenders. In the former case, chemical castration may be seen as a form of incapacitation that is expected to also have both specific and general deterrent effects. The evidence suggests that, properly implemented, pharmacological agents can be useful in the treatment of sexual offenders (Bradford 1995, 2000; Glaser 2003) as an adjunct to psychological treatment. There is, however, no evidence that chemical castration (i.e. the total elimination of testosterone) has any deterrent effects.

Dangerous sexual offender laws

Some sexual offenders, including some CSA offenders, are considered to be so dangerous that some jurisdictions have enacted specific laws to confine them beyond what would otherwise be a normal prison sentence for their crimes. In Canada the designation 'Dangerous Offender' can be applied to sexual offenders deemed so dangerous to public safety that they require special custodial sentences. A sexual offence that would otherwise result in a lengthy sentence can be overridden by Canadian prosecutors applying to the court for the application of the Dangerous Offender status. If successful the offender serves an indeterminate term of custody and is unlikely to be released until, on average, seventeen years has been served. Clearly the aim of this legislation is to deal with offenders when it is believed the usual laws governing sentencing would not provide sufficient protection to the public. The task facing the prosecutor is to demonstrate that the specific offender meets the criteria of presenting an imminent danger to the public. This requires a demonstration that the offender is at high risk to re-offend and that if he does so he will cause serious harm to the victim. A significant number of CSA offenders have been deemed to meet these criteria over the years, and very few have yet been released. This is true of similar laws in other countries.

In the US, many states have enacted what are called 'Sexually Violent Predator' (SVP) statutes (Schlank 2006). The procedures and rules determining whether or not a sexual offender meets criteria for SVP status are similar to those in Canada governing applications for Dangerous Offender status. However, the applications occur at quite different points in the judicial process. In Canada the applications occur immediately after the offender has been found guilty and prior to sentencing, whereas in the US the application process does not begin until the offender is about to complete his full sentence in prison. Similar provisions for post-sentence supervision or detention are now becoming available in New Zealand and in a number of Australian states.

In the US, as sexual offenders near the end of their sentence, prison authorities are required to identify those who they deem to be dangerous, and refer them to the District Attorney. The District Attorney then has the offender assessed by experts and on the basis of the assessment, decides to proceed or not with the SVP application. Of course, the offender's lawyer will also call experts in an attempt to refute the District Attorney's position. Once an SVP application is successful, the offender is placed in a special highly secure setting where he will be provided with treatment, the intention of which is to reduce his risk/dangerousness, so that he can be considered for release. Again the aim of these statutes is to reduce the threat to public safety posed by these offenders. Unfortunately, very few states of the US provide effective treatment for incarcerated sexual offenders (Shaw and Funderburk 1999), so potentially dangerous sexual offenders can do little or nothing to reduce their risk prior to being considered for SVP status. Despite this, and other issues, the US Supreme Court found these laws to meet constitutional requirements (*Kansas vs Hendricks* 1997). Just as with Canada's Dangerous Offender status, very few offenders meeting SVP rules are ever released despite the fact that extensive and comprehensive treatment programmes are in place in all SVP institutions.

There are numerous problems with these types of laws although most practitioners will readily agree that the behaviour of some sexual offenders, including some CSA offenders, is such that a normal prison sentence does not provide suitable protection to the public. In addition, some sexual offenders who enter prison-based treatment either do not participate effectively or are resistant to the best efforts of the therapists. In these circumstances it was thought necessary to create special laws or procedures to incapacitate these offenders.

One major problem with these laws concerns the ability of experts to determine future risk and, particularly, future dangerousness. Judgements of risk, even if they are based on sound evidence, simply indicate the probability that offenders of specific types will re-offend; they do not tell us what an individual might do or what harm he might cause. For example, a repeat exhibitionist with many victims over many years, is very likely to re-offend in the absence of treatment, but, without wishing to deny the distress he might cause to his victims, acts of exposure are not usually considered as devastating as are brutal rapes or violent acts of CSA. While research has provided reasonably adequate actuarially-based risk assessment tools, no satisfactory measure of the potential to harm has yet been developed.

Measuring risk

Doren (2002, 2006) has provided descriptions of the development of currently available risk assessment instruments. These instruments have all been developed in much the same way and follow procedures similar to those used by insurance companies. Insurance companies determine their fees for car insurance, for example, by examining the accident histories of several thousand drivers over many years. From these actuarial data, the insurance companies calculate the accident risk of drivers in various categories. The records indicate that the category of males under the age of twenty-five years has the greatest number of accidents and these accidents typically result in greater harm and, therefore, greater cost to the insurance companies. Accordingly, young male drivers are charged the highest car insurance fees. This may seem unfair to those young males who drive very carefully but unfortunately for them, the insurance companies cannot afford to take risks. The same is true for decisions about the disposition of sexual offenders; courts take the view that if an offender has the same characteristics as a group that has been shown to have a high number of recidivists, he should be treated as if he is at high risk.

Just as the insurance companies do, researchers developing risk assessment instruments have collected data on many sexual offenders and tracked their offending histories over many years. These data provide the bases for determining actuarially, the re-offence rates of various categories of offenders. From these studies, several different actuarially-based risk assessment measures have been developed and it has been claimed that they all produce much the same estimates of future risk (Hanson and Morton-Bourgon 2004). However, in a recent examination of the accuracy of five different actuarial risk instruments in predicting actual re-offences among sexual offenders, Barbaree, Langton and Peacock (2006) found significant differences across these commonly used instruments in predicting actual re-offences of sexual offenders. These findings indicate that clinicians attempting to assess risk will have to make a decision about which instrument is best suited to the purpose of the assessment, and for the client population under consideration. Fortunately, Doren (2002) has provided a multidimensional model of risk that guides clinicians in how to interpret differences among outcomes from different actuarial instruments.

Scores on these actuarial instruments should be seen as risk assessments rather than as predictors of risk. What the score does is indicate to which group of sexual offenders this particular client belongs. His scores can be seen to match that group of offenders for whom the actuarial data indicates either a low, moderate or high likelihood of committing another sexual crime. So it is inaccurate to say that, based on these measures, a particular offender has a low, moderate or high risk to re-offend. It is more accurate to say that he belongs to a category of sexual offenders who have been shown to have average re-offence rates that are deemed to be low, moderate or high. While a specific percentage (between, say, 40% or 50%) of sexual offenders in the so-called high-risk category are known to re-offend, we cannot say that a particular offender has the same percentage risk of re-offending; this is an error that some practitioners fall into driven, at least in part, by lawyers or judges demanding a specific statement about an individual. What courts often seem to demand is a precise statement about the probability that this person will or will not re-offend. In the high-risk category, as we have seen, a substantial proportion re-offend, but a reasonable number (even a high number if we are concerned about false positives) do not. Thus, while a specific offender may have the characteristics (e.g. past offence history features, dysfunctional lifestyle features, deviant sexual interests) that match those in the actuarially-determined high-risk group, he may never re-offend even without further interventions or sanctions. These are not problems that are easily explained to non-experts, and nor are they easily overcome.

At present the available risk assessment instruments have their limitations, not the least of which is their failure to indicate the likely harm that might befall a victim. One actuarial instrument, however, might assist in establishing likelihood of harm. The *Violence Risk Appraisal Guide* (VRAG), developed by Webster *et al.* (1994), is an actuarially-based instrument that specifically describes the features of men who belong to categories of risk for committing further violent acts. These categories are similarly said to indicate low, moderate or high probabilities of committing further violent offences. Like the risk instruments designed specifically for sexual offenders, the data on this scale have been replicated across several independent samples. Indeed Hanson and Morton-Bourgon (2004) found both the VRAG, and its sexual offender version (*Sexual Offender Risk Assessment Guide* [SORAG]), to accurately predict violent recidivism.

In SVP hearings, the laws not only demand the use of actuarial instruments to determine the risk category to which an individual CSA offender belongs, but they also require that the candidate for SVP status meets diagnostic criteria for a mental disorder. While in many commitment hearings various diagnoses are applied to particular individuals, the most common are one or another of the paraphilic disorders; in fact, some states require a diagnosis of paraphilia. This is particularly problematic since the reliability of any of the diagnoses of the paraphilias is, at best, questionable (see Marshall 1997, 2006, in press; and O'Donohue, Regev and Hagstrom 2000, for discussions). A specifically relevant study by Levenson (2004) demonstrates these problems.

In Florida SVP hearings, two independent clinicians are required to assess each person who has been referred to the courts to determine whether or not he meets criteria for indeterminate confinement. Among their other assigned tasks, these two clinicians are required to independently provide a diagnosis or set of diagnoses for the candidate. Since their diagnoses will be subject to rigorous scrutiny by the court and challenged by the defence attorney, we can expect the clinicians to very carefully arrive at their diagnoses. Levenson (2004) was able to obtain the court records of these diagnoses applied to 295 consecutive cases from July 2000 to June 2001. Comparing these independent diagnoses, Levenson found the inter-diagnostician agreement to be unacceptably low for even the category 'any paraphilia' (*kappa* = 0.47). For paedophilia it was unacceptably low for such an important decision (*kappa* = 0.65) and for sexual sadism it was similarly unacceptable (*kappa* = 0.30). Marshall *et al.* (2002) found that even 'internationally-renowned experts' in sexual sadism were unable to agree on the diagnosis in twelve detailed cases (*kappa* = 0.14).

While there appears to be some reasonable grounds for concern about how justice systems and sentencing laws fail to deal effectively with the highest risk and most dangerous CSA offenders, the development of Dangerous Offender laws or SVP legislation has not satisfactorily solved the problem. Until such time as various risk assessment instruments produce the same result, or until a specific risk instrument is shown to be superior to all others, clinicians undertaking risk assessments will have to choose among the various instruments guided by something like Doren's (2002) multidimensional model. Even then they will presently not have available any way of reliably estimating dangerousness. Finally, until the diagnostic reliability problems have been resolved, these laws will inevitably function with a high error rate. We have seen too many CSA offenders whose history reflects a dangerous level of behaviour overlooked by these laws, but the primary error has been for the courts to be far too over-inclusive by designating lower-risk offenders as dangerous.

Summary

Criminal justice interventions encompass the activities of police, the courts and corrections. Police activities are generally directed towards crime detection and investigation. Evidence concerning the effectiveness of policing in crime prevention suggests that there may be little to be gained in sexual abuse prevention by increasing police numbers, increasing random patrols, increasing police response times or giving increased attention to reactive arrest policies. On the other hand, sexual abuse prevention may be enhanced by focusing police attention selectively on persistent CSA offenders, by police and child protection authorities ensuring that they treat those suspected of committing CSA offences fairly and humanely (i.e. avoiding confrontational and punitive approaches), by generating intelligence about and directing police attention to possible sexual abuse 'hot spots', and by adopting 'problem-oriented policing' methods.

Leaving aside offender rehabilitation, which we will deal with separately in the next chapter, the main utilitarian goals of the courts and corrections are deterrence and incapacitation. Evidence from psychological experiments shows that, to deter a target behaviour, punishment must be perceived as certain, immediate, of sufficient severity and relevant. Because of delays and uncertainties associated with the punishments administered by criminal justice systems, and because of doubts about the relevance of criminal justice punishments particularly for committed offenders, the only element of effective punishment that can be readily controlled by criminal justice systems is severity. Unfortunately evidence suggests that, in the absence of certainty, immediacy and relevance, the influence of the severity of court-imposed punishments is generally negligible. In some cases, increasing the severity of court-imposed punishments can have the unintended effect of increasing re-offending.

Selective incapacitation policies targeting the highest risk offenders rely on assumptions that high-risk offenders can be reliably identified (and conversely that low-risk offenders can also be reliably identified). In practice, problems with diagnostic (e.g. concerning the presence of sexual disorders) and prognostic reliability (e.g. concerning the probability of recidivism) lead to large proportions of false-positive and false-negative predictions about risk and dangerousness. Thus many high-risk CSA offenders will avoid being targeted, and many low-risk offenders will be unnecessarily targeted, by selective incapacitation policies.

Chapter 6

Treating adult and adolescent offenders

In this chapter we consider how the treatment of adult and adolescent offenders can contribute to the prevention of CSA, by reducing recidivism among known CSA offenders. We begin by outlining the general principles that have emerged from a large volume of research that has sought to answer the question 'what works?' in offender rehabilitation. We then consider how these principles may be applied to the treatment of adult and adolescent CSA offenders. For the purposes of illustration we refer particularly to how these principles are applied in Marshall and his colleagues' work with adult sexual offenders in Canada, and in Smallbone and his colleagues' work with adolescent sexual offenders in Australia. These two programmes are very different from each other, although both are guided by similar theoretical principles. Neither is necessarily representative of mainstream treatment approaches for adult and adolescent CSA offenders. Rather, both represent innovative, evidence-based approaches in their respective fields. As numerous evaluation studies have attested, Marshall *et al.*'s programme makes the stronger claim for reducing recidivism among its sexual offender clients. Smallbone *et al.*'s programme is newer, and has yet to demonstrate its effectiveness in terms of recidivism outcomes. We conclude the chapter by reviewing evidence more generally for the effectiveness of treatment programmes for adult and adolescent CSA offenders.

General principles

A large body of research has accumulated on the effects of treatment targeting an array of offender problems, including violence and anger management, substance misuse and dependence, criminal thinking, impulsivity, mental and emotional disorders, coping skills, fire setting and sexual offending (Hollin 2001). Treatment outcome studies have been subject to meta-analytic reviews, with the better reviews restricting evaluations to those studies meeting reasonable methodological standards. From these higher quality meta-analyses it is apparent that treatment can reduce subsequent re-offence rates among diverse groups of adolescent and adult offenders (Andrews and Bonta 2003; Andrews *et al.* 1990; Davidson *et al.* 1984; Garrett 1985; Gendreau and Goggin 1996; Lipsey 1992; McGuire 2002; Lösel 1995; Redondo, Sanchez-Meca and Garrido 1999). It is also clear that it is cognitive-behavioural approaches for adult offenders, and cognitive-behavioural and multisystemic approaches for adolescent offenders, that generate these reductions in recidivism. Other approaches have negligible or negative effects. For example, nondirective, unstructured treatment approaches, shock probation and so-called 'Scared Straight' approaches, and wilderness challenge programmes, have consistently been found not to reduce recidivism (MacKenzie 2002).

The most important information derived from these meta-analyses, aside from the fact that they show that treatment can reduce recidivism, concerns the identification of what have become known as the *principles of effective offender treatment* (Andrews and Bonta 2003). The most important of these are the risk, needs and responsivity principles. The *risk principle* asserts that the greatest reductions in recidivism result from allocating resources in such a way that those offenders having the highest risk to re-offend are provided with the most intensive treatment. Of the three principles, the *risk principle* has shown the weakest effect size ($r = .07$), but this appears to be due to the varying bases across studies in the measures of future risk (Smith, Goggin and Gendreau 2002). It is important to note here that, although treating low-risk offenders may reassure the public that maximum efforts are being made to reduce re-offending, such treatment may not produce significant effects. This is partly due to the low base-rate of re-offending among low-risk offenders, which makes it statistically difficult to demonstrate any effect, but it may also be because of a tendency among some therapists to over-treat low-risk offenders. Over-treating low-risk offenders may inadvertently increase re-offence rates (Andrews *et al.* 1990), perhaps because overly intensive treatment convinces these low-risk offenders that their problems are far more serious and extensive than they believed.

The *needs principle* directs treatment providers to target those needs (so-called criminogenic needs) that have been identified in research as reliable predictors of re-offending. Until recently, risk assessment instruments were based on features that are static and unchangeable (e.g. past offending history). More recently, dynamic (i.e. potentially modifiable) risk predictors (e.g. antisocial beliefs, impulsivity, poor coping skills and relationship skills) have been identified. When these dynamic risk factors (or criminogenic needs) are appropriately addressed in treatment, reductions in future offending are significant (effect size $r = .20$; Andrews and Bonta 2003).

The final principle, the *responsivity principle*, directs treatment providers to attend to individual differences in their clients and to adjust interventions to the needs of specific client groups. For example, programmes for low intellectual functioning offenders should be adapted to the needs of these clients; such programmes should provide concrete examples, be repetitive and emphasise noncognitive (e.g. visual) ways of representing important concepts. In addition, the *responsivity principle* requires that treatment providers adjust their approach in a way that allows them to engage with the offender's learning style and in ways that accommodate day-to-day fluctuations in the offender's mood and motivation. Andrews and Bonta (2003) showed that appropriate adherence to the *responsivity principle* produced significant reductions in re-offending (effect size, $r = .19$).

Programmes that adhere to all three of these principles produce the most impressive reductions in recidivism (effect size, $r = .28$), whereas those that do not adhere to these principles produce negligible effects (effect size, $r = .05$) (Andrews and Bonta 2003). Although community-based programmes are generally more effective, both community-based programmes and residential or institutional programmes have been shown to produce significant positive effects (effect size, $r = .29$ and $r = .19$ respectively). The bases for these effects, other than adherence to the three principles, primarily involve programme characteristics. We have already noted the relative failure of approaches based on non-behavioural principles, but there are other features that influence outcome as well. The use of effective principles of reinforcement, for example, results in significant positive effects (effect size, $r = .24$), as does the presence in the treatment providers of good quality relationship skills (effect size, $r = .27$). Other behavioural principles, such as effective modelling by the therapist and structuring the skills training also contribute to reducing recidivism, as does the appropriate selection, training and supervision of staff (Gendreau *et al.* 2006).

Treatment for adult child sexual abuse offenders

Although there were many attempts over the last 100 years or more to apply treatment methods meant to reduce re-offending in identified CSA offenders (Laws and Marshall 2003) it was only towards the end of the 1960s and beginning of the 1970s that a systematic, research-based approach was developed (see Marshall and Laws 2003). Prior to 1970, the favoured approach was based on a simple conditioning model (e.g. McGuire, Carlisle and Young 1965). This model suggested that as a result of masturbating to images or fantasies of sex with a child, the future offender developed an irresistible urge to sexually abuse children. The exclusive target in treatment implied by this model was the fantasies of sex with children and the sexual arousal evoked by such images or thoughts (Bond and Evans 1967). Procedures were developed to achieve this goal (Abel, Levis and Clancy 1970; Marshall 1973, 1979), to which were later added procedures to enhance sexual interest in age-appropriate adult partners (Marquis 1970). However, it soon became apparent that these offenders had additional problems that needed to be addressed if treatment was to be successful (Barlow 1974; Marshall 1971). Over the subsequent years programmes for adult sexual offenders expanded the treatment targets (Abel, Blanchard and Becker 1978; Maletzky 1991; Marshall *et al.* 1983) in response to a broadening base of research findings.

From the 1970s on, the favoured approach to the treatment of these offenders has been group-based cognitive behavioural therapy (CBT) (Marshall and Fernandez 1998), and this has been complemented since the early 1980s by relapse prevention strategies (Marques 1982; Marques *et al.* 1989; Pithers *et al.* 1983) derived from Marlatt's work with addictive behaviors (Marlatt 1982). More recently, in response to Ward and Hudson's (Ward 1999; Ward and Hudson 2000) self-regulation model, the CBT approach has been expanded to include an emphasis on emotional expression during treatment so that both emotional and behavioural self-regulation can be acquired (see e.g. Marshall *et al.* 2006). In response to a series of criticisms by Ward and his colleagues (Ward and Hudson 1996; Ward, Hudson and Marshall 1994; Ward, Hudson and Siegert 1995) the relapse prevention approach has been markedly modified, although some elements have been retained (Laws, Hudson and Ward 2000). As a result a shift has occurred away from a standardised, modularised approach to one that is more flexible (Laws and Ward 2006), that involves collaboration between the client and therapist (Shingler and Mann 2006), that focuses on the development of the skills, emotions and attitudes necessary to meet a broad range of needs (Ward and Marshall 2004, in press), and that places far more emphasis on the therapists' skills (Serran *et al*. 2003).

Following developments in the more general field of offender rehabilitation, treatment programmes for sexual offenders have increasingly (but not universally) adopted the principles of effective offender treatment, namely the *risk*, *needs* and *responsivity* principles. Below we consider how these principles are currently applied in the treatment of adult CSA offenders, with particular reference to how this is done in Marshall *et al*.'s (2006) programme.

Risk principle

Marshall *et al*.'s (2006) programme operates under the auspices of the Correctional Service of Canada (CSC). The CSC has developed a model for the delivery of treatment programmes aimed at various problems (e.g. anger management, domestic violence, substance abuse, reasoning and rehabilitation, and sexual offending). This model is, at least in part, based on Andrews and Bonta's (1994, 1998, 2003) principles of effective offender treatment. Two of these principles (risk and need) guide the allocation of offenders to programmes, while an additional principle concerns institutional management and escape risk (both based on past history) and determines placement of offenders to different levels of security.

All sexual offenders entering the CSC system are thoroughly assessed at the induction centre before being sent to their 'home' prison. The results of these evaluations determine each sexual offender's risk to re-offend at three levels of intensity (high, moderate and low), and offenders are allocated to one of these levels based on their risk to re-offend and their treatment needs. Programmes for high-risk/needs sexual offenders target a broad range of issues and involve the offenders in at least three three-hour group sessions per week over a period of nine months. Additional individual sessions are programmed when necessary. Moderate-risk/needs sexual offenders are involved in two or three three-hour sessions per week over a four-month period covering much the same issues as the high-risk/needs programme but typically in less depth. For low-risk/needs sexual offenders treatment is limited to two three-hour sessions per week for three months; again there are similar targets but they are dealt with in less depth. In the Ontario region of CSC prisons, owing to the large number of sexual offenders in the low–moderate and moderate–high-risk ranges, separate programmes for offenders in these two groups have been established rather than placing them all in one, perhaps overly broad, programme.

This allocation to programmes reflects the need to distribute resources where the evidence suggests best meets the goal of maximising the reduction in re-offending. Evaluations of these programmes indicate that the high-risk/needs programme (Looman, Abracen and Nicholaichuk 2000), the moderate–high-risk/needs programme (Barbaree, Langton and Peacock 2004), and the low–moderate-risk/ needs programme (Marshall *et al.* 2006) are all effective in reducing post-release recidivism.

In Ontario, sexual offenders may also be referred to community-based programmes. Referrals to community-based programmes come from various sources, with a number coming from child protection agencies. Offenders referred from child protection agencies are often non-adjudicated and include some high-risk sexual offenders. Similarly some referrals come from parole and probation officers and included in this group are some sexual offenders who did not receive prison-based treatment (either because their prison sentences were too short or because they refused treatment). Again some of these are high-risk/needs offenders. Community programmes in Ontario therefore deal with sexual offenders at all levels of risk and needs, although the overall distribution is towards the lower end compared with prison-based programmes. An evaluation of 126 CSA offenders (sixty-eight treated vs fifty-eight untreated) from an Ontario outpatient community programme followed for an average of four years, revealed positive benefits for treatment (Marshall and Barbaree 1988). Nonfamilial CSA offenders who received treatment in this community programme re-offended at a rate of 5.1%, whereas 16.5% of the untreated nonfamilial offenders re-offended. Among familial CSA offenders, 2.6% of the treated subjects, and 8.3% of the untreated offenders, re-offended. Clearly Canadian-based treatment programmes for adult CSA offenders are effective whether this treatment takes place in prisons or in a community outpatient setting.

Needs principle

Meta-analytic reviews of the predictors of recidivism among (mainly adult) sexual offenders (e.g. Hanson and Bussiere 1998) have identified a large number of potential criminogenic needs specific to this offender population. Because no single predictor identified in these reviews has been shown to have more than modest predictive validity, there have been attempts to combine groups of predictors in ways that might be useful in applied settings (e.g. for the purposes of assessing short-term treatment effects). One such scheme, developed by Hanson and Harris (2000), is known as the STABLE. The STABLE includes six sets of dynamic risk factors (or criminogenic needs): social influences, intimacy deficits, sexual self-regulation, general self-regulation, offence-related attitudes and co-operation with supervision or remediation efforts. Consistent with the *needs* principle, schemes like the STABLE assist treatment providers to concentrate their attention on empirically identified criminogenic needs, as well as providing a standard method of assessing changes in these needs over the course of treatment.

In practice, treatment programmes must attend not only to empirically-identified treatment targets, but also to the therapeutic processes and techniques employed to engage with the offender and deliver treatment in a way that maximises its positive effects. Marshall *et al.*'s (2006) programme focuses on seven generic treatment targets: 1) acceptance of responsibility; 2) identification of offence pathways; 3) development of effective coping skills; 4) emotional self-management; 5) social and relationship skills; 6) generating appropriate sexual interests; and 7) development of self-management plans. The third, fourth, fifth and sixth of these targets (coping skills, emotional self-management, relationship skills and sexual interests) relate explicitly to known criminogenic needs for sexual offenders.

Training in appropriate coping skills, as well as developing an effective general coping style, is aimed at reducing the emotional ups-and-downs that CSA offenders typically experience and that may put them at risk to re-offend. Similarly, teaching them the skills, attitudes, perceptions and self-confidence necessary to develop effective adult relationships (romantic attachments and friendships), should also reduce stress in their lives as well as equip them to appropriately meet their needs for companionship, intimacy and sex. The provision of effective relationship skills also provides the offender with the chance to develop friends who will support him in his efforts to stop offending. Indeed, the provision of a post-treatment support group has been shown to enhance the effects of treatment (Barrett, Wilson and Long 2003; Stirpe, Wilson and Long 2001). CSA offenders frequently describe their inappropriate contacts with children in ways that suggest they are seeking comfort, self-reassurance and intimacy, as well as sex, with their victims, and many express reservations about fear of, or dissatisfaction with, adult romantic relationships. Consequently enhancing their adult intimate relationship skills is seen as crucial to effective treatment with these clients.

Assisting adult CSA offenders to develop effective self-management skills can build greater self-confidence. This is important. Poor emotional self-regulation is a predictor of offending (Hanson and Harris 2000), so its gradual development not only reduces risk but also facilitates treatment engagement. According to our integrated theory, positive emotional self-regulation is a key self-restraint mechanism, which we would expect to restrain a broad range of irresponsible social conduct, including CSA offending. Although there are specific strategies that encourage the development of self-regulation (Baumeister and Vohs 2004), unless emotional-regulation is developed behaviour-regulation will remain impaired (Gross 2007). Accordingly, in Marshall *et al.*'s programme a focus on the appropriate expression of emotions is maintained throughout treatment. All of these processes are also aimed at increasing the offender's acceptance of responsibility, and continue to be explored over the whole course of the treatment programme.

Although the modification of sexual interests (i.e. enhancement of sexual interests in adults and reductions or elimination of sexual interests in children) was the centrepiece of early treatment for CSA offenders, this has now been relegated to a more minor role. However, it is clear that some adult CSA offenders (particularly those who abuse other people's children and more particularly those who target male children) do experience persistent sexual arousal to children, and some (but fortunately few) display little sexual interest in adults (Marshall and Fernandez 2003). It is, therefore, necessary to employ procedures specifically to modify these responses for a small number of offenders. Various behavioural procedures have been developed to achieve this goal. Aversive procedures are rarely used anymore, presumably because they are likely to negatively affect the therapist–client relationship. Alternative procedures have been developed, with masturbatory reconditioning procedures having been shown to be effective (Laws and Marshall 1991). These procedures require the client to replace children with adults in his masturbatory fantasies, and to then, immediately after ejaculation, rehearse in detail any and all fantasies about children for approximately ten minutes (Marshall, O'Brien and Marshall, in press). While these procedures appear to be effective in many cases (Laws and Marshall 1991), there are certainly failures with this and pharmacological interventions may be the best recourse for these clients. There are also some clients for whom pharmacological interventions are the preferred strategy. Most treatment programmes introduce pharmacological strategies when behavioural procedures fail, but they also use medications for those who have extensive numbers of victims over several years (i.e. the true paedophiles) and with those who have enacted sadistic behaviours. Hormonal treatments (e.g. medroxyprogesterone acetate, or luteinizing hormone/releasing hormone) or an antiandrogen (e.g. cyproterone acetate) have been shown to be effective with such clients (Bradford 2000). Selective serotonin reuptake inhibitors (SSRIs) appear to have value with sexually preoccupied offenders (Greenberg and Bradford 1997).

The remaining targets in Marshall *et al.*'s programme involve assessment and therapeutic engagement processes (acceptance of responsibility, offence pathways), and planning for an offence-free future (development of self-management plans). These targets do not identify common additional problems (e.g. substance abuse) that may need additional interventions, and nor do they specify the very important therapeutic process issues that, as we have pointed out, markedly influence the effectiveness of sexual offender treatment.

Responsivity principle

As we saw in Chapter 1, adult CSA offenders are heterogeneous along several dimensions. Some have offended against family members, while others have abused children outside the family. Most know their victims prior to the onset of sexual abuse. Some offenders have selected boys as their targets, others have abused girls, and some have offended against both boys and girls. Pre-pubescent children are the targets of some CSA offenders (often, but not always accurately, called 'paedophiles'), while others (sometimes called 'hebephiles') have offended against post-pubescent children. Although recidivism base-rates vary according to these dimensions, these diverse offence targets appear to influence neither treatment needs nor treatment outcomes. Marshall *et al.* (2006) found no differences in outcome across the various types of CSA offenders and yet essentially the same programme was offered to all these offender-types. Of course, in keeping with the *responsivity principle*, the therapists in Marshall's programme adjust their approach, but not the content of treatment, to fit the idiosyncratic features of each client.

The therapeutic skills of those providing treatment needs to be ensured by careful selection, training and supervision. It has been demonstrated quite clearly that process issues in the treatment of sexual offenders, which are all dependent on the therapist's skills and style, are significantly related to effective reductions in post-discharge re-offending (Marshall and Serran 2004). In their studies of the influence of therapist features in adult sexual offender treatment, Marshall and his colleagues (Marshall *et al.* 2002, 2003a) demonstrated that therapists who were empathetic, warm and rewarding, and who also guided clients in the direction of prosocial attitudes and behaviours, produced the greatest positive changes on all treatment targets. Those therapists who adopted a strongly confrontational style, however, failed to produce any treatment benefits. Indeed, confrontational therapists appear to produce either lip-service agreement among offenders with what the therapist demands, or hostile opposition and withdrawal. Drapeau (2005) examined the attitudes of sexual offenders undergoing treatment and found that they identified as effective and helpful essentially the same therapist features as Marshall *et al.* reported.

Group psychotherapy appears to be the most effective method of treatment for adult sexual offenders. An examination of the characteristic features of treatment groups in sexual offender programmes was reported by Beech and his colleagues (Beech and Fordham 1997; Beech and Hamilton-Giachritsis 2005). Their studies revealed that groups that were cohesive (i.e. all participants worked together and supported one another) and expressive (i.e. each client actively participated and was appropriately emotionally expressive) produced significant positive gains, while groups that did not have these features failed to achieve the goals of the programme.

Underpinning these positive therapist features and group process features is the ability of the therapist to adjust to the ever-changing characteristics of the group and of each individual (Marshall *et al.* 2003b). Flexibility is a well-established feature of all types of effective psychotherapy with all types of client populations (Corsini and Wedding 1995; Kottler, Sexton and Whiston 1994). This need for flexibility on the part of the therapist is consistent with Andrews and Bonta's (2003) *responsivity* principle. Both of these important therapist features (i.e. flexibility and adherence to the *responsivity principle*) are achievable only when the therapist is allowed to exercise them. This may seem so obvious as to be tautological, but apparently it is not evident to the designers of many sexual offender programmes. Many sexual offender programmes are instead guided by highly detailed treatment manuals that are often so restrictive of therapeutic flexibility that they are more accurately described as 'psychoeducational' (Green 1995) than as 'psychotherapeutic'. It would be surprising if psychoeducational programmes generated much in the way of beneficial changes, and certainly the evidence suggests that some sexual offender programme evaluations have shown either no benefits or at best marginal effect sizes (Hanson *et al.* 2002; Lösel and Schmucker 2005). Indeed, the overall effect size for sexual offender treatment programmes (essentially the difference in post-release recidivism rates between treated and untreated groups, or between actual and expected recidivism rates for a group of treated clients), while statistically significant, is within the small range (i.e. effect size, $r = .28$).

Marshall and his colleagues have consistently argued for a more flexible and positive approach to the treatment of sexual offenders that includes an emphasis on therapist qualities and the development of an effective group climate (Marshall *et al.* 2006; Marshall *et al.* in press; Marshall *et al.* 2005). In this programme, the therapists do not adhere to a detailed manual, but rather follow a 'guide' that specifies treatment targets and suggests some procedures. Weekly case conferences keep therapists from straying too far from this guide but these conferences also encourage innovations. One aspect of these innovations has been the progressive move over the past twenty years in Marshall's programme to reduce the emphasis on offenders developing plans to avoid future risks. The shift has been towards developing skills and attitudes (both towards others and towards themselves) that would allow clients to meet their needs in prosocial ways, thereby reducing their need to offend. While this is in line with Ward's (Ward and Stewart 2003a, 2003b) 'Good Lives Model', Marshall's programme does not use that as a structural guide (it appears to be beyond the intellectual grasp of most sexual offenders), and nor does it focus exclusively on developing a better life. Although Marshall's programme continues to incorporate some, albeit limited, avoidance plans, the programme is significantly different from the typical cognitive behavioural, relapse prevention programmes offered in most sexual offender treatment centres (see Burton and Smith-Darden 2001 and McGrath, Cumming and Burchard 2003 for surveys describing North American programmes).

Conventional relapse-prevention programmes emphasise the identification of comprehensive offender-specific risks based on detailed analyses of the client's past offences, and for these identified risks each client generates an extensive set of plans to avoid these risks. One problem with this approach is that future risky situations cannot always be anticipated and some may be entirely novel to the client.

Second, this generates a negative focus in the client and involves strictly avoidance plans. General psychological research shows that avoidance plans are more difficult to sustain than approach plans (e.g. engaging in rewarding, prosocial activities) (Emmons 1996; Gollwitzer and Bargh 1996). More specifically, Mann *et al.* (2004) showed that among adult sexual offenders only those who were guided to develop approach goals fully engaged in treatment and were judged to be the most motivated to stay offence-free. Marshall *et al.*'s (2006) programme emphasises the development of approach goals and encourages sexual offenders to believe that they can achieve a fuller, more satisfying life. A recent evaluation of Marshall's programme (Marshall *et al.* 2006) demonstrated that it produced a reduction in offending that was almost five times greater than the reductions reported in meta-analyses of sexual offender treatment outcome studies. Apparently Marshall's programme is more effective in reducing recidivism than are most other programmes for sexual offenders.

Treatment for adolescent child sexual abuse offenders

When treatment programmes for adolescent sexual offenders were first introduced in the 1980s, they focused on the same treatment targets and used the same treatment methods as those that had been developed for adult sexual offenders (see Becker and Kaplan 1993 for comments). As adult sexual offender programmes moved from narrow behavioural models to more comprehensive, group-based, cognitive behavioural approaches, programmes for adolescent sexual offenders generally followed suit. The rationale for treating adolescent sexual offenders in much the same way as adult sexual offenders was based on assumptions that adolescent sexual offenders were generally at high risk of chronic, life-long sexual offending, and that adult sexual offenders typically began offending in adolescence. As evidence began to emerge that questioned these assumptions, and as treatment providers became more sensitive to the unique developmental needs of adolescents, programmes for adolescent sexual offenders began to be modified accordingly. However, it was not until the late 1990s that the logic and efficacy of modelling adolescent sexual offender programmes on adult sexual offender programmes came to be widely questioned (see e.g. Chaffin and Bonner 1998; Freeman-Longo 2003; Letourneau and Miner 2005). In recent years it has become more widely acknowledged that a more developmentally sensitive

123

approach that included attention to peer and family relationships was essential (Print and O'Callaghan 2004; Thomas 2004). While some programmes for adolescent sexual offenders still retain many of the features derived from adult programmes (see, e.g. Worling 2004), others have moved closer to treatment models that have been shown to be effective with other (i.e. nonsexual) youth offenders, giving a greater emphasis to parental training, functional family therapy and relationship skills training (O'Reilly and Carr 2006).

Perhaps the most well established of these newer approaches with adolescent sexual offenders is multisystemic therapy (MST) (Henggeler *et al.* 1998). MST is a family-based treatment that targets both proximal (individual, family, peers and school) and distal elements (neighbourhood, community and child/adolescent service agencies) of the youth's social ecology. The behaviour of the adolescent sexual offender, as with other adolescent offenders, is seen as nested in a network of these interconnected systems and emerges as a product of the interaction between the youth and these systems. Interventions, therefore, target the specific interactions of the adolescent offender within and between his family, peers, school and community. MST is a pragmatic, outcome-focused approach that draws from a wide repertoire of evidence-based therapeutic techniques. There is an emphasis on 'home-based, family-focused services that are intensive, time-limited, and goal-oriented' (Henggeler *et al.* 1995: 112).

Below we consider how the risk, needs and responsivity principles can be applied in the treatment of adolescent CSA offenders, with particular reference to how this is done in a treatment programme developed by Smallbone and his colleagues at Griffith University: the Griffith Youth Forensic Service (GYFS) (Rayment *et al.* in press). GYFS draws explicitly from the integrated theory outlined in Chapter 2 of this volume, and from a broad evidence-base in developmental criminology, developmental psychopathology, environmental criminology and adult and adolescent sexual offending. Assessment and treatment methods draw from cognitive behavioural and especially multisystemic models.

Risk principle

GYFS is the only dedicated assessment and treatment service for adjudicated adolescent sexual offenders in Queensland, Australia. As in other Australian states, there has been a sustained effort in Queensland to minimise the number of young offenders in detention centres. With a general population of about 4.2 million, on average only about 100 young offenders are in Queensland detention centres on any given day. The majority of these are remanded in custody, and many of these are later sentenced to community orders. While GYFS provides treatment services to a small number of adolescent sexual offenders serving detention orders, most of its clients are serving community orders. GYFS is a field-based service, with staff travelling throughout the state (an area of some 1.7 million square kilometres), sometimes to remote communities, to conduct assessments and deliver treatment. Queensland has a geographically dispersed and culturally diverse population, and the limited resources available to GYFS require a prioritising of treatment services. Consistent with the risk principle, GYFS treatment services are prioritised towards the highest risk cases.

Valid application of the risk principle of course requires reliable and accurate individual risk assessment. This presents special problems for adolescent sexual offender programmes. First, the development of standardised, empirically-guided risk assessment instruments for adolescent sexual offenders is much less advanced than it is both for other youth offenders and for adult sexual offenders. Two specialised instruments are available – the Juvenile Sex Offender Assessment Protocol (J-SOAP) (Prentky and Righthand 2003) and the Estimate of Risk of Adolescent Sexual Offense Recidivism (ERASOR) (Worling 2004) – but neither of these has yet been adequately tested for predictive validity.

A second problem is that, whereas a history of offending is widely recognised as one of the most important predictors of future offending, early intervention with adolescent offenders is likely to involve adolescents who may have no significant history of offending but who may nevertheless pose a significant risk of recidivism. After all, even the most persistent offenders were once first-time offenders, and identifying valid risk profiles that do not rely on prior offending histories is therefore critical for effective early intervention. False-negative prediction errors are especially problematic when they lead to inadequate or no intervention for high-risk offenders. On the other hand, false-positive prediction errors can lead to young offenders and their families being unnecessarily drawn into intensive and sometimes highly intrusive interventions.

A third, more general, problem is that conventional approaches to recidivism risk assessment with sexual offenders are based more or less exclusively on individual-level conceptions of risk. By contrast, a social ecological perspective locates risk and protective factors at multiple levels of the young offender's social ecosystem. His relationship with a parent, peers or school community, for example, may be more relevant to a youth's risk of further sexual offending than, say, his failure to express remorse for a previous offence. Risk assessment, and of course efforts to reduce risk, therefore require attention to the presence of risk and protective factors at all levels of the young offender's social ecology, including but not limited to the offender himself.

GYFS clinicians undertake highly individualised, but not exclusively individual-level, risk assessments. These assessments are guided by our integrated theory and a broad evidence-base. The starting point for an initial assessment is the index offence(s) itself, with a functional analysis that aims to specify hypothesised causal factors at the situational, individual and ecosystemic levels. This is then considered in terms of the strengths and needs within the youth's social ecosystem at the present time, and, to the extent it can be anticipated, for the immediate and longer term future. Youth are either allocated to one of three treatment categories, or are referred back to standard (non-specialised) youth justice services. If the referral is accepted, a treatment plan is developed and efforts are made to establish both a multi-system team (comprising professionals and other significant persons within the youth's social ecosystem, such as a parent or responsible friend) and a collaborative (usually multi-disciplinary) treatment team. High-risk/needs youth are provided with intensive treatment, with (often extensive) direct therapeutic input by a GYFS clinician. Moderate-risk/needs youth are provided with medium-intensity treatment, with direct therapeutic input sometimes being provided by a local professional or para-professional. In these cases a GYFS clinician provides a high level of supervision and support. Low–moderate-risk youth receive low-intensity treatment, usually provided by youth justice and other workers with a GYFS clinician providing a monitoring and supervision role. Youth assessed as low risk are generally referred back to standard youth justice services, with advice about risk management offered by a GYFS clinician.

Needs principle

Prescriptive, manualised programmes for adolescent sexual offenders rely on assumptions of homogeneity among these young people, and on preconceptions about universal criminogenic needs that should be targeted in treatment. Evidence shows instead that adolescent sexual offenders are a heterogeneous population. While a number of recurrent themes emerge in risk/needs assessments for adolescent CSA offenders, each young person presents with a unique set of personal circumstances.

Once again, GYFS assessments begin with the index offence itself. A systemic case formulation is then developed that seeks to explain how and why the offence occurred. Situational assessment involves a micro-level analysis of the situational features of the offence setting, and generating inferences about how these situational factors may have interacted with the youth's offence-related motivations. Attention is thus given both to the structural features (e.g. how the offender and victim came to be at the offence setting, the whereabouts and capabilities of the offender's and victim's guardians) and to the dynamic features of the immediate offence setting (e.g. how the pre-offence interaction between the offender and victim may have evoked offence-related motivations in the offender). Situational analyses may inform interventions at various levels of the youth's social ecosystem. For example where the sexual abuse has occurred in a domestic setting (e.g. involving a biological, step- or foster-sibling), understanding the offence situation may allow for specific safety rules to be developed and facilitate effective parental monitoring. More generally, situational assessment provides a good starting point for understanding offence-related motivations, and therefore for identifying individual-level treatment needs.

At an individual level the emphasis is on understanding the young offender's motivations at the point of the onset CSA offence, and how these motivations may have changed following that offence. As predicted by our integrated theory, we often find that the onset offence involved an acute disorganisation of attachment-related (care-seeking, care-giving and sexual) motivations, sometimes associated with overt aggression. In many, but not all, cases we find chronic attachment-related problems (50% of GYFS clients have substantiated child protection histories), and also often chronic self-restraint problems (many have a documented history of conduct problems, nonsexual offences, substance use and mental health problems). Sometimes by the time of the referral the young offender has engaged in repeated sexual offending, and may already have established strong CSA-related pre-occupations or compulsions. In other cases the young offender shows no particular psychopathology or behavioural problems other than the CSA offence behaviour itself. As a general rule, the more chronic and diverse the offence-related individual-level problems, the more extensive the individual-level treatment needs.

127

Family-focused interventions vary according to the strengths and needs identified in the assessment and case formulation. Some families are very stable and supportive, but may nevertheless require assistance to re-establish secure emotional bonds, engage in ordinary positive family activities and develop the capacity for effective guardianship. Others have serious and longstanding problems, and may require assistance to establish positive social supports and to access social resources (e.g. mental health care). Behavioural family interventions may be employed to increase positive family interactions and decrease negative interactions. In some cases, particularly for older youth, relationships with parents and siblings are seemingly irretrievable. While GYFS clinicians often go to significant lengths to locate and engage with their clients' families, sometimes the emphasis is turned instead to assisting the youth in his transition to independent living, including assisting him to establish intimate peer relationships.

Peer relationship problems for adolescent CSA offenders sometimes involve attachments to antisocial peer groups, but more often involve peer isolation (Righthand and Welch 2001). Peer-level interventions are therefore generally directed towards maximising opportunities for the young offender to develop and maintain secure attachments to prosocial peers. Parents or other guardians are encouraged to take a central role in these efforts by engaging more directly with the youth's peers and by more closely monitoring his peer associations and activities. Others in the multi-system team are often aware of local community resources that might be used to engage the youth in positive social activities, such as work, sports and hobbies. One of the greatest challenges is to work towards increasing the social inclusion of the young CSA offender in a social environment where others tend to react to his offending by negative labelling and exclusion. For example, we have seen instances where a young CSA offender has been excluded from his school, even when his offending was unrelated to the school community and when school inclusion is more likely to decrease than to increase risk. Including school personnel and other community stakeholders in multi-system teams provides opportunities for education as well as multi-systemic intervention and sensible risk management.

Responsivity principle

Just as flexibility and therapeutic responsiveness have been shown to be important features of effective programmes for adult CSA offenders (Marshall *et al.* 2006), so too are these features important in the treatment of adolescent CSA offenders. As we have already noted, programmes for adolescent sexual offenders were originally modelled on programmes designed for adult sexual offenders. One aspect of this has been the widespread use of manualised, group-based treatment models with adolescent sexual offenders. Indeed, group-based treatment for adolescent sexual offenders is recommended both by US National Adolescent Perpetrator Network (NAPN 1993) and by the American Academy of Child and Adolescent Psychiatry (2000). Recent surveys of adolescent sexual offender treatment providers show clearly the popularity of group-based treatment, with significantly more hours being spent on group interventions than on individual or family interventions (Burton, Smith-Darden and Frankel 2006).

GYFS does not offer group-based treatment. Although as we have noted it is possible to introduce a high level of flexibility and therapeutic responsiveness into group-based programmes for adult sexual offenders, we think there are particular reasons to be cautious about group-based interventions with adolescent offenders. First, it is widely recognised that adolescent attitudes and behaviour are more directly influenced by peers than is the case for adults. This is often used as a rationale for group-based interventions with adolescent sexual offenders, with the assumption that relationships among groups of youth sexual offenders can be controlled and made positive in a therapeutic setting. However, it is also widely recognised that promoting associations with *prosocial* peers is very important for serious adolescent offenders (Loeber and Farrington 1998), including adolescent sexual offenders (e.g. Miner and Crimmins 1995). GYFS therefore aims to promote positive peer associations for its youth clients, and to reduce their contact with other problem youth (especially with other youth who have also committed sexual offences). A second, related concern is that group-based interventions with high-risk youth offenders have been shown in some circumstances to be related to increased problem behaviour and with negative life outcomes in adulthood (Dishion, *et al.* 1999). Finally, group-based programmes are unlikely to have any direct effects on the social ecology of the young offender. While some group-based programmes also include family interventions (e.g. Worling and Curwen 2000), these seem often to be more concerned with enlisting the support of parents for individual-level treatment of the adolescent's behaviour than with targeting the behaviour of the family itself.

Attrition rates for adolescent sexual offender programmes are often alarmingly high, with many programmes reporting attrition rates of 50% or more (Righthand and Welch 2001). This is of special significance, because research with both adult (Hanson and Bussière 1998) and adolescent sexual offenders (Hunter and Figueredo 1999) consistently shows that those who begin but drop out of treatment are more likely to re-offend than those who decline to participate in the first place. Attrition rates may be exacerbated by the length of time young sexual offenders are required to participate in a programme. NAPN (1993) recommends that treatment for adolescent sexual offenders should involve a minimum of twelve to twenty-four months. This seems a very long time, especially considering that programmes for adult sexual offenders ranging from three to nine months have been found to be effective. It is also likely that attrition rates are exacerbated when young offenders are required to 'fit' into an inflexible, prescriptive programme. GYFS in fact aims to do the reverse – to take the youth's offending and personal circumstances as the starting points, and to design a customised programme around the young offender himself. Therapeutic engagement itself often becomes a key point of focus. Our research (Schaeffer 2008) shows that therapeutic engagement is more difficult with older youth, indigenous youth and those with versatile criminal histories, and this research has led GYFS staff to develop new methods for engaging with these youth. For example, we have given additional emphasis to engaging with and enlisting the support of indigenous adults when we are working with indigenous youth, particularly in small remote communities. Despite the difficulties of engaging with some young people, their families and their communities the attrition rate for the GYFS programme is virtually zero, although this may say as much about the patience, skill and dedication of GYFS clinicians as it does about the format of treatment.

In addition to its direct therapeutic work, GYFS aims to build professional and community capacity to respond effectively to sexual violence and abuse by young people through its formal training and collaborative treatment partnerships. Preliminary evaluations (Dadds *et al*. 2003; Rayment *et al*. in press) have demonstrated significant and sustained effects for increasing skills and confidence in collaborative partners, who play critical roles in the interventions with the youth sexual offender clients and their families. Plans are well established to evaluate recidivism outcomes, but formal recidivism outcome data are presently unavailable.

Treatment outcomes

Several recent meta-analytic reviews of treatment outcome studies with adult sexual offenders have come to quite positive general conclusions (Alexander 1999; Dowden, Antonowicz and Andrews 2003; Gallagher *et al.* 1999; Hall 1995; Hanson *et al.* 2002; Lösel and Schmucker 2005). Unfortunately, some of these meta-analyses did not carefully select studies, and included some that had serious methodological problems. In the better-designed meta-analyses (Dowden *et al.* 2003; Hanson *et al.* 2002; Lösel and Schmucker 2005), outcomes for treated offenders have been compared with groups of untreated offenders. When these meta-analyses examined the effects of those programmes that were cognitive behavioural and had some elements of relapse prevention, they found statistically significant benefits for treatment. Lösel and Schmucker (2005) extracted data from the sixty-nine studies they examined and determined that the programmes were particularly effective with CSA offenders.

In the evaluation noted earlier by Marshall *et al.* (2006), 534 sexual offenders were followed for 5.4 years after release to the community. Among these only seventeen (3.2%) re-offended with a sexual crime. The expected rate of sexual re-offending based on actuarial risk levels of Marshall *et al.*'s subjects was 16.8%. What is also interesting is the fact that only 13% of the treated subjects also committed a nonsexual offence, against an expected rate of 40%. Thus treatment not only directly reduced sexual offending, it also reduced rates of more general antisocial conduct. These same effects were observed in both Hanson *et al.*'s (2002) report and in the meta-analysis of Lösel and Schmucker (2005). Although their study included sexual offenders with adult victims, Marshall *et al.* extracted the recidivism data for nonfamilial CSA offenders (evaluated separately for male victim and female victim offenders) as well as for incest offenders; neither group had a sexual re-offence rate over 4%. Clearly there is good evidence pointing to the effectiveness of treatment for adult CSA offenders.

Since treatment programmes for adolescent sexual offenders have been implemented rather more recently than programmes for adult sexual offenders, there is considerably less evidence on their effectiveness. What evidence is available, however, is less convincing than it is for the outcome evaluations of adult sexual offenders. Marshall and Fernandez (2004) reviewed the treatment outcome literature on youth sexual offender programmes. They identified eleven reports that evaluated treatment for these offenders. Unfortunately, eight of these did not include a comparison group of untreated offenders, and did not provide actuarially-based estimates of the expected recidivism rates. This latter failure to report expected re-offence rates is not surprising since at the time of these evaluations, actuarially-based risk assessment instruments had not been developed for this population. In addition, most of the reports employed a quite limited follow-up period.

Reitzel and Carbonell (2006) surveyed the available literature, including a number of unpublished reports, on the effects of adolescent sexual offender treatment. Setting standards that required, among other things, a comparison group (either untreated or treated by some supposedly inferior programme) with which to compare the treated subjects, Reitzel and Carbonell identified only nine studies. Unfortunately, only five of these employed an adequate comparison group. Three others assigned offenders to treatment based on risk and needs, suggesting that the comparison group was both less risky and less needy, thereby biasing outcome in favour of treatment. One study provided no information on how subjects were assigned to groups. Furthermore, one study used only the clients' self-reports as a basis for inferring recidivism while two others used only local information rather than national databases. Finally, three studies failed to provide recidivism data on their comparison groups, meaning no credible comparisons were possible.

Reitzel and Carbonell (2006), nevertheless, examined all nine studies and compared recidivism rates between treated subjects and comparison groups. They reported a sexual recidivism rate of 7.4% for the treated subjects (including those in the 'alternative' comparison treatment programmes) and 18.9% for the untreated groups. However those treated in the alternative programmes had a recidivism rate almost identical to the overall treated groups' rate (i.e. 7.63%).

Summary

Research on offender rehabilitation has led to the identification of a number of key principles, the most important of which are the risk, needs and responsivity principles. According to the risk principle, the greatest reductions in recidivism are achieved by providing the highest intensity treatment programmes to those offenders who present the highest risk for recidivism. Involving low-risk offenders in high-intensity programmes may risk iatrogenic effects. According to the needs principle, offender treatment is most effective when it targets those factors that are empirically or theoretically related to recidivism (i.e. criminogenic needs). According to the responsivity principle, offender treatment is most effective when the treatment is tailored to the individual characteristics of offenders in ways that maximise therapeutic engagement (and thus offenders' responsiveness to the treatment). The CSC presents a good model for how these principles can be applied to the treatment of convicted adult sexual offenders. Here, the risk and needs principles inform decisions about the allocation of sexual offenders to treatment programmes of high, moderate and low intensity. The responsivity principle is applied within the programmes themselves.

Treatment programmes for adult CSA offenders generally have been highly prescriptive, requiring treatment providers to strictly adhere to manualised instructions. Consistent with the responsivity principle, recent evidence suggests that the best results are achieved with a more flexible approach, which requires a range of both positive therapist (e.g. empathic and rewarding) and group process features (e.g. cohesion and expressiveness). Group-based cognitive behavioural approaches have been associated with more positive outcomes. CSA offenders vary widely in their baseline risk of recidivism, and yet well designed and implemented treatment programmes have been shown to produce similar reductions in recidivism for different offender subtypes (e.g. for both familial and nonfamilial offenders). Sexual offence specific programmes have consistently been shown to reduce both sexual and nonsexual recidivism.

Treatment programmes for adolescent CSA offenders have emerged only since the 1980s, and were originally modelled on programmes for adult sexual offenders. It is only in the last few years that the logic and efficacy of using methods developed for adult sexual offenders in the treatment of adolescent sexual offenders has been widely questioned. Rather than borrowing directly from the work with adult sexual offenders, some adolescent sexual offender programmes (Borduin and Schaeffer 2001; O'Reilly and Carr 2006; Rayment *et al*. 2007) have drawn from a wider evidence-base in developmental psychopathology and adapted methods found to be effective in the treatment of serious youth (nonsexual) offenders. Evidence for the effectiveness of programmes for adolescent sexual offenders generally, and for adolescent CSA offenders in particular, is less clear than is the case for adult sexual offender programmes.

Chapter 7

Victim-focused prevention

In this chapter we shift our attention from prevention strategies targeting offenders and potential offenders, to those targeting victims and potential victims. Intervention with victims of CSA can occur at two points. First, as a primary or secondary prevention strategy, efforts may be directed at potential victims to minimise the chances that they will be sexually abused. To date, personal safety programmes, which seek to teach children self-protective skills, are the usual way of operationalising this strategy. Second, as a tertiary prevention strategy, interventions with known CSA victims may minimise their chances of ongoing or future abuse. This may involve facilitating the role of victims in the disclosure and prosecution of sexual abuse cases, and addressing factors that may lead to their re-victimisation in the future. We argue in this chapter that interventions with victims form a crucial part of CSA prevention. However, too often victim-focused approaches have pushed responsibility for prevention onto children. Victim-focused interventions should not be interpreted as interventions *by* victims. Rather, we need to consider ways that responsible adults can more effectively intervene on behalf of victims to prevent their abuse.

Interventions with potential victims

According to routine activity theory, a suitable target is one of the three minimal elements – along with a likely offender and the absence of a capable guardian – in any crime (Cohen and Felson 1979). One way to prevent crime is to 'harden' potential targets to make them less vulnerable to criminal attack. In routine activity terms, this section considers ways to turn children from 'suitable' to 'unsuitable' targets for CSA. Before we examine attempts to achieve this aim through personal safety programmes, we begin by considering what makes a child a suitable target and how their victimisation occurs.

Victims and victimisation

Victim risk factors

The appearance, behaviour and demeanour of children may increase their risk of sexual victimisation. In Chapter 1, we examined the gender and age characteristics of CSA victims. We reported that girls are more likely to be victimised than boys (around twice as often); and that younger children are more at risk of familial abuse while older children have a greater risk of non-familial abuse. We can add here that, in comparison to non-abused children, abused children are more likely to have poorer academic performance (Paradise *et al.* 1994), lower IQ scores (Manion *et al.* 1996) and more behavioural problems (Paradise *et al.* 1994). They also tend to come from more dangerous neighbourhoods; to come from unhappy families characterised by divorce, separation or discord; and to have histories of neglect, physical abuse and prior sexual victimisation (Boney-McCoy and Finkelhor 1995; Finkelhor *et al.* 1990; Finkelhor *et al.* 1997; Mian *et al.* 1986). There emerges a close statistical association between CSA and other forms of child abuse and neglect. Sexual abuse is both predicted by, and predictive of, more general maltreatment of the child, and both are predicted by the same family and environmental risk factors.

Interviews with offenders provide further information on preferred victim characteristics. Conte *et al.* (1989) asked perpetrators what they looked for when selecting victims for CSA. Most perpetrators had a specific preference for certain physical characteristics, but were generally attracted to friendly and vulnerable children. Similarly, Elliot *et al.* (1995) found that perpetrators are most likely to target victims who are alone, who have family problems and who are physically small, pretty and 'provocatively' dressed. Perhaps more tellingly, they also looked for children who appear to lack confidence and have low self-esteem, and who seem innocent, curious and trusting. Such children may crave attention and affection from adults leaving them open to emotional exploitation.

The victimisation process

The sexual abuse of children typically occurs within a broader relationship between the victim and the perpetrator and as the culmination of an incremental process. As we reported in Chapter 1, Smallbone and Wortley (2000) found that around 95% of offenders already knew their victim prior to the abuse, and almost half (47%) were related to, or lived with, the child. The child is likely to have established emotional ties and loyalties to the offender that may compromise his or her ability to identify sexual abuse and the illegitimate use of adult authority. This is particularly so when the adult has a guardianship or supervisory role with the child. Under these circumstances, it may be difficult for children to distinguish between appropriate and inappropriate care-giving activities that may be associated with sexual abuse (bathing, dressing and so forth).

Moreover, as we noted above, children may develop relationships with perpetrators in order to satisfy unmet emotional needs. Offenders typically build non-sexual, emotional bonds with victims prior to engaging in sexual contact. In terms of our integrated theory, relationship-building may be employed as a deliberate grooming strategy by offenders, or sexual attraction for the child may arise as a consequence of the relationship. In any event, Smallbone and Wortley (2000) found that prior to sexual contact most perpetrators invested a lot of time with the child, touching him/her non-sexually (67%), giving him/her a lot of attention (65%), and playing with him/her (57%). In most cases, sexual contact was introduced gradually and rarely involved overt coercion or violence. The perpetrator said nice things about the child (51%), touched him/her sexually more and more (49%), and talked lovingly to him/her (45%). Similarly, offenders relied on the emotional bonds established with the child to prevent disclosure of the abuse. The most commonly used methods of keeping a child from disclosing was saying he (the offender) would go to jail or get into trouble if the child told anyone (61%), and relying on the child not wanting to lose the offender because of the affection he provided (36%).

It should not be assumed, however, that victims are necessarily oblivious to the sexual nature of the relationship or that they recognise it as immediately traumatic. For example, Wolak, Finkelhor and Mitchell (2004) investigated sexual offences against minors that had begun with online encounters. The most common victims in these circumstances were females between the ages of thirteen and fifteen and the most common offenders were males aged over twenty-five years. Contrary to media stereotypes that emphasise the deceptive nature of online grooming, in most cases the perpetrator made few efforts to disguise his age or his sexual intentions. Victims generally went to the meeting fully expecting a sexual liaison with an older man. More generally, many offenders, as part of their modus operandi, try to engage the sexual curiosity of children by talking explicitly about sex and showing the children pornography (Smallbone and Wortley 2000). Sanderson (2004) makes the perhaps uncomfortable point that victims may well experience sexual contact with the perpetrator as stimulating and pleasurable, and that hypersexualisation is sometimes a consequence of sexual abuse. The sexualisation of victims is more likely to occur if the sexual relationship with the perpetrator develops gradually over time (Berliner and Conte 1990).

Personal safety programmes

Personal safety programmes seek to reduce CSA by equipping potential victims with knowledge and skills to recognise and avoid sexually risky situations, and with strategies to physically and verbally resist sexual advances by offenders. Personal safety programmes began in the early 1970s and have emerged as the most common primary prevention strategy for CSA. A literature search using the key words 'child sexual assault' and 'prevention' will produce an overwhelming majority of articles describing programmes of this sort. They are, however, a controversial strategy. While there is good evidence that programmes can achieve significant increases in children's knowledge about CSA concepts and self-protection strategies, there is almost no available research that can demonstrate behavioural transfer of knowledge to real-life situations and resultant reductions in CSA for participants. Moreover, there has been criticism of both the content and conceptual foundations of the programmes, with concerns expressed about the appropriateness of shifting the burden of prevention onto children. We begin this section with a description of personal safety programmes, and an assessment of the empirical evidence of their success. We then summarise the criticisms of personal safety programmes. We conclude that ultimately adults must be responsible for the safety of children, and that situational and developmental prevention approaches offer more appropriate models of intervention with potential victims.

Description of programmes

Programmes are designed primarily for school children from kindergarten to sixth grade (twelve years old), and most are delivered in schools by visiting experts (Roberts and Miltenberger 1999). Finkelhor and Dziuba-Leatherman (1995) estimated that two-thirds of US school children have been exposed to a programme at some stage. Typically, programmes seek to teach children three things: 1) definitions of sexual abuse and the ability to recognise sexually inappropriate behaviour; 2) strategies to avoid risky situations and to resist sexual advances of perpetrators; and 3) the message that they should tell a trusted adult if any inappropriate advances have been made or if actual abuse has occurred (Sanderson 2004; Taal and Edelaar 1997). In their review of thirty published studies on personal safety programmes, MacIntyre and Carr (2000) identified the following core concepts contained within the curricula: the child's body belongs to him/her and he/she has a right to control access to it (body ownership); there is 'good', 'bad' and 'confusing' touch, and the child has the right to reject bad or confusing touch (touch); a child has the right to say no to an adult if the adult suggests something inappropriate (saying no); the child should try to get away if in danger (escape); there are appropriate secrets and inappropriate secrets, and the child should tell someone if he/she is asked to keep an inappropriate secret (secrecy); the child should trust his/her instincts if he/she believes something is wrong (intuition); the child should identify adults who can be turned to for help, and should be prepared to be persistent if the first adult does not believe him/her (support systems); the child is never to blame (blame); and the child should be assertive with bullies and help friends who are bullied (bullying).

While the exact format of personal safety programmes varies, most are delivered within a Behavioural Skills Training (BST) model (Wurtele 1986). BST is based on social learning principles and emphasises skill acquisition through instruction, modelling, rehearsal and feedback. MacIntyre and Carr (2000) identified three modalities of programme delivery. The first was group training. This essentially involved standard classroom instruction and discussion, which may be supplemented with handouts. Twenty-eight programmes evaluated included this technique. The second method of delivery was behavioural practice, included in twenty-one programmes. This typically involved role plays and behavioural rehearsal of safety skills. The third method of delivery was video training, found in fourteen programmes. This involved video presentation of programme content and the use of video in modelling exercises. Programmes may also utilise live plays with actors (Taal and Edelaar 1997) and puppet shows (Roberts and Miltenberger 1999). However, there is wide variation in programme 'dosage'. MacIntyre and Carr found that the shortest programme was twenty-five minutes in total, and the longest was 1.5 hours per week for a term. Most interventions comprised three sessions of between fifteen minutes and 1.5 hours.

Outcomes of personal safety programmes
Most published programmes utilise some form of evaluation, usually involving a pre-test/post-test design. The follow-up period varies from between one week to one year, with one to three months typical (MacIntrye and Carr 2000). Five outcome measures have been variously employed – knowledge gains, skill gains, disclosures, negative effects and subsequent incidence of CSA.

There is good evidence that personal safety programmes are successful in imparting sexual abuse concepts and skills to children. Rispens *et al.* (1997) conducted a meta-analysis involving sixteen studies. They found that all studies yielded positive post-treatment gains (effect size, .71) although effect sizes varied widely. While there was evidence of decay over time, overall significant gains were maintained for the specified follow-up period (effect size .62). MacIntyre and Carr's (2000) evaluation produced similar results. Gains in knowledge were found in twenty of twenty-five training conditions examined, and gains in skills in seventeen of twenty training conditions. In all programmes for which gains occurred, these gains were maintained over the post-testing period. As an alternative to meta-analysis, Finkelhor and Dziuba-Leatherman (1995) conducted a national telephone survey of 2,000 children who had participated in various personal safety programmes. They found that two-thirds of respondents reported that the programmes covered key safety skills training, and three-quarters reported that they found the programmes were helpful. Forty per cent of respondents said that they had used skills learnt in the programme to get out of fights or avoid suspicious strangers and 5% said they had said 'no' to an adult as result of what they had learnt.

There is more limited evidence that victim-focused programmes increase disclosure rates. MacIntyre and Carr (2000) found disclosure rates after participating in a programme of between 4% and 8% across four studies. Finkelhor and Dziuba-Leatherman (1995) found that 14% of their telephone respondents said they told an adult about an incident as a result of programme participation. The interpretation of findings is restricted by the lack of comparative data.

The issue of collateral negative impacts has also been less extensively investigated and available evidence is mixed. MacIntyre and Carr (2000) found slight increases in anxiety and wariness about being touched among participants in four studies. Taal and Edelaar (1997) found older children developed discomfort about being touched. Finkelhor and Dziuba-Leatherman (1995) found that 2% of their telephone sample worried more as result of the programme. However, other studies have found little evidence of collateral negative effects (Sarno and Wurtele 1997).

Finally, few studies have examined whether programme participation results in a lower incidence of CSA, and fewer still have reported positive results. As part of their national telephone survey, Finkelhor and colleagues (Finkelhor and Dziuba-Leatherman 1995; Finkelhor *et al.* 2005) found that, while respondents who had participated in victim-focused programmes reported that they were more likely to utilise self-protective strategies, there was no evidence of any decrease in the percentage of threatened victimisations that were actually completed or in the level of injury reported. The only study to date to have found evidence of reduced victimisation was by Gibson and Leitenberg (2000). They surveyed 825 female undergraduates on their prior participation in victim-focused programmes and their self-reported experience of child sexual victimisation. Eight per cent of programme participants had been subsequently sexually abused, compared with 14% who had not participated in a programme.

In sum, much of the supportive evidence for personal safety programmes is confined to the learning of key self-protection concepts. The evidence for the long-term retention of those concepts, and more importantly, behavioural transfer into the adoption of successful self-protective strategies in real-world settings, is at this stage largely lacking. The evidence that the programmes cause harm to participants is mixed.

Criticisms of personal safety programmes

Personal safety programmes have been criticised at two levels. At a surface level, some criticisms are directed at the content of particular programmes. For example, programmes have been criticised for having an undue focus on girls as victims and neglecting the needs of boys (Sanderson 2004). Such criticisms accept the basic validity of personal safety programmes as a prevention strategy and are directed at improving them. Other criticisms, which we will focus on here, challenge the conceptual foundations of personal safety programmes. According to this view, children both cannot and should not bear the burden of preventing their own child sexual abuse.

From a purely evidence-based perspective, the objectives and methods of personal safety programmes are at odds with the realities of most CSA. Personal safety programmes are based on a resistance model of prevention. They assume that children can be taught to recognise sexual contact with an adult as unwelcome, and will have the personal resources to rebuff sexual advances. In fact, as we outlined earlier in this chapter, grooming strategies by offenders are often subtle and incremental, and the child is gradually desensitised to the sexual nature of the advances. This, coupled with the child's lack of sexual knowledge and sophistication, means that the sexual intentions of the offender may not always be obvious to the child. Moreover, the child may come to feel a special emotional attachment towards the perpetrator and it can be difficult for him/her to separate the sexual and non-sexual aspects of that relationship. Perhaps more challenging is the fact that children may enjoy 'bad touch' and become sexually precocious as a result of their abuse. This both limits the effectiveness of the prevention message (e.g. if it doesn't feel bad then it can't be abuse), and may increase feelings of shame in abuse victims who assume that there is something wrong with them if they enjoyed being touched.

Even if children recognise 'bad touch' when it occurs, they are ill-equipped to negotiate with adults about their safety. As we have discussed, the most vulnerable children are those who lack confidence and have low self-esteem. These are also the children who benefit least from personal safety programmes and are likely to be the least resourceful in implementing self-protection strategies (Bagley *et al.* 1996; Fryer, Kerns-Kaiser and Miyoshi 1987). But even resourceful children face an overwhelming power imbalance. Children are physically smaller than their abuser, naturally submissive to adult authority and are cognitively and socially immature. Personal safety programmes require them to make complex decisions about the appropriate use of adult authority and to challenge that authority when it is judged to be illegitimate. Should the child decide to report the abuse, there is then the dilemma of deciding to whom it should be reported. This is especially so where the perpetrator is the primary care-giver, but even in other cases the child may judge that the perpetrator has an unchallengeable position of trust within the family.

Just the same, there remains the fact that some children are more likely to be sexually abused than others, and any attempt to 'target-hardening' these children by changing the factors that put them at risk is intuitively appealing. But of course in other areas of crime, targets do not harden themselves. If a person wants to prevent their car from being stolen, then it is that person's responsibility to ensure that the car is adequately protected. Likewise, a more appropriate way to target-harden children is to provide for them more effective guardianship and safer environments in which to live. We consider such strategies at length in the following chapter on situational prevention.

This does not mean we should ignore the personal characteristics of children that increase victimisation. However, the question we should be asking is not how to teach children to rebuff sexual advances, but rather why some children get into relationships with adults that put them at risk of sexual abuse. An alternative to strengthening victim resistance is bolstering victim resilience. This approach involves developing the protective factors that make children less vulnerable to the attentions of perpetrators, and this fits much better with what we know about the dynamics of victimisation. When perpetrators are asked to provide advice on prevention of CSA, among the most common suggestions involve providing children with a loving home environment that allows them to feel confident and secure (Elliott *et al.* 1995). Interventions may directly target at-risk children – for example, providing them with self-esteem programmes (Daro and Salmon-Cox 1994) – or operate indirectly by providing services and resources to at-risk families (Larner, Stevenson and Behrman 1998). In Chapter 4 we discussed developmental prevention with potential offenders, pointing out the long-term benefits of early intervention. The same logic applies to interventions with potential victims. In fact, prospective victims and perpetrators of CSA share many developmental risk factors, and, given the intergenerational nature of much CSA, developmental interventions may be simultaneously targeting both populations. We will return to the issue of resilience later in this chapter.

Interventions with known victims

There is an extensive literature on responding to victims after they have been sexually abused. A good deal of the available research is conducted within a harm reduction model. It focuses on the identification of the short- and long-term negative psychological outcomes of CSA for victims, and the provision of services to ameliorate these outcomes (e.g. Briere and Elliott 1994; Kendall-Tackett, Williams and Finkelhor 1993; Molnar, Buka and Kessler 2001). Much of this research falls outside the scope of our analyses. We will focus here instead on interventions with known victims that are directed at the prevention of further CSA. We examine two issues: stopping the abuse that the victim is currently suffering, and ensuring that the victim is not re-abused at a later date.

Ending the current abuse

Victims may be involved in stopping their abuse at four stages of a disclosure process. First they may disclose to another trusted adult that they are being abused. Second, they, or someone on their behalf, may formally report the abuse to the authorities. Third, they may provide evidence against the offender as part of the formal investigation of the case. Fourth, they may testify in court against the offender. In this section we examine the how each of these stages contribute to the prevention of CSA, and what can be done to facilitate the victim's participation in these activities.

Initial disclosure

The protection of children from continued abuse begins with the awareness by others that the abuse is occurring. The sexual abuse may become known to someone close to the child – a parent, neighbour or family friend – or may be uncovered by a teacher, doctor, social worker or the like in the course of their professional work. The child may disclose the abuse to that person, or that person may observe direct physical or behavioural evidence of abuse. In one study (Sauzier 1989), just over half of substantiated CSA cases came to light through disclosure by the victim, with the rest through discovery by an adult. However, most victims do not tell others about their abuse. In their review of the literature, London *et al.* (2005) report a modal self-disclosure rate of 33%. Even when self-disclosure does occur, it may not be immediate. For example, Ussher and Dewberry (1995) found that only about half of disclosures occurred during the victim's childhood, with the mean age at disclosure of twenty-six years, a delay of some twelve years on average from the time of the abuse.

We have already discussed in this chapter some of the reasons why a child may not disclose abuse. It can be extraordinarily difficult for the child victim to first recognise sexual abuse and then find a trusted adult to whom to report. The child may also be deterred from reporting because of the loyalty felt to the offender, or the shame and embarrassment felt about the sexual abuse. Lawson and Chaffin (1992) found that disclosure increased with the level of support towards the child provided by care-givers. In an examination of cases where sexual abuse had been discovered accidentally by the diagnosis of a sexually transmitted disease, children were nearly four times more likely to deny that they were sexually abused if care-givers would not concede that sexual abuse was a possibility or if they otherwise displayed a punishing attitude towards the child. However, there are few other reliable predictors of disclosure. As might be expected, several studies have found disclosure decreases the more closely the victim is related to the offender (e.g. Hanson *et al.* 1999; Wyatt and Newcomb 1990), but others have not supported this finding (e.g. Arata 1998; Kellog and Hoffman 1995). Likewise, victim age, gender and ethnicity, and abuse severity, do not seem systematically related to the likelihood of disclosure (see London *et al.* 2005, for a review).

Psychologically, disclosure of the abuse that is accompanied by a supportive response is associated with more positive subsequent adjustment (Arata 1998; Harvey *et al.* 1991; Testa *et al.* 1992). Indeed, victims who receive a non-supportive response can fare worse than those who do not disclose in the first place (Everill and Waller 1994). However, there is surprisingly little research on the extent to which the revelation of CSA alone (i.e. without formal intervention from child protection or the police) puts a stop to the abuse. It seems likely that in many cases the exposure of the abuse will be sufficient to deter the offender, at least in the short term, but we do know that there are some exceptions to this. Where the perpetrator is a family member, other family members may take the perpetrator's side against the victim. Classically, this occurs when the accusation of abuse is made to a non-abusing mother about her partner. Heriot (1996) found that in approximately a quarter of substantiated familial CSA cases, the child's mother did not believe the accusation. Almost one-third of mothers failed to take action to protect the child (e.g. making the perpetrator move out of the home) and approximately the same number withdrew maternal support from the child (e.g. became hostile towards the child). The most powerful predictors of the mother's reaction were her feelings towards the perpetrator, and the severity of the abuse. Less protection and support were provided when the mother had positive feelings towards the perpetrator and, surprisingly when the abuse involved penetration.

Undoubtedly, disclosure by victims is a positive step in the prevention of abuse and should be encouraged. However, most CSA is not self-disclosed at the time of the abuse, and almost half of cases that come to light are detected by means other than self-disclosure. We saw in the section on personal safety programmes that directly schooling children to disclose abuse has a limited effect. The strongest predictor of disclosure is a supportive family response, suggesting again the need to invest in family-level interventions to create the environment in which children feel confident to talk about sensitive issues. Even so, we cannot rely on victims to protect themselves by reporting their own abuse. Like the protection of children generally, responsibility for the discovery of CSA ultimately depends upon the vigilance and the diligence of adults.

Reporting to authorities

Self-report victimisation surveys indicate that between 3% (Finkelhor and Dziuba-Leatherman 1994) and 15% (Kilpatrick and Saunders 1997) of all CSA cases are reported to authorities. Non-reported abuse includes cases that were not disclosed by the victim to anyone, and those that came to the attention of an adult but were not on-reported. In this latter category, Finkelhor (1984) found that only 42% of sexual abuse cases known to parents were reported to police. We have mentioned one reason for this above. In addition, parents might elect to deal with the matter informally in the belief that this is in the best interests of the child. The parents may predict that the child will be doubly traumatised by having the abuse investigated and made public. A recent study found that two-thirds of legal professionals involved in CSA cases would not put their own child through the legal process if the child was sexually abused because they judged that it was not worth the emotional cost (Eastwood 2003). Even among mental health professionals who work in the area of CSA, it has been estimated that between 30% (Besharov 1994) and 54% (Pence and Wilson 1994) of known CSA cases are not reported to authorities. The main reasons given by professionals for not reporting (apart from a lack of evidence) are concerns that the case will not be properly dealt with by the authorities, and that reporting may deter victims and perpetrators from seeking treatment (Pence and Wilson 1994).

In an effort to increase reporting rates, most jurisdictions have mandatory reporting laws, in some cases dating back to the 1970s. In some jurisdictions these laws apply only to certain professionals dealing with children (e.g. doctors and teachers), while in other jurisdictions all citizens are obliged to report suspected CSA (Higgins, Bromfield and Richardson 2007; Pence and Wilson 1994). Where mandatory reporting has been introduced it has generally led to an immediate increase in notifications (Besharov 1994). However, mandatory reporting has also attracted some criticism. One unintended consequence has been an increase in unsubstantiated cases, suggesting that it may encourage reports based on weak evidence. Besharov reported that unsubstantiated cases rose from 35% to 65% following the introduction of mandatory reporting in the US. Over-reporting not only taxes child protection resources, but also has the potential to unfairly stigmatise innocent people.

The other main criticism, to which we have already alluded, is that reporting abuse does not always lead to positive outcomes for victims. In fact, the research on the experiences of child victims after reporting their abuse is mixed, and no doubt depends on the way cases are handled in the particular jurisdiction in which the report is made. In recent years there have been efforts by many police departments, child protection services and courts to deal with victims of CSA in a more compassionate and professional manner, and research from the last ten years or so tends to paint a more positive picture than that from the 1970s and 1980s. Berliner and Conte (1995) found that while children experienced various aspects of the reporting process as daunting and humiliating, they mostly felt that they were being treated with respect and accepted the process as a necessity. Victims described the main benefits of reporting as stopping the abuse and ending the emotional distress. In a pattern that is becoming consistent in this chapter, positive experiences with reporting were associated with the level of family support. Ninety-seven per cent of children said that they were glad that they reported the abuse and all but one in the sample would advise other children to tell. Henry (1997) found that victims had more positive views on reporting if they were not required to give multiple interviews, and if they developed a trusting relationship with the investigating professional. Eastwood, Patton and Stacy (2000) found that negative experiences of reporting were lessened if victims were interviewed by female officers and if empowering interviewing techniques were employed.

One advantage of formal reporting, of course, is that child welfare agencies can act to secure the protection of the child if required. Where the alleged perpetrator is a member of the household, in-home risk-management strategies may be offered (see Chapter 8), or if necessary the child or offender may be removed from the home. In Berliner and Conte's (1995) sample of CSA cases, 38.5% of which involved abuse by a care-giver or another relative, the offender left the home in 21% of cases and the victim was removed in 8% of cases. The reaction of victims in these cases was mixed but most victims were relieved that the abuse would end.

On balance, reporting abuse would seem to have positive psychological and practical outcomes for most victims. While reporting sexual abuse will unavoidably be an emotionally difficult experience for victims, with sensitive handling, the trauma can be minimised.

Providing evidence

We have discussed reporting sexual abuse from the point of view of victims. From the perspective of the interviewing officer, a key concern is how to elicit reliable accounts of the abuse from victims.

Whether children are prone to deny abuse in the face of physical evidence, and to recant disclosures once they have been made, have proven to be contentious issues. Early research suggested high rates of denial and recantations. Sorenson and Snow (1991) proposed a five stage disclosure process: 1) initial denial; 2) tentative disclosure; 3) active disclosure; 4) recantation; and 5) reaffirmation of disclosure. They found that 78% of victims initially denied the abuse, and 22% recanted their disclosure, with 93% of those who recanted later reaffirming the allegations. However, the objectivity of this and similar research has since been criticised, with the suggestion that in many cases there was insufficient evidence to objectively substantiate abuse, and that children were led by the researchers to make false allegations (see London *et al.* 2005). In other words, many of the initial denials may well have been true, thus accounting for the high level of recantation. Studies with more rigorous substantiation criteria typically produce lower rates of denial and recantation. Lawson and Chaffin (1992), who used the presence of a sexually transmitted disease as the substantiation criterion, found a denial rate of 57%. However, this figure is likely to be inflated since to qualify as a participant in the study the child had to have previously denied being abused. Thus these children were by definition already deniers. Bradley and Wood (1996) examined a sample of case files in which sexual abuse was substantiated after a thorough investigation by child protection services, they found denial and recantation rates of 4% and 6%, respectively. In all cases, the denial or recantation was associated with external pressure from the victim's care-giver.

On the other side of the coin, there are also concerns about the accuracy of children's allegations of abuse. Concerns have been expressed that children's developmental limitations leave them more suggestible, more prone to lying and fantasy, and more likely to forget facts, than are adults. Research suggests that there are grounds for some of these concerns. Goodman and Aman (1990), for example, found that a quarter of five-year-olds gave inaccurate answers to the question: 'Did he touch your private parts?' In a review of the extensive literature, Ceci and Bruck (1993) concluded that young children are especially vulnerable to suggestibility, that children (like adults) will lie when it is in their self-interest and that generally children have good recall for information, although young children do not recall as much detail as do older children.

To improve the accuracy of children's accounts, a number of forensic interviewing techniques have been suggested. Open-ended questions have been found to elicit more accurate responses than closed or focused questions, especially where the questions are repeated (Memon and Vartoukian 1996; Sternberg *et al.* 2001). However, an examination of interviews conducted in the field reveal that practitioners rarely adhere to interviewing best-practice. Many interviewers rely heavily on asking suggestive questions, or posing options for interviewees that potentially contaminate the accuracy of responses (Hershkowitz *et al.* 1997). Interviewing practices and victim accuracy can be substantially improved with the use of structured interview protocols (Sternberg *et al.* 2001).

Testifying

The end stage of the disclosure process is prosecution of the case. There is a heavy attrition of cases before this stage is reached. In an Australian study of 3,351 cases substantiated by child protection authorities, 2,143 were reported to police, 630 accused were charged, and 404 (12% of substantiated cases) were found guilty of at least one charge (Gallagher, Hickey and Ash 1997). This pattern seems fairly typical across jurisdictions (Goddard and Hiller 1992; Hood and Boltje 1998; Parkinson *et al.* 2002). These figures highlight the different standard of proof required for the purposes of intervention by child protection services, and that required to satisfy a court of law. There is also evidence that while prosecution rates for CSA are increasing, conviction rates are dropping (Cashmore 1995). This suggests that while people are being encouraged to report more incidents of CSA, and police are more inclined to charge those against whom allegations are made, they are doing so on less legally-rigorous grounds.

Testifying in court is potentially the most stressful event for victims who have reported CSA. In an adversarial system the victim may be forced to come face-to-face with the accused, and be put through a gruelling cross-examination (Eastwood 2003; Myers 1994). Some jurisdictions have introduced reforms to courtroom practices to accommodate CSA victims. These include reducing waiting times to go to trial, allowing victims to testify via closed-circuit television (CCTV), the use of pre-recorded testimony and limits to cross-examination (Eastwood 2003; Myers 1994; Sas, Wolfe and Gowdey 1996). Typically, modifications to courtroom procedures are available but not necessarily utilised, and it is unclear how widespread changes have actually been. For example, CCTV may be an option reserved for 'special' cases (Eastwood 2003). The experiences of victims are varied, and depend upon the particular court-room practices they encounter. Eastwood (2003) describes abusive and intimidating experiences of victims under cross-examination. In these cases victims and their parents regretted their decision to take the matter to court. Participants in Berliner and Conte's (1995) study, on the other hand, generally found the court-room experience was not as bad as they had expected and were glad that they had the opportunity to testify.

Preventing re-victimisation

The phenomenon of repeat victimisation is commonly reported in the general criminological literature. It is known that for a wide variety of crimes – including burglary, domestic assault, bullying and credit card fraud – being a victim on one occasion significantly increases the chances of being a victim again some time in the future. Repeat victimisation has obvious crime prevention implications. For example, victims of burglary can be given advice on how to improve security in the event that the same or another burglar returns. We begin by reviewing the available research on the serial victimisation of children, then go on to consider protective factors that might reduce the risk of re-victimisation.

Repeat victimisation

There are two main ways that sexual re-victimisation of children has been studied, each of which examines a slightly different aspect of the issue. Some studies have used self-reported experiences of sexual victimisation. In most cases, re-victimisation is operationalised as incidents of unrelated incidents involving different perpetrators. Various samples have been examined, producing different re-victimisation rates, but showing a consistent pattern of more severe symptomology for repeat victims. Long and Jackson (1991) surveyed female college students. They found that 5% of the sample, representing 10% of those reporting childhood sexual abuse, had been abused by multiple perpetrators. When compared to single-perpetrator victims, repeat victims were younger at the onset offence, were more likely to be abused by a familial perpetrator and experienced greater levels of family discord. Children abused by a familial offender on the first occasion tended to be abused by familial offenders on subsequent occasions, with a similar level of consistency for non-familial abuse. Kellog and Hoffman (1997) surveyed adolescent waiting-room patients at four clinics, including a sexual abuse clinic. Thirty per cent of the sample reported unwanted sexual experiences by a single perpetrator and 18% of the sample reported multiple perpetrators. Those reporting multiple perpetrators experienced higher levels of family violence, had greater self-blame and were more likely to delay disclosure of the abuse due to shame. Boney-McCoy and Finkelhor (1995) conducted telephone interviews with 2,000 children between the ages of ten and sixteen. They found that 29% of respondents who were sexually abused prior to the previous year, were also sexually abused during the previous year. (Note that in this study prior victimisation may have included the same perpetrator, and so re-victimisation rates are likely to be inflated.) Both sexual and non-sexual victimisation increased the likelihood of future sexual victimisation and led to higher levels of post-traumatic stress, even when controlling for demographic and offence-related factors.

The second method of investigating repeat victimisation is the analysis of substantiated CSA cases recorded in official hospital and child-welfare files. Because intervention by authorities is the measure of victimisation, repeat victimisation may or may not involve a different perpetrator. Fryer and Miyoshi (1994) followed children on a state abuse and neglect registry for four years. Sexual re-abuse was greater for females (8.5%) than for males (7.1%), and decreased with the age of the victim. Levy *et al.* (1995) followed a sample of children for five years after their discharge from a child abuse inpatient assessment programme. The sexual re-abuse rate was 16.8%, with greatest risk occurring in the first two years. Re-abused children were more likely to live in public housing, and have unmarried or unemployed parents. Swanston *et al.* (2002) took a sample of substantiated CSA cases over a designated time period, then determined if there were other substantiated notifications prior to, and during the six years following, the reference notification. One in six had subsequent notifications and one in ten had prior notifications for sexual abuse. Sexual abuse was a marker for family dysfunction and also predicted subsequent non-sexual abuse and neglect.

There are three possible explanations for repeat victimisation. First, there may be stable, pre-existing characteristics of the child (e.g. low self-esteem) that make him/her particularly vulnerable to abuse, and account for both the initial victimisation and subsequent victimisations. Second, there may be stable environmental or sociodemographic factors (e.g. family dysfunction) that similarly put the child at a higher risk across time. Third, the initial victimisation may somehow contribute to subsequent victimisations. With respect to this last explanation, the experience of victimisation may exacerbate both victim and environmental risk factors. Feelings of shame and a sense of one's self as 'spoilt goods' may deplete already low levels of self-esteem and emotional security. Sexual abuse can also lead to premature sexualisation that may expose the child to increased risk. Compared to non-victims, victims of CSA have been found to begin consensual sexual activity earlier, to have more sexual partners, to have higher rates of teenage pregnancy and to have higher rates of sexually transmitted diseases (Browne and Finkelhor 1986; Fergusson, Horwood and Lynskey 1997; Krahe *et al.* 1999). Additionally, the disclosure of the abuse may contribute to further family dysfunction and reduce the quality of guardianship available to the child. Where the perpetrator was the father or stepfather, the family may be reduced to a single parent. As we noted earlier, it is also not uncommon for the non-abusing mother in these circumstances to withdraw emotional support for the victim (Heriot 1996).

Resilience among CSA survivors

Most interventions with victims of CSA are designed to help victims and their families deal with the immediate impact of the abuse, and to reduce negative psychological sequelae. While interventions may be driven largely by a therapeutic concern with harm minimisation, there are clear overlaps between this objective and re-victimisation prevention. The uncovering of sexual abuse gives child protection workers the opportunity to address some of the personal and environmental risk factors that caused the initial abuse, and which, if left unchanged, may also facilitate re-victimisation. Additionally, many of the negative consequences of abuse, which may be the focus of harm minimisation interventions, may also increase the risks of re-victimisation. Treating issues such as feelings of powerlessness, diminished self-esteem, self-blame, early sexualisation, stigmatisation and social isolation, all of which may follow the experience of sexual abuse, is likely to have both harm minimisation and prevention benefits.

Unfortunately, there is a dearth of research that specifically evaluates the success of post-abuse interventions on preventing re-victimisation. However, there is a promising line of research examining the relationship between resilience and victimisation that may have prevention implications. Earlier in this chapter we reported that victims of CSA often lack confidence and emotional security, and we suggested that resilience in children might be a protective factor against becoming a victim of sexual abuse. Research also shows that resilience may be a protective factor that minimises the negative impacts of sexual abuse for children who have been victimised. As we outlined in Chapter 1, there is considerable variation in the psychological reactions of victims to their abuse, with 25% of maltreated children in one study showing no detectable long-term symptoms (McGloin and Widom 2001). It is theoretically plausible – and there is some suggestive research to support the proposition – that these resilient children are also at a lower risk of re-victimisation. There have been two main areas of research in this area – resilience as a function of social support and resilience as a function of cognitive style.

Resilient survivors of CSA report closer relationships with their parents than non-resilient survivors (Romans *et al.* 1995; Spaccareli and Kim 1995). Unfortunately, one of the possible consequences of sexual abuse, as we have seen, is that even greater stress is placed on what is often an already vulnerable family. In particular, at the very time that the child requires greatest emotional support, that support may be withdrawn by the non-abusing care-giver. However, social support does not have to come from the care-giver. In cases where the child is taken from the home, then valuable support may be provided by relatives or by foster parents (Egeland *et al.* 1993). Having at least one supportive person to whom to turn at the time of the abuse reduces the likelihood that the victim will perpetuate child abuse into the next generation (Egeland, Jacobitz and Sroufe 1988). Non-familial support can also be provided by structured social institutions such as schools and churches, and through involvement in extracurricular hobbies and activities (Heller *et al.* 1999). For example, adult survivors of CSA who had positive school experiences, an active social life and were involved in sports had higher self-esteem and fewer psychological problems than did other survivors (Romans *et al.* 1995).

The other area of research has examined dispositional features of resilient survivors. Heller *et al.* (1999) identified four key adaptive cognitive styles. The first is positive self-concept. A number of studies have reported positive associations between measures of self-esteem and resilience among adult survivors of CSA (Moran and Eckenrode 1992; Valentine and Feinauer 1993). The second is a belief in personal control over life events. Females are generally prone to have an external locus of control (i.e. they hold factors outside themselves responsible) for positive events, but an internal locus of control (i.e. they hold themselves responsible) for negative events. Resilient survivors of CSA have been found to buck this trend by having relatively a high internal locus for both positive and negative events (Moran and Eckenrode 1992). The third is an external attribution of blame. While resilient CSA survivors do not have a generalised external locus of control for negative events, they do attribute greater blame to the perpetrator than do non-resilient survivors (Moran and Eckenrode 1992). Some research has shown higher levels of re-victimisation among children who blame themselves for their abuse or rationalise the offender's behaviour (Berliner and Conte 1990; Kellog and Hoffman 1997). The fourth is ego control. This refers to the ability to insulate oneself from adverse environmental influences and stressors. Ego control is associated with self-assertion, persistence, emotional expressiveness and self-reflection. Cicchetti *et al.* (1993) argue that ego-controlling individuals are more attuned to cues that may put them at risk of victimisation.

Himelein and McElrath (1996) make the point that resilient cognitions are not necessarily realistic, and in fact, there can be psychological advantages to possessing distorted beliefs. They found that CSA survivors who displayed 'unrealistic optimism' about their abuse fared better than survivors who had no such illusions. Optimism manifested in a number of ways. Resilient survivors tended to minimise the seriousness of their abuse, and downplay the impact that it had on their lives. They may have even reframed the abuse in positive terms, for example, claiming that they became stronger through the experience. They also were less likely to dwell on the experience, and rather, tried to put it out of their minds. At the same time, resilient abuse survivors were more likely than non-resilient survivors to have confided in someone about their abuse, and to openly discuss their abuse histories with family and friends. Himelin and McElrath conclude that these findings do not indicate that resilient survivors are in denial about their abuse, but rather that they have 'worked through' their experiences. The research calls into question the wisdom of challenging rationalisations just because they seem unrealistic.

Summary

The popular stereotype of CSA is of a cunning and predatory offender who makes sudden and overt sexual advances to unsuspecting and reluctant victims, who in turn invariably suffer psychological trauma as a result of their victimisation. This view fails to acknowledge the complexity of CSA and, in particular, the emotional component of the victim–offender relationship. Without suggesting that children are complicit in their victimisation, or diminishing the negative psychological consequences of sexual abuse for many victims, we need to frankly acknowledge that victims often have, or develop, close emotional ties with offenders. Interventions that target potential CSA victims must begin with this understanding.

Only a small proportion of CSA cases become known to adults other than the perpetrator, and of those that do come to light, very few result in the conviction of the offender. However, while we may desire a conviction to satisfy our sense that justice has been done, worthwhile protection for the child can be achieved in its absence. Informal measures by non-abusing care-givers, and formal interventions by child protection services, can end the abuse for the child. Clearly it is desirable that as many cases of CSA as possible should be brought to light, although whether all cases should be subject to mandatory reporting is less clear-cut. A recurring theme as we progressed through the stages of the disclosure process was that few of the predictors of disclosure resided within the victim. The most important factors were the support the victim received by his/her family, and the way the victim was treated within the child welfare and criminal justice systems. Again the responsibility for children's safety must be accepted by adults.

Children who have once been victimised are at an increased risk of repeat victimisation. As such, they are a group of children who warrant special attention. At present, most post-abuse treatment is directed at the amelioration of the psychological distress. We believe that intervention at this time also provides the opportunity to address factors that might decrease the chances of re-victimisation. While the evidence at this stage is somewhat speculative, one promising approach is to develop interventions that increase resilience among CSA survivors.

In conclusion, as one of three necessary elements of any crime, victims are an obvious target for prevention efforts. However, we have argued from both philosophical and empirical positions that we should not expect children to be responsible for their own safety. At both the pre-abuse and post-abuse stages, we have highlighted the critical role in protecting children played by supportive adults, be they care-givers, family and friends or professionals within the child protection and criminal justice systems. We may strive to make children more confident and resilient in order to give them the best chance of avoiding abuse, or, if they have been abused, surviving the experience with minimal psychological damage. But at the end of the day, we must provide safe environments where all children are protected. How this goal might be achieved through situational interventions is the topic of the following chapter.

Chapter 8

Situational prevention

In Chapters 4, 5 and 6 we examined various ways in which preventing CSA might be achieved by targeting offenders and potential offenders. In the previous chapter (Chapter 7) we examined alternative approaches focused on victims and potential victims. In the present chapter we consider how CSA can be prevented by targeting the immediate environments in which it occurs. We borrow the situational crime prevention model from criminology and show that the same prevention principles can be applied to the problem of CSA. Situational crime prevention does not aim to change offenders in any permanent way, but rather to eliminate or reduce their inappropriate behaviour in prescribed settings. It does this by systematically identifying and modifying aspects of potential crime scenes that encourage or permit misbehaviour. Situational prevention, then, is about creating safer environments rather than creating safer individuals.

Advocates of situational prevention frequently face resistance from other social scientists who doubt the efficacy of their interventions. The situational approach is accused of neglecting the 'root' causes of problem behaviour, namely (depending upon one's discipline) social disadvantage and the antisocial dispositions of offenders. In comparison to these factors, critics contend, situations play a trivial role in behaviour and, at best, situational prevention will only succeed in displacing the problem to another location or victim. We begin by addressing these concerns, reviewing the conceptual and theoretical foundations of situational prevention. We show that situations have as much claim to the label of 'root' cause of CSA as do traits and social structures. We go on to suggest situational crime prevention strategies that may be used to combat CSA in domestic, institutional and public settings.

Conceptual and empirical foundations

As any introductory psychology text book will tell us, all behaviour is a result of the interaction between the characteristics of the actor and the circumstances in which the action takes place. Despite this fundamental principle, the discipline of psychology is heavily biased in favour of person-centred explanations of behaviour. Except in some notable exceptions (radical behaviourism and social psychology, for example), the contributions of the immediate contexts of behaviour are generally given short shrift in favour of the intrapsychic forces (attitudes, values, personality, mental disorders, and so forth) that are assumed to drive the individual to act. This theoretical bias parallels (and is probably the result of) the way human beings intuitively account for events. We have a natural proclivity to see individuals as the authors of their own fate, particularly where the outcomes are negative. Fundamental attributional error, as this cognitive bias is called, involves the over-estimation of personal deficits and malevolent intentions, and the discounting of immediate environmental pressures, when assessing others' (though not our own) responsibility for undesirable behaviour. In short, in both the academic literature and broader public policy debates, the role of situations in initiating and shaping problem behaviour, and the implications that this role has for preventing that behaviour, are rarely given the attention they deserve.

Still the most forceful and persuasive rebuttal of this person-centred bias in psychology is Mischel's (1968) classic articulation of the principle of behavioural specificity. Mischel took aim at the presumed stability of human traits. He weighed in to the cross-situational consistency debate, pointing out that an individual's behaviour can vary dramatically from one situation to the next. For example, someone can be extroverted in some circumstances and introverted in others. Even when a behaviour is thought typical of an individual, its performance is nevertheless situationally dependent. A person described as aggressive is not universally aggressive, but becomes so relatively infrequently and only under specific conditions. It follows, too, that given the right circumstances people are capable of atypical and at times reprehensible conduct. Rape, for example, is a frequent occurrence in war zones, carried out by soldiers who in other circumstances may never contemplate such behaviour. Like all species, then, human beings are best understood from an ecological perspective, as enmeshed within, and in dynamic relationship with, their immediate environment.

The person–situation interaction provides the theoretical basis of situational prevention. If behaviour is non-trivially mediated by immediate environments, then, in addition to treating dispositions, problem behaviour can be changed by altering the environmental conditions that initiate and maintain it. Clinically, this principle has been applied to relapse prevention and other stimulus-control interventions, in which clients are counselled to avoid or manage provocative situations (see Chapter 6). However, as adjuncts to treatment, these strategies remain tertiary interventions that must be applied on a case-by-case basis. The scope of situational prevention is far wider than this. The alternative to advising selected individuals to avoid risky environments is to purposely design those environments in ways that minimise their problem-evoking potential for all who encounter them.

Situational crime prevention

To see how situational principles might be operationalised as primary or secondary prevention we need to turn to criminology and the situational crime prevention model (Clarke 1997; Cornish and Clarke 2003). Situational crime prevention seeks to reduce crime, not to cure criminality. This is not merely a semantic distinction but requires a fundamental shift in the way we typically think about prevention in person-centred terms. In situational prevention, the crime event and not the offender is the object of interest. The focus is on the proximal rather than distal causes of crime; for practical purposes, how the offender came to be the way they are when they enter the crime scene is of little immediate relevance. The implementation of situational crime prevention begins with a detailed analysis of the problem in question – what is the crime? Where does it occur? When does it occur? Who is involved? Why do they do it? And how do they go about it?

Situational crime prevention tackles specific crimes in specific locations. For example, it will seek to reduce fights in nightclubs rather than the amorphous problem of 'youth violence'. Further, situational crime prevention is aided by the fact that crime is not randomly distributed in time and space but is patterned according to the criminogenic qualities of the environment. Not all nightclubs will be experiencing violent incidents, and for those that are, violence is likely to peak on certain days of the week and certain times of the day. Prevention practitioners can concentrate their efforts at crime clusters that will yield greatest return for effort. Still further analysis can be undertaken to reveal what makes certain locations hotspots for crime. Some nightclubs might attract patrons with pre-existing animosities (for example, supporters of rival football teams), the premises might be poorly designed and engender violence, or patrons might have developed strategies for circumventing existing security measures.

Once the target crime has been analysed, a comprehensive array of techniques is available to apply to the problem. As we noted in Chapter 2, these are of two main sorts. Original formulations of situational crime prevention emphasised opportunity-reduction. Offenders were assumed to be rational decision-makers who committed crime in order to benefit themselves in some way (Cornish and Clarke 1986). Situational interventions were designed to tip the cost–benefit analysis against the performance of crime. Contemplated crimes could be made to require more effort, to entail more risks, to deliver fewer rewards or to be less excusable (Clarke 1997). For example, violence-prone nightclubs might employ stricter patron screening procedures that make it more difficult for troublemakers to enter (increasing effort); they might install CCTV to identify troublesome patrons (increasing risk); patrons involved in violence might be banned from the premises (reducing rewards); and clear rules might be posted to leave no doubt about expected standards of behaviour (removing excuses).

Later, Wortley (2001) proposed additional prevention strategies that targeted crime precipitators. Criminogenic environments were conceptualised not just as locations that enabled motivated offenders to carry out intended crimes, but also as places that actively stimulate criminal behaviours by individuals who might not have otherwise considered committing a crime. Strategies for countering these situational precipitators included controlling environmental cues that prompt criminal responses, controlling social pressures on individuals to offend, reducing perceived permissibility to commit crime (similar to Clarke's concept of removing excuses) and reducing provocations for crime. Thus, dilapidated nightclubs might be gentrified in order to send out expectancy cues that violence is no longer appropriate (controlling prompts); security staff might be trained in non-confrontational management techniques to avoid encouraging crowd defiance (reducing social pressures); server-intervention policies might be vigorously enforced to reduce patron dis-inhibition associated with excessive alcohol consumption (reducing permissibility); and crowding levels might be reduced in order to alleviate patron stress (reducing provocations). Cornish and Clarke (2003) subsequently incorporated a modified version of Wortley's classification into their own classification under the heading of reducing provocations.

There is an accumulating catalogue of case studies attesting to the efficacy of situational crime prevention (Clarke 1992, 1997). It is true that situational crime prevention has been most commonly applied to property crimes (and thus, say critics, works best with 'rational' behaviour), but there are also examples of successful interventions with behaviours that might be regarded as 'psychological' in their origins. Clarke and Mayhew's (1988) *British Gas Study* is illustrative in this regard, albeit that the intervention in this case was not explicitly devised with a crime prevention outcome in mind. Clarke and Mayhew tracked two sets of data – British suicide rates and the uptake of domestic natural gas, which gradually replaced coal gas. Unlike natural gas, coal gas is toxic and, prior to its replacement, accounted for 40% of all suicides in Britain. The study revealed that suicides fell as the carbon monoxide content of gas reduced. Over a period of twelve years as the changeover took place, annual suicides fell from 5,714 to 3,693. Gassing is a relatively convenient and painless method of suicide. When this avenue was denied, a significant proportion of potential suicide victims abandoned their suicide attempt, rather than seek out alternative (less desirable) methods. The study neatly demonstrates that changing situational dynamics can have a net preventative effect even for desperate, deeply motivated behaviour.

Situational bases of CSA

Nevertheless, it might be objected that CSA is a special case – that CSA offenders are so peculiarly driven to sexually abuse children that they are immune to situational influences and will readily thwart any interventions put in their way. As we have argued in detail elsewhere (Smallbone and Wortley 2000; Wortley and Smallbone 2006a), we have several reasons for disputing this assumption. In Chapter 1 of this volume, we set out what is known about the demographic characteristics and offending patterns of CSA offenders. The research we cited there challenges many of the stereotypic assumptions about the relentlessness of CSA offenders. First, many CSA offenders do not begin sexually offending until a relatively late age (Smallbone and Wortley 2004a, reported a mean onset age of thirty-two years), suggesting both a lack of entrenched deviancy and a crucial role for opportunity. Early thirties is an age when men typically have greater access to children through childcare duties and as employees and volunteers in youth organisations. Second, and following from the previous point, CSA overwhelmingly occurs between offenders and victims who know each other. Sexually abusing strangers requires a degree of planning, effort and skill; offenders instead prefer to target victims to whom they have ready access. Third, the majority of CSA offenders are criminally versatile rather than sexual offending specialists, suggesting that they may possess generalised self-restraint problems rather than specific sexual deviancy. Many are opportunity-takers who succumb to criminal temptations in many forms. Finally, CSA has a relatively low official recidivism rate (around 13% after five years according to Hanson and Bussiere's [1998] meta-anlaysis), much lower than would be expected from individuals irresistibly driven to offend. It seems that detection and its consequences, including the reduced opportunity to access children once parents and guardians learn of the arrest, are sufficient to deter the majority of CSA offenders.

These data are consistent with a control model of CSA (see Chapter 2). They suggest that the capacity to view children as sexual objects is not confined to a few dedicated 'paedophiles', but may lie dormant in many men. In most cases, a combination of internal and external controls, including natural situational barriers, ensures that sexual attraction towards children is kept in check. However, when these controls break down, and opportunities are available, the potential for CSA may be activated in a broad spectrum of men. Unfortunately, situational controls on the victimisation of children are often deficient. Simon and Gzoba (2006) found that over half of all forcible rape arrests in the US involve child victims. This does not mean that most males have a sexual preference for children over adults, but it does suggest that children are convenient targets for sexual behaviour. From an offender's point of view, raping an adult woman may be a relatively difficult and risky proposition. In comparison to a child, she is less trusting and naïve, she is physically stronger and more likely to offer resistance, and there is a greater probability that she will report the offence and be able to present a coherent account of what happened. One of the prime reasons that many offenders sexually abuse children is because they can. It is not just the good fortune of CSA offenders that children are vulnerable and make easy targets: it is the fact that children are vulnerable and make easy targets that in large part drives CSA.

The stereotype of the persistent, specialist offender has no doubt contributed to a resistance to fully consider the role of situational factors in CSA. But – and this needs to be emphasised – the situational perspective does not depend upon a view of offenders as hapless victims of circumstance. All behaviour, even the most determined, cannot exist without a conducive immediate environment in which to occur. We outlined in Chapter 2 a three-category CSA offender typology based around the role of situational variables. Committed offenders actively manipulate the environment in order to seek out and groom victims; opportunists are sexually indiscriminate and are quick to exploit sexual opportunities presented to them; and situational offenders are not primarily attracted to children but are stimulated to offend by specific behavioural cues and/or environmental stressors, often in association with care-giving duties. It is easy to see how opportunists and situational offenders fit within the situational/ control model outlined above. However, the behaviour of committed offenders is no less situationally dependent. A committed CSA offender does not offend arbitrarily. On the contrary, he carefully selects vulnerable targets who offer least resistance and pose fewest risks (Elliott, Browne and Kilcoyne 1995). In fact, of the three offender types, committed offenders are arguably the most discriminating and sophisticated consumers of situational cues.

Situational prevention of child sexual abuse

In this section we will propose situational prevention strategies for CSA suggested by the classifications outlined by Cornish and Clarke (2003) and Wortley (2001). However, without further qualification, CSA is too broad for the implementation of situational crime prevention; it needs to be broken down into setting-specific subcategories. The situational strategies required to prevent CSA by a stranger at the local swimming pool will be quite different to those required to prevent familial CSA in the home. As a first step, we can differentiate between three main settings for CSA – public, institutional and domestic (see Chapter 1). The hypothesised interaction between the three settings and the three offender categories outlined in the previous section is shown in Table 8.1.

It should be noted before we proceed that our proposals, while based on well-established principles, are necessarily speculative. There is little existing research that tests the efficacy of situational interventions in CSA on a pre-test/post-test basis. Moreover, because

161

Table 8.1   The intersection of offender characteristics and offence settings

Setting	Situational	Offender Opportunistic	Committed
Public	Stimulated to offend in the course of short-term contact with a child encountered in generally accessible locations.	Exploits sexual opportunities when encountering children in generally accessible locations.	Frequents generally accessible locations where children are likely to be in order to access those children.
Institutional	Stimulated to offend in course of routine quasi-parental duties while working or volunteering in an organisation or agency that caters to children.	Exploits sexual opportunities while working or volunteering in an organisation or agency that caters to children.	Joins organisations or seeks employ-ment in agencies that cater to children in order to access those children.
Domestic	Stimulated to offend in the course of routine childcare duties.	Exploits sexual opportunities when left alone in the home with children.	Establishes relationships with single mothers or befriends neigh-bours with children in order to access their children.

each crime site has unique features, each requires tailor-made interventions. Our proposals, therefore, are not intended as ready-made solutions that will work in all circumstances and nor are they intended to be an exhaustive list of all possible strategies. Within each of the three offence site locations discussed below, there is still enormous variation. The more precisely the potential abuse setting can be described, the better. What the situational approach offers is a problem-solving methodology that will help researchers and practitioners develop their own prevention responses.

Public settings

Public settings for CSA are generally accessible spaces in the community, either where children typically congregate or where a child might be found alone. Smallbone and Wortley (2000) found that the most common public settings for accessing CSA victims were public toilets, isolated places, shopping malls, swimming pools, parks and playgrounds; similarly, Elliot *et al.* (1995) identified schools, shopping malls, arcades and playgrounds. Public settings are the stereotypical sites for 'stranger-danger'. Committed offenders are the most likely of the three offender categories to access children in public places, although situational and opportunistic offenders may take their victims to isolated locations to carry out their offences (Wortley and Smallbone 2006a). Overall, however, public places are the least likely of the three settings for CSA.

Public spaces are at one level the easiest of the three crime settings in which to implement situational strategies, in that these areas typically come under the control of some governmental or corporate authority that has the power to make any necessary changes to the environment. However, there is a wide range of potential public offending sites and the baseline of offending in any one location is extremely low, so knowing where to concentrate prevention strategies can be problematic. Moreover, there is a risk that if situational measures are too broadly or vigorously applied, they may be perceived as intrusive and may unnecessarily generate public fear and suspicion. We do not think that these are inevitable consequences of situational intervention, but this balance between adopting sensible safety precautions and fuelling a moral panic is a theme that we will return to a number of times in the remainder of this chapter. Notwithstanding these concerns, a number of situational prevention strategies for public places may be suggested. Of the available situational crime prevention strategies outlined earlier, we will highlight two as most applicable to reducing CSA in public settings – increasing effort and increasing risks.

Increasing effort
All other things being equal, offenders will choose soft targets that involve minimal deviation from their routine activities. Increasing the effort involved in offending may be particularly successful in deterring impulsive or ambivalent offenders. However, even highly motivated, persistent offenders will seek to minimise the amount of effort expended in committing crime. While committed offenders

will be the most difficult offender-type to deter, interventions that make CSA more difficult may reduce the overall frequency of their offending. Several of the methods suggested by Cornish and Clarke (2003) for increasing effort may be applied to CSA.

Perhaps the most widely known technique for increasing effort is *target hardening*. Ordinarily in crime prevention target hardening involves the use of bars, locks and toughened materials to protect vulnerable objects of crime. In the case of CSA, the teaching of self-protective behaviours to potential victims may be conceptualised as a type of target hardening. This is a controversial strategy that we dealt with in detail in Chapter 7. To briefly summarise here, it is assumed that perpetrators select victims who appear to lack confidence and who will offer least resistance. Children who are assertive, who are alert to the grooming strategies of perpetrators and who have been taught a repertoire of protective responses will be more difficult to victimise (Elliott *et al.* 1995). Smallbone and Wortley (2000), for example, found that, when perpetrators were asked to nominate what potential victims could do to deter their advances, the most common response was for the victim to assertively declare 'no'.

Another technique of particular interest for increasing the effort of CSA is *controlling tools/weapons*. In this technique, attempts are made to restrict the use of objects that support offending. When applied to CSA, the main target for intervention is the Internet and associated digital technology. There are three main ways that the Internet may support CSA. First, the Internet can provide direct access to potential victims. Committed offenders have been known to enter child-oriented chat rooms in order to set up meetings with children (Aftab 2000), or to engage in cyber-stalking (Finklehor, Mitchell and Wolak 2000). The Internet can also provide direct contact with children overseas who may be used in sex tourism (Aloysius 2001). Second, the Internet is now the major method for the distribution and acquisition of child pornography. While the relationship between child pornography and CSA is far from straightforward, it can be said that at least some offenders use pornography either to stimulate themselves to offend (Marshall 1988), or as part of the grooming process with victims (Goldstein 1999). (And of course, the very production of child pornography necessarily involves CSA.) Third, the Internet facilitates networking among some committed offenders, helping to create a virtual community that offers social and psychological support, as well as technical advice to its members.

There is a range of tactics available to help combat the use of the Internet to support CSA. Reputable Internet Service Providers routinely scan server content and take down illegal sites. Filtering software is also available for home and work computers that can block certain keyword searches or access to offending websites. In addition, most police departments now have dedicated units devoted to preventing and investigating Internet sex crime. Police may enter chat rooms posing as children in order to arrange meetings with offenders (US Department of Justice 2004). Similarly, phoney 'honey-trap' websites purporting to contain child pornography have also been set up to capture the IP address or credit card details of people trying to download illegal images (BBC News 2003). As well as resulting in the arrest of offenders, these strategies are designed to have a general deterrent effect by shaking the confidence of Internet users in the apparent anonymity and safety of online transactions. For a detailed coverage of the complex task of combating the use of the Internet to support CSA, see Wortley and Smallbone (2006a).

Increasing risks

Cohen and Felson (1979) have argued that any crime requires three minimal elements – a suitable target, a likely offender and the absence of a capable guardian. CSA offenders are most likely to select locations where the supervision of children is absent or inadequate and where the chances of being interrupted or getting caught are minimal. Consequently, an obvious generic strategy for combating CSA in public settings is to improve surveillance at possible crime sites.

Cornish and Clarke (2003) list several ways that the risk of detection can be increased. The first is by *extending guardianship*. CSA offenders are known to target children who are unaccompanied (Elliott *et al.* 1995). Clearly a child is safest if there is someone specifically looking out for their welfare, and parents and care-givers therefore have a primary responsibility to ensure that children are properly supervised outside the home. Not surprisingly, most 'stranger-danger' public education programmes include advice to care-givers on the effective guardianship of children.

Of course, one problem is that not all parents will heed such advice, and in any case, it is perhaps unrealistic to expect that children can be watched at all times. (Do we, for example, never allow children to walk to school?) Extending guardianship also includes strategies that increase the chance that neighbours or even strangers will assume guardianship roles and will intervene to stop possible crimes. Newman (1973) introduced the concept of 'defensible space' to crime prevention. Newman argued that urban living produced in residents a sense of anonymity and a lack of personal investment in community welfare. He advocated increasing the control residents have over the areas around their homes as a method of increasing public safety. One way of doing this is to increase their sense of territoriality. If residents feel ownership of public spaces they will be more likely to take care of those spaces and to vigilantly defend them against intruders. Many of the responses to increasing territoriality involve design of the built environment. For example, Newman suggests subdividing housing estates in ways to create 'zones of influence' that signal to both strangers and residents that the grounds are for the private use of residents. Extensions of this principle include programmes such as neighbourhood watch and safety-house programmes that similarly aim to involve residents in the crime prevention task (Beyer 1993; Salcido, Ornelas and Garcia 2002).

Formal and informal authority figures can also contribute to increased surveillance. *Strengthening formal surveillance* refers to the use of police patrols, security guards and CCTV coverage to watch over high-risk areas. More routinely, *utilising place managers* involves encouraging employees – such as pool attendants, shopping mall staff and park maintenance workers – to be on the look-out for possible crimes. In the case of CSA, it may be useful to provide staff with training to help them better recognise grooming behaviour. On some occasions employees, or someone purporting to be an employee, may in fact be the perpetrator. Staff uniforms and identification badges can *reduce anonymity* and make it easier to identify offenders.

Finally, the risk of detection can also be increased for offenders by making physical changes to potential crime sites. *Assisting natural surveillance* (another element of Newman's defensible space) involves improving visibility and removing blind spots so that potential crimes may be observed by passers-by. This may include installing better lighting, trimming hedges that obscure sightlines and regulating traffic flow in ways that increase natural interaction among pedestrians. For example, Cockfield and Moss (2002) make a number of recommendations for the design of public toilets to reduce sexual offending. These include building toilets in busy locations, facing entry doorways onto pedestrian thoroughfares, and ensuring they are well lit.

Institutional settings

Institutional settings are establishments, organisations and clubs that cater to children for some specific purpose. They include residential centres such as orphanages, juvenile detention facilities, boarding schools and hospitals and community centres that children attend as day visitors, such as local schools, youth groups, church organisations and sporting clubs. CSA offenders in institutional settings are likely to be staff or volunteers. Committed offenders who offend in institutional settings are likely to have joined the organisation with the express purpose of accessing children for sexual abuse. However, opportunists and situational offenders may also offend in institutional settings, responding to the opportunities and temptations that are presented. In particular, as we pointed out in Chapter 2, the quasi-parental roles adopted by many employees and volunteers may encourage attachments with children that find expression in sexual behaviour.

CSA in institutional settings has received a great deal of academic and media attention in recent years. Cases of CSA have been reported in residential children's homes (Colton, Vanstone and Walby 2002; Forde 1999; Gallager 2000; Utting 1997), in hospitals (Kendrick and Taylor 2000), within the church (Dunne 2004; Gallager 2000; Gartner 2004; Lothstein 2004; Saradjian and Nobus 2003; Shepard 2003), in schools (Anderson and Levine 1999; Gallager 2000; Trocmé and Schumaker 1999), in sporting and recreational clubs (Trocmé and Schumaker 1999) and in childcare centres (Gallager 2000; Kelley, Brant and Waterman 1993; Williams and Farrell 1990). Like public settings, institutional settings provide considerable scope for intervening in CSA, in that those in charge have the authority to dictate and enforce expected standards of behaviour of employees and volunteers. The main problem in implementing CSA prevention in institutional settings has been the secrecy within the offending organisations and a reluctance to tackle the problem (Colton, Vanstone and Walby 2002; Dunne 2004; Finkelhor 2003). In some cases, more than turning a blind eye to the problem, those in charge are among the perpetrators. We discuss three main strategies here for reducing CSA in institutions – increasing effort, increasing risks and the combined removing excuses/reducing permissibility.

Increasing effort

A logical response to abuse within institutions is to restrict who comes into the institution (*controlling access to facilities*). In crime prevention, this strategy is usually directed at outsiders. Thus, to prevent CSA, schools may require visitors to report to the office before they enter the grounds, or may keep a register of who is entitled to pick children up after class. However, given that most CSA offenders in institutions are insiders, it is tempting to think of this strategy more in terms of risk assessments designed to screen staff and volunteers. Obviously, screening-out known CSA offenders makes common sense. However, there are limitations to relying on this strategy. Smallbone and Wortley (2000) found that more than three-quarters of their sample of CSA offenders did not have previous sexual offence convictions. Screening alone will therefore not make institutional environments safe and may create a false sense of security. From a situational perspective, it is better to develop interventions that can be generally applied, rather than to assume that we can accurately identify risky individuals.

As an alternative (or supplement) to individual risks assessments of staff and volunteers, risk assessments may be performed on the institutional setting itself. An example of this strategy is being developed in Australia by the New South Wales Commission for Children and Young People (2008). One of the roles of the Commission is to oversee a system of employment screening for persons wishing to work with children. In addition to a screening instrument developed for this purpose, the Commission has developed two risk assessment instruments that seek to identify opportunities and temptations for child maltreatment that are made available through inappropriate environmental design and workplace practices. One instrument focuses on characteristics of the institution (Organisation Risk Estimate instrument) and the other on the characteristics of the specific staff role (Position Risk Estimate instrument). For example, an organisation is rated on the basis of factors such as whether it has formalised job descriptions that include appropriate and inappropriate behaviour towards children, whether there is a position in the organisation dedicated to managing risks of harm to children, whether the organisation has a formal action plan for minimising risks of harm to children, whether staff are formally made aware of the organisation's action plan and whether there is a process for the regular review of the organisation's action plan. A specific position within the organisation is rated on the basis of factors such as whether it involves working with children out of sight or hearing of other staff, whether training is provided to the supervisor on how to identify and respond to risky behaviour by staff, whether there are specific rules associated with the position about regulating interactions with children, whether the position involves contact with children outside the normal workplace, whether the children involved have particular vulnerabilities (e.g. disabilities) and whether the job involves emotional closeness to and/or physical contact with children. In developing these instruments, the Commission recognises that risks for children in institutions do not reside solely within the individual. This is one of the few attempts of which we are aware that a holistic approach to risk assessment has been adopted, and where organisations are given guidance on managing situational risks.

Increasing risks

Except in cases where there is conspiracy among staff, for there to be an opportunity for CSA in institutional settings requires a staff member to be alone with a child or children. Gallagher (2000) found that 92% of cases of institutional CSA involved lone perpetrators. One strategy to address CSA in institutions, therefore, is to minimise opportunities for staff to be alone with children. This may be done under the umbrella of *extending guardianship,* by developing formal protocols that set out the conditions under which staff and children may interact (Anderson and Levine 1999; Trocmé and Schumaker 1999). Teachers may not be permitted to keep a child back in class alone, excursions may be required to have a minimum of two teachers, sporting teams may require two coaches, and so on.

Opportunities may also be reduced through physical redesign of the environment. For example, interview rooms may be required to have glass viewing panels that allow people outside to observe activities within (an example of *assisting natural surveillance*). We are aware, of course, that such measures must carefully balance the potential benefits of preventive interventions against the potential risks of increasing unwarranted suspicions about physical and emotional contact between adults and children.

Perceived risks may also be increased by facilitating the detection and punishment of CSA. CSA has been allowed to flourish in some institutional settings because the perpetrator has been confident about the silence of victims, other staff and those in charge. *Formal surveillance* may be increased in a number of ways. Children should be given opportunities to make complaints if abuse occurs (Trocmé and Schumaker 1999). This can involve formal complaints procedures (especially in residential institutions) or through the provision of telephone and Internet helplines. Similarly, other staff should be encouraged to report abuse of which they become aware. Formal whistleblower support policies and procedures are a way to encourage this (Kendrick and Taylor 2000). Finally, institutions should be opened to outside scrutiny, including regular independent inspections and reviews (Kendrick and Taylor 2000; Trocmé and Schumaker 1999).

Removing excuses/reducing permissibility

Situations can sometimes contribute to blurring for offenders of the link between their behaviour and its consequences. The human conscience is highly malleable and sensitive to feedback from the environment and immediate social groups. Distorted feedback may assist offenders to make excuses or neutralisations (Sykes and Matza 1957) that portray their behaviour as an exception to the usual moral rule. Techniques to *remove excuses/reduce permissibility* aim to challenge these exculpatory cognitions that might permit otherwise self-proscribed behaviour.

The capacity of residential institutions, in particular, to engender abuses of power by staff has been well documented. Goffman (1959), in his classic sociological analysis of the 'total institution', outlined the inevitable divisions that develop between residents and staff. Institutional regimes divest residents of human qualities and individuality, facilitating neutralisations by staff that justify abuse ('they're all just numbers'). Staff, on the other hand, develop a sense of superiority and righteousness, and may justify brutal treatment through euphemistic labelling that redefines behaviour in terms of noble goals ('it's for their own good'). Later research by Zimbardo and colleagues (Haney *et al.* 1973; Haney and Zimbardo 1998; Zimbardo 1970) further fleshed out the psychological processes underpinning institutional behaviour. They described the pressures on staff to conform to the expectations of colleagues and to submerge their identity within the group. In this de-individuated state they are afforded a degree of anonymity and a cloak of collective responsibility that minimise their sense of personal accountability for their actions ('everybody's doing it').

Official inquiries and reports on CSA in residential institutions are replete with harrowing case studies describing the actions of staff who have clearly given themselves licence to do as they please (Forde 1999). In many cases the abuse is endemic and sustained over many years. Offending occurs not just because staff are secure in the belief that they will not be caught; there is a pervasive culture of abuse that has a distorting effect on individual moral judgement. From a situational prevention perspective, it is more productive to think in terms of pathological institutions than pathological individuals. Under *increasing risks* we suggested that formal protocols might be used in institutional settings to manage the interactions between staff and the children under their care. Such protocols not only increase the risks for offenders, but they are also a method of *rule-setting*. Rule-setting techniques seek to reinforce moral codes by making clear acceptable standards of conduct. For example, guidelines may be provided setting out the limits of physical contact between staff and residents (Trocmé and Schumaker 1999). Staff inductions, formal codes of conduct, posters, regular training, explicit directions from management and the vigorous prosecution of known offenders are designed to deny staff the opportunity to make excuses for their behaviour by exploiting ambiguity about what is expected of them.

It is also apparent from official inquiries that the sexual abuse of children in residential institutions often occurs against a background of a more general pattern of dehumanisation. Forde (1999) describes humiliating admission procedures, regimentation and suppression of individuality, crowded and substandard accommodation, drab and poor-quality institutional clothing and denial of access to basic standards of hygiene. Such treatment reinforces the image of residents as objects and prepares them for victimisation. *Personalising victims* seeks to make it cognitively more difficult to mistreat individuals by investing them with human qualities. As far as possible, institutional environments need to be normalised and residents must receive the physical care and individualised attention that afford them human dignity.

Domestic settings

Domestic settings for CSA are the home of either the victim or the perpetrator, which in many cases may be the same. This is by far the most common setting for CSA, with Smallbone and Wortley (2000) finding that 69% of cases occurred here. This is the most likely setting for opportunistic and situational offending, although committed offenders may also engineer relationships with single mothers or neighbours with the express intention of gaining sexual access to their children. It is in this setting that the potential for the conflation of attachment (care-seeking), nurturing (care-giving) and sexual motivations and behaviour is most likely to occur.

While many offenders in this setting may not have ingrained deviant motivations, and therefore are most likely to be responsive to environmental strategies, these offenders are also the most difficult to reach through situational prevention. The home is by definition a private space. Behaviours are largely hidden from outside scrutiny and social relationships within the home often militate against reporting abuse. Further, unless child protection or community corrections agencies are for some reason involved, there is no authority to ensure that situational prevention strategies are implemented within the home. Indeed, in some cases the person who might be relied upon to protect the child is in fact the perpetrator of abuse. Moreover, it is in domestic settings in particular where the dangers of implementing counterproductive measures become most acute. Notwithstanding these difficulties, we believe there is scope to implement situational strategies in the home. We will discuss increasing effort, increasing risks and controlling prompts.

Increasing effort

Given the difficulties noted above in accessing domestic settings, most situational strategies must be implemented through the primary care-giver. One risk factor for CSA in domestic settings is the presence of a stepfather or boyfriend of the child's mother (Finklehor *et al.* 1997; Fleming, Mullen and Bammer 1997; Kendall-Tackett and Simon 1992). Single mothers, therefore, need to think carefully about whom they invite into their home to share parenting duties (*controlling access to facilities*). At the same time, most stepfathers do not sexually abuse their step-children, and indeed they can provide crucial adult male role models and other emotional support. Again, the issue comes down to exercising judgement on a case-by-case basis.

In some cases, accommodation pressures can create the temptations and opportunities to offend. Sexual offending by adolescents often involves sibling abuse, which may be more common when siblings share beds or bedrooms (Finkelhor 1984). Similarly, a high prevalence of CSA has been reported in some remote Australian Aboriginal communities (Aboriginal and Torres Strait Island Task Force on Violence 1999) and this may be partly facilitated by cramped, open-plan housing where families are forced to share sleeping quarters (Smallbone, Wortley and Lancefield 1999). Providing single-room accommodation where possible is a means of *deflecting offenders.*

Increasing risks

Strategies to increase risks likewise usually require the co-operation of primary care-givers. Increasing risks may be operationalised by bolstering parents and other care-givers in their duty to safeguard the children in their care (*extending guardianship*). As Simon and Zgoba (2006) have estimated, parents are perpetrators in just 15% of sex offences against children. That is, parents may potentially play a preventative role in up to 85% of CSA cases. A number of public education programmes provide advice to parents on how to protect their children in the home (Darkness to Light 2005; Wyles 1988). The most common suggestion is to avoid as far as possible allowing the child to be in a one-to-one situation with an adult, even other family members. If this cannot be avoided, then parents are advised to require explicit information about planned activities from the adult or to drop in on the pair unexpectedly. There is obviously a potential danger that the blanket implementation of such rules may create unnecessary suspicions and ultimately interfere with healthy child–adult relationships. Nevertheless, applied judiciously such rules may provide appropriate safeguards. For example, parents and other care-givers may be better educated to recognise danger signals such as an offender's repeated or seemingly over enthusiastic attempts to seek opportunities to be alone with a child (Elliott *et al.* 1995).

Controlling prompts

According to learning theory, behaviour must be prompted, or cued, by a stimulus in the immediate environment. Some environmental cues – eliciting stimuli – can trigger reflexive responses such as sexual arousal. Sexual offences against children may be stimulated by the observation of children in 'provocative' (from the perspective of the offender) or vulnerable situations. In domestic settings, offending often occurs while the offender is engaged in some intimate activity with the child, such as giving the child a bath (Smallbone and Wortley 2000). *Controlling triggers* involves identifying and removing such arousal-evoking cues (Wortley 2001). This strategy may be particularly important in managing offending by situational and opportunistic offenders, but even committed offenders are sensitive to environmental cues.

Controlling triggers is a central rationale for relapse prevention treatment with known sexual offenders. Where offenders are re-turning to the family home under treatment after their abuse has been exposed, they may be required to conform to a number of house rules that seek to minimise stimulating situations. Typical rules might include: not to undertake intimate parenting roles such as dressing children; not to allow children to come into their bed; to avoid physical 'horseplay'; to make sure that bathroom doors are locked when in use; not to walk around the house in underwear; not to enter children's bedrooms; not to invite children to sit on their lap; not to require children to give kisses; not to have pornography in the house; and so on. Such rules, of course, are very restrictive and it is not suggested that they should be applied to family members in situations where there is no suspicion of sexual abuse. Again, the potential for such interventions to create undue suspicion and to inhibit desirable adult–child interaction is obvious. However, some of these rules may be appropriate for visitors to the home. There may also be circumstances where a household member may impose these restrictions on themselves. As we note in the next chapter, almost one-quarter of all calls to a sexual abuse prevention hotline programme were from otherwise undetected offenders concerned about their sexual urges (Chasan-Taylor and Tabachnick 1999). It may be possible to use such opportunities to educate men to recognise and manage situations that they might personally find tempting. The current media focus demonising sexual offenders may leave many men who are struggling with these temptations confused about their urges and left without guidance. While perhaps controversial, a franker approach that acknowledges that many men may from time-to-time become aroused by children may nevertheless prove more productive.

Summary

Situations are a neglected component of most current theoretical formulations of CSA. We have argued in this chapter that this neglect should be redressed. The situational context is not a passive backdrop to CSA; it plays an active role in the initiation and maintenance of the behaviour. Situations give an additional point of leverage in the task of preventing CSA. If CSA is mediated by opportunities and triggers presented by the immediate environment, then altering immediate environments can potentially have a significant impact on the performance of the behaviour.

We acknowledge that implementing situational interventions to prevent CSA is not without difficulties. Public settings, and to an even greater degree institutional settings, provide considerable scope for implementing situational strategies. Theoretically, situational factors are also crucial in CSA in domestic settings. However, accessing homes to ensure situational strategies are implemented is technically problematic, and the responsibility for prevention in most cases must be carried by the primary care-giver. Moreover, in all settings, but most particularly in the home, care needs to be taken that strategies are not too intrusive and do not ultimately cause more harm than good. We are not advocating a siege mentality where fathers feel they are unable to show affection to their children, where people are reluctant to baby-sit their friends' children or where teachers feel that they cannot comfort a distressed pupil, for fear of raising suspicions that they were involved in sexually abusive behaviours.

We have emphasised in this volume the need for evidence-based prevention. In the case of situational interventions, there is evidence that these strategies work for crimes other than CSA, and there is evidence that the incidence of CSA is significantly affected by situational factors. There is as yet little direct research evidence of situational interventions that have reduced CSA. Providing that direct evidence is now the challenge for researchers.

Chapter 9

Community-focused approaches

Thus far we have considered how CSA might be prevented by targeting offenders and potential offenders (Chapters 4, 5 and 6), victims and potential victims (Chapter 7) and the situations in which CSA occurs (Chapter 8). We now turn our attention to how CSA might be prevented by targeting prevention efforts on communities. We begin here by outlining the conceptual and empirical foundations of community-focused approaches to crime prevention and considering how these approaches could contribute to CSA prevention. We then examine community-focused approaches to preventing child maltreatment, and again consider how these approaches could contribute more specifically to CSA prevention. Finally, we examine community-focused approaches aimed specifically at preventing CSA.

Community-focused approaches to crime prevention

Compared to developmental and situational crime prevention and to modern approaches to offender treatment, community-focused crime prevention tends to be much more eclectic in its conceptual and empirical foundations and more diverse in its applied focus and methods. Indeed, modern community crime prevention programmes typically draw on a wide range of other proven or promising crime prevention methods as part of a menu of options that can be selected and applied to specific crime problems found to exist at a local community level. The overarching rationale for community crime prevention has historically been that social structures and other social conditions can both produce and sustain crime in residential communities, and that reducing or eliminating the presumed criminogenic features of these social conditions should lead to crime reduction. Although social ecological models have provided the conceptual basis for some community crime prevention projects, sociological models such as community disorganisation (Shaw and McKay 1942) and community disorder (Wilson and Kelling 1982) theories, which have arguably been less clear about the specific mechanisms linking social factors to individual behaviour, guided the early work and continue to influence thinking about community crime prevention. More recently, community crime prevention has also embraced conceptual and applied developments in environmental criminology, which attaches particular importance to the immediate settings in which crime occurs and is thus more concerned with reducing opportunities for criminal conduct than with reducing individual criminality (see Chapter 8).

Hope (1995) distinguished six approaches to community crime prevention according to their methods and main points of focus: community organising; tenant involvement; resource mobilisation; community defence; preserving order; and protecting the vulnerable. The earliest of these – the *community organising* approach – is exemplified in the Chicago Area Project (CAP) (Shaw and McKay 1969), which was originally implemented in the 1930s and is generally regarded as the first systematic attempt to implement community-based crime prevention. The CAP aimed to reduce delinquency in disadvantaged neighbourhoods by improving recreational activities for children and youth, providing informal counselling and mentoring of at-risk and delinquent youth by concerned and capable adults, and improving general social conditions. The project was based on the assumption that local residents themselves could be organised in a self-sustaining way to provide opportunities for the positive socialisation of children and youth, through the co-ordination of local institutions, groups and agencies.

The *tenant involvement* approach is exemplified in the responses in Britain in the 1970s to the social problems that had emerged in many public housing estates. As with the CAP these responses included a concerted effort to involve local residents, in this case in the management of the housing estates themselves and in consultation about local crime problems and potential solutions. These projects have typically aimed to improve residential maintenance and security, and to involve local residents in caretaking and property guardianship roles. *Resource mobilisation* initiatives grew in part from the recognition that even with sufficient capacity, commitment and organisation within local communities, the ability to solve local crime problems remained dependent to a significant extent on the ability of communities to secure access to the resources needed to improve local social and economic conditions. This approach is exemplified in the Mobilisation for Youth (MFY) Project in New York City (Short 1975), which sought to redress the inequitable allocation of central government resources to programmes affecting poor (mainly African American) youth and their families who had migrated to inner city neighbourhoods in the 1940s and 1950s. The MFY Project placed a greater emphasis on the co-ordination and resourcing of formal youth social, employment and welfare services, and (despite its initial plans to do so) placed less emphasis on building community institutions, than its predecessors (Hope 1995).

Community defence approaches to community crime prevention became popular in the 1970s and 1980s, following concerns about rising crime problems and a lack of hard evidence for the effectiveness of programmes that aimed to reduce delinquency by improving social conditions. Community defence approaches have relied on providing residents with security advice and on the co-ordinated involvement of residents in conducting routine surveillance in their neighbourhoods (e.g. Neighbourhood Watch programmes). Community defence approaches also include Crime Prevention through Environment Design (CPTED) (Wallis and Ford 1980), which aims to 'design out crime' in the built environment by removing obstacles to natural surveillance and the expression of natural territorial guardianship.

Community crime prevention approaches aimed at *preserving order* developed from the recognition that serious crime problems in high density urban settings were related to, and reflected in, a wide range of lower-level 'incivilities', such as vandalism, drug dealing, uncollected rubbish, run-down public facilities, and so on. Community policing and problem-oriented policing (Moore 1992), where police adopt a collaborative, preventive approach with local residents and other local agencies, are examples of this approach. Finally, and most recently, approaches aimed at *protecting the vulnerable* developed from the recognition that the incidence (not just the prevalence) of crime victimisation is unevenly distributed, even within high-crime areas. That is, within high-crime areas there are not only more victims, but there are also more individuals who are victimised more often. Thus, prevention efforts should be directed to reducing victimisation among the most vulnerable – those most at risk of repeat victimisation. An example of this approach is the 'cocooning' of recently victimised households by a small group of immediate neighbours (Forrester *et al.* 1990).

Although macro-level social and economic conditions are acknowledged as likely to contribute to crime problems at a local community level, in practice community crime prevention typically aims to intervene at the local level itself. Thus community crime prevention typically concentrates on building the capacity of local social institutions (families, friendship networks, clubs, associations and organisations) to reduce crime in residential communities. Three features typically characterise well-organised community crime prevention programmes: 1) a sustained and carefully co-ordinated effort involving key stakeholders and service delivery agencies (e.g. local government and non-government service agencies, police and other criminal justice agencies, business and community leaders); 2) the systematic identification and targeting of specific crime problems (e.g. street violence, residential burglaries) within defined locations; and 3) the utilisation of established theory and evidence to guide the selection, implementation and evaluation of prevention strategies. To illustrate how these features guide current approaches to community crime prevention, we will briefly describe two applied community crime prevention projects – Communities That Care, and Safer Cities.

Developed in the US by Hawkins and Catalano (1992), and later implemented in the UK (Communities That Care 1997), Communities That Care (CTC) is a rational, systematic approach to identifying and measuring local crime problems and crime-related risk and protective factors, and to selecting, implementing and evaluating proven or promising preventive interventions for specific crime-related problems. Individual projects are overseen by a management board comprising key community leaders (e.g. elected local government representatives; leaders of community groups and organisations; head teachers of local schools; probation and court officials; and the police), and managed by a paid co-ordinator. CTC itself provides overall guidance, including a range of training and technical support services. Risk and resource audits are undertaken by the local management board to systematically measure selected crime problems, to identify existing projects and services in the area, and to identify needs for new resources and services. CTC recommends that individual projects prioritise between two and five specific problems to be targeted, and provides a 'menu' of evidence-based individual-, school-, family- and community-level interventions for each selected target. Process and outcome evaluations are built in to each project design.

Like CTC, the Greater Newark Safer Cities Initiative (Safer Cities) (Kelling 2005) involves an oversight board, a systematic process of local crime problem analysis, a range of intervention modalities and a systematic approach to outcome evaluation. Unlike CTC, which leaves decisions about prioritising prevention targets to the communities themselves, Safer Cities emerged as a response to particular concerns about violent crime. Safer Cities gives a much greater emphasis than does CTC to policing and other criminal justice interventions, and accordingly gives more explicit attention to managing active offenders than to primary or secondary prevention interventions. Indeed, Safer Cities intervention modalities – notification sessions, accountability sessions, 'rev-up' sessions, enhanced supervision of known offenders and a gun-control programme – are all associated with a traditional criminal justice-led approach to crime control. Nevertheless, its credentials as a community prevention initiative are established both through its inclusion of community representatives on its oversight board and its emphasis on problem-oriented and community policing. Further developments are anticipated in this regard with the planned addition of community outreach and public education components (Kelling 2005).

Although some evidence has been marshalled to support these kinds of community-focused crime prevention approaches, on the whole the evidence for their effectiveness has been less convincing than for the other major (e.g. developmental and situational) crime prevention models (Tonry and Farrington 1995; Welsh and Hoshi 2002). Part of the problem is that the complexity of community approaches makes systematic, controlled evaluation very difficult. At a practical level, because community-focused approaches generally aim to establish genuine collaborative partnerships with community members themselves, their original aims may be diluted or redirected by divergent interests. For our present purposes, an additional problem is presented by the fact that community crime prevention approaches have generally not been directed towards the prevention of child maltreatment, much less CSA; instead, their typical focus has been on property and violent crime and other 'external' threats to public safety.

Applying community crime prevention to the prevention of CSA

The history of community crime prevention as described by Hope (1995) illustrates the various strategic approaches that might inform the overall focus of individual community crime prevention projects, and applied community crime prevention models such as CTC and Safer Cities provide practical frameworks for the organisation and implementation of individual projects. CTC in particular is designed to be transportable, with central support services provided but with a strong focus on local 'ownership' and management of crime prevention projects. Intervention techniques themselves can be selected from an extensive menu of proven or promising methods, depending on identified priorities, including those targeting: 1) the development of individual criminality; 2) the ecological factors that produce or sustain specific crime problems; and 3) the physical environments that obstruct routine community surveillance and guardianship. Thus community crime prevention does not derive from any particular theoretical conception of crime or method of intervention, but rather offers a pragmatic organisational framework for involving local communities in taking action concerning a broad range of potential crime and crime-related problems, in a broad range of ways.

Because of common developmental and ecological risk factors for general offending and for CSA offending, any community crime prevention programme that succeeds in reducing individual criminality is likely to also reduce CSA offending. Moreover, while the specific situational factors associated with CSA are likely to be very different than for other kinds of crime, situation-focused analytical methods (see Chapter 8) could nevertheless be employed to analyse local problems concerning child maltreatment, including CSA. However, apart from its potential generic effects that may include reductions in CSA offending (along with general reductions in crime and disorder), community crime prevention may have rather limited direct application specifically to the prevention of CSA. First, local community action is probably more likely to be evoked in circumstances where significant external threats, such as high rates of residential burglary or 'street crimes', are identified. Community perceptions that CSA is either committed by a small number of highly deviant individuals, or otherwise that it only occurs in 'other people's families', may be unlikely to evoke sufficient self-interest to generate wide participation in community prevention initiatives targeting CSA. Second, because of its very low official base rates CSA may be unlikely to be identified as a local community priority, especially in circumstances where much more visible crime problems present more immediate concerns. In England and Wales, for example, property offences comprise around 80%, and violent offences around 16%, of all offences reported to police (Maguire and Brookman 2005), and it is these kinds of offences that have typically been the priority targets of community crime prevention. By contrast, sexual offences comprise less than 1% of all crimes reported to police, with probably around half of these involving CSA offences. It would therefore be unlikely that crime audits undertaken by community prevention oversight committees, especially if they were to rely on official data, would identify CSA as a community crime prevention priority.

This is not to say that community prevention efforts could not be directed specifically to preventing CSA. Indeed, notwithstanding the difficulties of obtaining accurate prevalence figures, there is no compelling reason why applied community prevention models could not be used in circumstances where there are particular local concerns about CSA. These concerns could of course arise from community concerns about the potential harm of CSA even for a small minority of children and their families, rather than simply from high prevalence rates. But community crime prevention models may be especially applicable in social settings where the prevalence of CSA is particularly highly concentrated, where local social conditions are more directly implicated in its causes, where local communities see themselves as being directly and significantly affected by the problem, and where traditional criminal justice approaches have failed to produce any enduring solution. All of these conditions apply, for example, in some remote Australian Aboriginal communities (Aboriginal and Torres Strait Islander Women's Taskforce on Violence 1999).

In the US and the UK, from where much of the academic and applied work in community crime prevention has originated, social disadvantage and high crime rates are often concentrated in high-density urban areas, and accordingly it is in these settings where most community crime prevention projects have been conceived and implemented. But in Canada and Australia, for example, some of the highest rates of crime and disorder, including CSA, are concentrated in small regional and remote communities, many of which may be literally thousands of kilometres away from the major cities where most social service agencies are based. Both logistical and cultural barriers obstruct the provision of routine education, justice, health and welfare services, let alone the level of services commensurate with the breadth and depth of social problems found in many of these remote communities. Community-level preventive interventions may present a viable option in these settings.

As Homel, Lincoln and Herd (1999) have noted with respect to the Australian situation, involvement with criminal justice agencies is especially problematic for many Indigenous people because of social and historical associations with police racism and violence, deaths in custody, dispossession and colonisation. Thus, despite an increasing willingness in some remote communities to work alongside local police (Homel *et al.* 1999), criminal justice-led community programmes like those modelled on projects such as Safer Cities are unlikely to be embraced, and may even be actively resisted, by some Indigenous communities, especially if they are seen as yet another imposition from non-Indigenous social control agencies. Programmes guided by models such as CTC may be more appropriate in these circumstances, particularly if genuine community partnerships can be established and maintained. The alarming extent of CSA in some of these communities occurs in a wider context of pervasive physical and mental health problems, alcohol dependence and violence (particularly family-related violence), and many of these problems are likely to present serious constraints on the capacity for wide community involvement. However, giving particular attention to CSA might give some impetus to a broader child-focused prevention strategy which may over time produce a diffusion of benefits. A child-focused approach may also allow for community prevention programmes to build on some of the cultural strengths in Indigenous communities, such as extended, multi-generational family networks, strong social bonds to family, and traditions of reciprocity and sharing of social and material goods.

Community-focused approaches to preventing maltreatment

Social ecological models (Belsky 1980; Garbarino 1977) have had a wide and enduring influence on thinking and practice in the field of child maltreatment. However, recognition of the influence of wider community factors on child maltreatment has been more apparent in planned prevention initiatives than it has in the day-to-day operation of child protection services. Many commentators point to the problem that, in the face of limited resources, overwhelming demand and complex family problems, child protection services in practice are often drawn towards highly coercive, individual-level intervention approaches (Cook, Reppucci and Small 2002). Community-focused prevention programmes, on the other hand, generally aim to provide non-coercive, non-stigmatising, neighbourhood-based, family-focused, child-centred interventions. Cook *et al.* (2002) conducted a narrative review of the efficacy of community-focused maltreatment prevention programmes, identifying three main approaches: family life (or parenthood) education; family support; and home visiting programmes.

Parenthood education approaches may target school-aged children, adolescents, expectant or new parents, or 'at-risk' parents. Programmes typically aim to provide education about child development and positive child rearing practices, and to explore perceptions and attitudes about parenting (O'Connor 1990; Wekerle and Wolfe 1991). Interest in universal parenthood education, as an addition or alternative to the historical emphasis on intervening with high-risk groups (including maltreating parents), has increased in the last two decades (Cook *et al.* 2002; Luster and Youatt 1989). On the whole, evaluations of universal parenthood education programmes have reported positive outcomes, including reductions in authoritarian parenting strategies, and increases in parenting confidence, responsible decision-making, conflict resolution skills, social competence and social support (Cook *et al.* 2002). Additionally, behavioural parent training programmes (e.g. Patterson, Reid and Dishion 1992; Sanders 1999) have been shown to be effective in reducing coercive parent–child interactions and in improving parental monitoring.

Cook *et al.* define *family support* approaches to maltreatment prevention as '... programmes located in neighbourhoods where families seek and take part in a comprehensive variety of services and activities designed to strengthen families and neighbourhoods through social networking' (Cook *et al.* 2002: 72). Family support approaches typically include some combination of child development education, health screening and advice, support groups, drop-in centres, home visits, parenting skills education and training, and childcare assistance, with programmes typically staffed with a combination of professionals, paraprofessionals and volunteers. Evaluations of family support approaches have reported improved parenting attitudes and knowledge, improved parent–child interactions and reductions in child abuse and neglect reports (Lutzker, Wesch and Rice 1984). Cook *et al.* (2002) argue that family support programmes are most likely to be effective when they: 1) are designed to work at multiple ecological levels (individual, peer, family, school and neighbourhood); 2) target multiple developmental (e.g. cognitive, emotional, social and physical) outcomes; 3) focus on the entire family, rather than on individual children or parents; 4) aim to produce sustained changes to the family dynamics and environment; 5) are of sufficient length and intensity, with higher intensity interventions available for at-risk families; 6) are culturally sensitive; and 7) target appropriate risk and protective factors, at appropriate times to maximise family responsiveness.

Because *home visiting* programmes offer in-home services, these programmes may reach families who may otherwise not take advantage of or may not have access to neighbourhood-based family support services. Cook *et al.* (2002) list three assumptions underpinning home visiting services: 1) as the most consistent care-givers of children, parents should logically be the key target of maltreatment prevention efforts; 2) parents can respond positively and effectively to their children when they (parents) are given appropriate knowledge, skills and support; and 3) effective parenting is optimised when their own emotional and physical needs are met. Home visitors may be health professionals (often attached to hospitals or community health facilities), paraprofessionals (e.g. parent coaches and aides) or trained volunteers. The services offered in these programmes depend on the level of expertise of the home visitors, but a similar range of services to those offered in neighbourhood-based family support programmes may be offered as in-home services.

Olds and Kitzman (1990) reviewed home visiting programmes that were aimed at families at risk of health problems or child maltreatment, and concluded that the most effective programmes were those that: 1) were based on ecological models; 2) incorporated material, social, behavioural and psychological services; 3) focused on intervening during pregnancy and early childhood; 4) involved extended contact; and 5) concentrated on universal application in communities with low resources (e.g. poor or young single parents), rather than risking stigmatisation by selecting individual at-risk families. Importantly, and consistent with social ecological models, home visiting services may include efforts to assist families to access formal and informal services and other social supports in the wider community, rather than simply intervening in the home environment itself.

Applying community-focused prevention of maltreatment to CSA prevention

Parenthood education, family support and home visiting services – the mainstays of community-level efforts to prevent child maltreatment – have explicitly targeted physical and emotional abuse and neglect, but have tended to give less explicit attention to CSA. It is not entirely clear why this is the case. Some commentators argue that the causes of CSA are so different from those of other forms of child maltreatment that an entirely different approach is warranted. For example, although they do not point to any evidence to support their claims, Tomison and Wise argue that the community-level factors related to child maltreatment, such as poverty, culture and parenting practices, are simply not relevant to CSA, noting that 'community-level approaches, particularly those designed to create healthy communities … are not designed to prevent sexual abuse' (Tomison and Wise 1999: 7). Other commentators argue that, while the causes of each form of child maltreatment are likely to be somewhat different, parent education and support programmes, for example, could nevertheless make important contributions to the prevention of CSA (Donnelly 1997; McMahon and Puett 1999). The WHO makes no special distinction in this regard, asserting that 'common features, as regards their epidemiology and risk factors, shared by different forms of maltreatment suggest that similar approaches to prevention might be adopted for physical abuse, sexual abuse, emotional abuse and neglect' (WHO 2006: 43). While we are inclined to accept the position of the WHO in this regard, we would argue that differences between CSA and other forms of child maltreatment nevertheless need to be taken into account for community-level prevention to be effective in preventing CSA.

One important difference between CSA and other forms of maltreatment lies in the different patterns of perpetration by men and women. US child protection data show that women are identified as perpetrators in the majority (58%) of combined child maltreatment incidents (US Department of Health and Human Services 2006). By contrast, adolescent and adult males are implicated as perpetrators in the vast majority of reported *sexual* abuse incidents. Community-focused maltreatment prevention programmes are, for a variety of reasons, typically oriented more to engaging with women than with men. For example, home visiting programmes often exclusively target vulnerable young women (e.g. Olds 2002). As Finkelhor and Daro (1997) have noted, men have traditionally been considered more difficult to recruit into seeking or accepting help generally, and it may be these perceived difficulties that have maintained the more or less exclusive focus in maltreatment prevention on women. A significant shift in strategy is therefore required to engage effectively with men in community-level prevention programmes, and especially in programmes targeting the prevention of CSA. For example in a report commissioned by the Australian government, Russell *et al.* (1999) recommended that child and family focused service agencies should establish more father-inclusive policies and practices, that the ambivalent and negative attitudes towards fathers held by some professionals and service providers need to be addressed and that community-based prevention targeting fathers should be directed to the places where men spend much of their time (e.g. in the workplace).

Another difference between CSA and other forms of maltreatment is that parents are less likely to be implicated as perpetrators in CSA. Again with reference to US child protection data, 63% of parents who are identified as perpetrators in child maltreatment incidents are implicated in neglect cases, whereas only 3% of maltreating parents are implicated in sexual abuse. By contrast, where family friends or neighbours are identified as perpetrators, 73% are implicated in sexual abuse. Thirty per cent of 'other relatives', and 11% of the unmarried partners of the parents of maltreated children, are identified as perpetrators of sexual abuse (US Department of Health and Human Services 2006). These and other prevalence data suggest that community-level CSA prevention needs to assist parents to protect their children from the risks presented from non-parents, including friends, neighbours, boyfriends, stepfathers and occasional visitors to the home. One approach may be to assist vulnerable young mothers to reduce their emotional and economic dependence on men, and to be better able to make careful, informed decisions about involving unrelated men in primary childcare responsibilities. Rather than concentrating on mothers and fathers as potential abusers, as some maltreatment prevention approaches at least implicitly do, for CSA prevention the emphasis may need to be shifted to assisting parents to understand from where the risks to their children might arise and to improving their capacity for and commitment to parental monitoring and supervision.

Finally, assisting parents to establish secure attachment bonds with their children is widely considered to be a sensible strategy for preventing many kinds of maltreatment, and there are some additional reasons why this may be important particularly in the prevention of CSA. First, secure parent–child attachment bonds are thought to diminish risks for CSA by enhancing the quality of parental supervision and by reducing emotional neediness in children (and thus decreasing vulnerability with respect to the attentions of sexual offenders) (Alexander 1992). Second, secure father–daughter attachment in particular has been identified as an important protective factor for familial CSA (Williams and Finkelhor 1995). Third, insecure father–son attachment has been identified as a potential risk factor in terms of the son himself later engaging in irresponsible sexual conduct (Smallbone and Dadds 1998, 2000). Once again, these observations underscore the need for CSA prevention to promote secure attachment bonds between adults and both male and female children.

Community-focused approaches to preventing sexual abuse

While community-focused approaches to preventing crime and child maltreatment have tended to adopt rather different prevention strategies, both have been guided by a recognition that social conditions influence individual behaviour and that improving social conditions is therefore likely to lead to reductions in the targeted behaviours. Both have drawn from a long history of theoretical and empirical research to identify specific prevention targets and to develop applied prevention strategies. Community-focused approaches to preventing CSA have also been guided by a recognition that social conditions influence the occurrence of CSA. However, there are several important differences in the ways that community-focused CSA prevention has proceeded.

First, whereas community-focused prevention projects in the crime and child maltreatment fields tend to have been led by researchers and practitioners, until very recently there has been less direct involvement by researchers and practitioners in community-focused prevention specifically targeting CSA. Most of the academic and applied work in the field of CSA has instead been directed towards understanding and treating identified CSA offenders and victims. Community-focused CSA prevention projects have tended to be led instead by politically engaged advocacy groups. One result of this seems to be that while community prevention of CSA has a very prominent presence in the popular media (e.g. the Internet), there is little research on community CSA prevention reported in the peer-reviewed literature. At this stage we still know very little about either the positive or negative effects of community-focused CSA prevention. Second, the links between theoretical and empirical knowledge and the design of community-focused CSA prevention strategies are much less clear than is the case for community crime and maltreatment prevention. Community-focused CSA prevention programmes make very little reference to established scientific theory, and tend to be selective in their use of empirical evidence. Publicity materials tend to present the highest defensible prevalence estimates, avoid controversies concerning the resilience of many children to the otherwise harmful effects of CSA and say little about the low observed recidivism rates among CSA offenders. This may be partly because it is difficult to convey complex ideas and incomplete knowledge to the general public. Third, advocacy-led prevention campaigns identify CSA as a more or less wholly distinct problem. Whereas researchers and practitioners concerned with preventing child maltreatment include sexual abuse as part of the broader problem of child abuse and neglect, CSA prevention programmes typically present CSA as a unique problem, with its own unique causes and requiring its own unique solutions. Finally, whereas community approaches to preventing crime and child maltreatment have generally adopted direct community engagement strategies, community-focused approaches to preventing CSA have instead tended to concentrate on universal social awareness and education strategies and have generally given less attention to direct community engagement.

As CSA advocacy groups became better organised in the 1980s and early 1990s, these groups increasingly embraced mass media technologies, especially television and the Internet, as the main method of disseminating their ideas about CSA to the public at large. This shift towards the use of sophisticated mass media technologies has allowed for these groups' messages about CSA to be presented to a much wider, adult audience. As we saw in Chapter 7, unlike prevention strategies for other kinds of child maltreatment, CSA prevention has tended to target children themselves, usually through school-based education and skills training. This focus on educating and training children continues to be promoted in many of the current community-focused prevention programmes. At the same time, a prominent message conveyed in these programmes is that adults, not children, should take responsibility for preventing CSA. At one level this presents an apparent contradiction, since these programmes typically call upon adults to themselves engage in educating children about CSA. The aims of these campaigns therefore seem to be to widen, rather than reduce, children's roles in the prevention of CSA. However, encouraging adults to educate children about CSA is just one of a broad range of activities that are suggested for adults to contribute to preventing, detecting and responding to CSA. Two of the more prominent community-focused CSA prevention programmes that seem to have made this shift towards engaging with adults are the US-based Darkness to Light and Stop It Now! campaigns.

The Darkness to Light campaign was established in 1997 by a group of activists in Charleston, South Carolina. According to its promotional materials, within a few years this group had established a significant media presence, with public service announcements being broadcast on major television networks, wide dissemination of print materials, training programmes for concerned individuals and organisations and a sophisticated website providing a range of information and resources. While continuing to promote child-focused education and skills training, the campaign's stated mission is to shift the responsibility for CSA prevention from children to adults through education and awareness. Visitors to its website are advised, for example, to eliminate or reduce one-child/one-adult situations, to talk openly with children about sexual abuse (including telling children that abusers may be an adult friend or family member), and to act on their suspicions by immediately reporting them (the site includes information about how to contact child protection and law enforcement agencies).

Arguably the most ambitious and sustained community-focused CSA prevention campaign has been the Stop It Now! programme, which was founded in Vermont in 1992 and is now also operational in the UK and the Republic of Ireland. The original Vermont programme aimed to use the media to increase public knowledge and awareness about sexual abuse, engaged directly with individuals and organisations who work with at-risk families, provided a toll-free helpline to provide information and referral advice, and sought to implement a 'systems change strategy' designed to influence the development of relevant public policy (Chasan-Taber and Tabachnick 1999). Like the Darkness to Light campaign, Stop It Now! asserts that adults, not children, should be responsible for preventing, recognising and reporting CSA. At the same time, Stop It Now! argues that children should be warned about CSA and trained to prevent their own victimisation. Stop It Now! provides a range of resources and information intended to enable adults to recognise 'grooming' and sexually abusive behaviour in adolescents and other adults, as well as the behavioural and physical symptoms of sexual abuse in children.

One of the most significant developments in community-focused CSA prevention programmes has been the implementation of confidential telephone helplines targeting adults concerned with their own or others' behaviour. The Stop It Now! helpline in Vermont received 657 calls in its first four years from 1995 to 1999. About half of these calls were reported to have been from adults who knew either a suspected abuser or a suspected victim. An additional ninety-nine calls (15%) were reported to be from self-identified sexual abusers themselves (Stop It Now! 2006). While these numbers are quite small (fewer than three calls per month from self-identified abusers), they do suggest that it is possible to engage with some actual or potential CSA offenders before more formal investigative responses are activated. More detail is reported in an evaluation of the helpline service operated by Stop It Now! (UK and Ireland) (2006). Here, 4,013 helpline calls (from 2,076 callers) were received in the three-year period from June 2002 to May 2005. In this case the largest group, representing 45% of all calls and 32% of all callers, was adults concerned about their own be-haviour. Of the 674 callers who were concerned about their own behaviour, 37% were identified as not yet having sexually abused a child and as wanting assistance to refrain from doing so. A further 27% were identified as having already committed an undetected CSA offence and wanting assistance to prevent further offending. Of the 254 self-identified potential or actual abusers who identified their relationship with a (potential) victim, 176 (69%) stated that this was a family member. The remainder (31%) stated that the victim was a friend or family acquaintance. Two hundred and eighty-four callers asked for assistance with Internet sexual offences. Of these, 214 (75%) had already been arrested for an Internet offence. The remaining seventy of these callers (25%) had not been arrested but had either accessed child pornography or were concerned that they might do so.

The availability of a confidential telephone helpline that aims to provide information and assistance particularly to people who have either already engaged in CSA, who are concerned that they might do so, or who have concerns about others' behaviour, is a very significant development in community-focused CSA prevention. This development also represents an important shift towards direct community engagement, and thus towards the involvement of professional services, in CSA prevention. Evidence that at least some members of these key target groups will make use of these helplines is very encouraging, but raises important questions about how best to organise the information and support services attached to the helplines. One pressing issue is the capacity and willingness of these services to maintain confidentiality. At present, while callers are able to exercise their choice to remain anonymous, any face-to-face contact that may be offered is subject to agency policies and laws concerning the reporting of CSA offences. The helpline operated by Stop It Now! (UK and Ireland), for example, allows callers to remain anonymous, but informs callers of the limits to confidentiality if they provide identifying information. Specifically, helpline operators routinely advise callers that information will be passed on to relevant child protection or law enforcement authorities if the caller identifies themselves or anyone else suspected of engaging in CSA or related (e.g. Internet pornography) offences. While these conditions still allow anonymity for helpline calls themselves, callers are advised that face-to-face contact with qualified counsellors is not possible without the involvement of police. Presumably in most cases this will deter those who have already committed an offence, and perhaps also those who fear being identified as potential offenders, from seeking face-to-face assistance. Paradoxically, then, perhaps the single most important prevention opportunity presented by these helplines – to engage directly with actual or potential CSA offenders – may effectively be denied through policies such as mandatory reporting that are themselves ostensibly designed to prevent CSA. We think an open and informed debate is needed about whether the potential benefits of allowing for confidential professional services to be made available for actual or potential CSA offenders may outweigh the benefits of policies that require formal notification to police and other authorities. We think this should be part of a broader debate about the stigmatisation of CSA offenders which, as other commentators (e.g. Finkelhor and Daro 1997) have noted, presents significant obstacles to engaging with undetected or potential CSA offenders.

While some of the advice offered by these CSA prevention campaigns – whether it is provided through their print materials, radio and television activities, helplines or websites – has at least face validity, its efficacy nevertheless remains untested. For example, the Darkness to Light website advises parents to minimise opportunities for CSA, and that minimising one-adult/one-child situations is one way to achieve this. This kind of advice is consistent with situational prevention models (see Chapter 8). The Stop It Now! website advises adults to be suspicious if, for example, another adult 'is overly interested in the sexuality of a particular child or teen' or 'frequently walks in on children or teenagers in the bathroom', which is broadly consistent with evidence concerning CSA offenders' clinical presentation and modus operandi research. However, if a key strength of this universal dissemination of 'preventive' advice is that it reaches many more people than would ever be possible with direct community engagement, a key weakness is that it contains fewer important safeguards. An important advantage of direct engagement strategies is that it is possible to provide advice and assistance while taking account of individual circumstances. Trained home visitors or helpline counsellors, for example, are potentially able to assist people to weigh the risks and benefits of certain safety measures concerning their children and to consider these in the context of their life circumstances. Clearly universal education strategies are not able to do this, but instead rely on the public making sensible use of the advice. Of particular concern would be if these education strategies were to raise unnecessary suspicions, to decrease healthy intimacy between adults and children or more generally to increase public anxieties, without contributing to prevention. Evaluation studies are needed that systematically test for the possibility of negative, as well as positive, outcomes of these universal education campaigns.

Although community-focused CSA prevention campaigns have in recent years extended their aims well beyond increasing community awareness, current approaches nevertheless continue to focus on community awareness as a key prevention strategy. From an ecosystemic perspective, this may contribute to a clarification of sociocultural norms and values about the importance of child protection and particularly about the dangers of sexual abuse. However, as we noted in Chapter 3, social ecology theory suggests it is the more proximal levels of their social ecosystems that exert the most powerful influences on individuals' behaviour. Accordingly, we argued in Chapter 3 that targeting the more proximal elements of individuals' social ecosystems, such as schools, workplaces and institutions, may be more effective and more efficient than universal community awareness and education strategies. So far as universal community-wide education campaigns are concerned, these should be accompanied by valid information and effective services that can contribute to prevention outcomes. Increasing awareness without specifying the nature of the problem and how parents and guardians can protect children risks increasing public anxieties without contributing to prevention.

There is clearly an urgent need for more involvement by researchers in community-focused approaches to CSA prevention. Perhaps at the most basic level it is important for researchers themselves to do what they can to engage with the media and to provide balanced and informed perspectives to the public on both the extent of the problem and what might be done in terms of prevention. One immediate opportunity for researchers is to engage in rigorous evaluations of current community-focused prevention strategies. But there is also an important role for researchers to play in establishing the conceptual and empirical foundations of community-focused CSA prevention, and perhaps in the design, implementation and evaluation of community-focused prevention projects.

Summary

Modern community-focused approaches to crime prevention are able to draw from a long history of thinking, practice and applied research dating from the late-nineteenth and early twentieth centuries. A variety of approaches, including community organising, tenant involvement, resource mobilisation, community defence, preserving order and protecting the vulnerable, have emerged over time in different social and political contexts. A common theme has been direct engagement with (often socially disadvantaged) communities to identify and respond to local crime problems. Unfortunately, the evidence for the effectiveness of community crime prevention itself is weak, although the absence of evidence may at least partly be explained by the complexities of the interventions and associated difficulties presented in controlled evaluations. On the other hand, there is evidence to support the use of many of the component interventions used in community prevention projects.

The sustained involvement of communities in crime prevention projects is no doubt motivated by collective interests in public safety and security. Community crime prevention efforts have generally been directed towards property and violent crime, probably because these present more immediate and pressing concerns. The low official prevalence of CSA, together with community perceptions that CSA is a remote problem for most individuals, make it unlikely that most communities would identify CSA as a prevention priority. Community crime prevention strategies may nevertheless make an important contribution in community settings where the prevalence of CSA is highly concentrated, where local social conditions are more directly implicated in its causes, where local communities see themselves as being directly affected by the problem and where criminal justice approaches have been ineffective, such as in some disadvantaged remote communities.

Modern community-focused approaches to preventing child maltreatment are also able to draw from a long history of thinking, practice and applied research. Current approaches focus on parenting education, the provision of neighbourhood-based family support services and home visiting programmes. There is evidence that parenting education can improve parenting attitudes and knowledge, improve parent–child interactions and reduce the incidence of child abuse and neglect reports. Family support services have been shown to reduce authoritarian parenting strategies, and to improve parenting confidence, responsible decision-making, conflict resolution skills, social competence and social support. Home visitation programmes, which are able to reach families who may otherwise not have access to neighbourhood-based services, have been associated with a wide range of positive outcomes, including the reduction of child abuse and neglect. Researchers and practitioners concerned with the prevention of child maltreatment tend to include CSA alongside other forms of maltreatment (physical abuse, emotional abuse and neglect), although the effects of community prevention specifically on CSA are presently unknown. Some shifts in focus may be needed for these approaches to be effective in preventing CSA, including giving more attention to engaging men in prevention programmes, to enhancing attachment bonds between children and both male and female parents and to educating parents and guardians about the risks for CSA presented by non-parents.

Community-focused approaches aimed specifically at preventing CSA have arisen only since the 1980s, and thus far have generally been neglected by researchers and practitioners. Instead, a variety of advocacy and interest groups have developed and implemented CSA prevention campaigns designed to raise community awareness and to provide a range of public education resources. Many of these have made use of mass media (e.g. television and Internet) technologies that have allowed the dissemination of information and prevention advice to a very wide audience. While a common stated aim of these campaigns is to shift the burden of responsibility for preventing CSA from children to adults, they nevertheless continue to promote universal child-focused sexual abuse education. The involvement of researchers in community-focused CSA prevention is urgently needed to establish the conceptual and empirical foundations of these approaches and to evaluate their outcomes. Evaluation studies are needed that systematically and objectively test for both negative and positive outcomes.

Chapter 10

Towards a comprehensive prevention strategy

We set out in this book to analyse what might be done, and what is currently being done, to prevent CSA. We can conclude with some optimism that in fact a great deal can be done, that the problem can be confronted in many ways and in a variety of settings. However we must also conclude that current approaches are generally inadequate in scope, often poorly targeted and sometimes, frankly, misguided. Our aim in this final chapter is to draw together the various lines of inquiry we have pursued in this book, and in doing so to stimulate discussion and debate about how current and emerging knowledge and expertise concerning CSA, and related social problems, can be translated into effective sexual abuse prevention policy and practice.

In Chapter 3 we proposed four essential targets for preventing child sexual abuse: offenders (or potential offenders); victims (or potential victims); the situations in which sexual abuse has occurred (or is more likely to occur); and communities. In the intervening chapters we examined how prevention strategies might be organised to address each of these targets. We now return to the public health model (see Chapter 3) and consider how offenders, victims, situations and communities might most appropriately be targeted at the primary, secondary and tertiary prevention levels. This yields twelve points of focus for preventive action (four targets x three prevention levels). For each of these we comment briefly on current approaches and, where appropriate, propose new directions for prevention policy and practice. The model is set out in Table 10.1, together with some examples of the kinds of interventions that may be associated with each point of focus. The model is intended to serve as a heuristic device, and we acknowledge some conceptual overlaps and slippage between categories. Ultimately, whether a particular intervention qualifies as primary or secondary prevention, or as victim-focused or situation-focused prevention, for example, is immaterial. What matters is that prevention policy is comprehensive in its scope, clear in its aims and based on the best available evidence and theory.

Primary prevention

There will surely be no disagreement that the most desirable goals for preventing CSA are to prevent potential offenders from first sexually abusing a child and to prevent potential victims from being sexually abused in the first place. Perhaps the most obvious ways in which these goals could be approached is by targeting potential offenders and victims themselves. However, since CSA occurs within (and is influenced by) specific situational contexts and broader social ecosystems, a comprehensive approach to primary prevention also needs to target the situations in which children are more likely to be exposed to sexual abuse, as well as the more distal elements its social ecology.

Offender-focused approaches

Current approaches to preventing potential offenders from first sexually abusing a child rely very heavily on formal general deterrence strategies. General deterrence in turn relies on the assumption that public dissemination of successful prosecution outcomes for known offenders will dissuade would-be offenders from first committing such an offence themselves. Where general deterrence is seen to fail, as it obviously does whenever a new offence is committed, it is often further assumed that existing penalties must be inadequate and that increasing the severity of penalties will therefore remedy the problem. 'Getting tougher', 'sending a stronger message' and the like have become very familiar catch-cries in political law and order debates, which have, incidentally, increasingly singled out sexual offenders for particular attention.

The public dissemination of relevant laws and penalties undoubtedly serves an important declarative function, and the removal of laws prohibiting sexual engagement with children would presumably result in a substantial increase in the prevalence of sexual abuse. We would also expect to see an increased prevalence of sexual abuse in

Table 10.1 Twelve points of focus for preventive action

	Primary prevention	Secondary prevention	Tertiary prevention
Offenders	General deterrence	Confidential helplines	Early detection
	Developmental prevention	Counselling for at-risk individuals	Specific deterrence
		Developmental prevention	Selective incapacitation
			Offender treatment
Victims	Personal safety programmes	Counselling and support for at-risk children	Early detection
	Resilience-building		Harm minimisation
			Preventing repeat victimisation
Situations	Extended guardianship	Situational interventions in at-risk places and organisations	Safety plans
	Situational prevention in institutional and public setting		Relapse prevention
			Situational interventions with organisations where CSA has occurred
Communities	Public education	Support for at-risk families	Interventions with high-prevalence communities
	Community services	Interventions with at-risk communities	
	Community capacity-building		

communities where these laws are poorly enforced or where there are serious breakdowns in law and order. Nonetheless it is very doubtful that continuing to increase formal penalties for sexual offenders will contribute anything further to primary prevention. For the already-motivated potential offender, the immediate prospects of self-gratification may be much more compelling than the distant and uncertain risk of criminal justice sanctions. The effectiveness of general deterrence could theoretically be improved by increasing the perceived immediacy and certainty of formal sanctions, but, as we observed in Chapter 5, in practical terms criminal justice systems are not well placed to do this. For those with positive personal and social attachments, informal social controls (e.g. threats to personal relationships and reputation) may serve as a more reliable general deterrent, but the effectiveness of informal social controls will also depend to a large extent on the perceived risks of detection and sanction. Fortunately, in the vast majority of circumstances robust internal controls (e.g. empathy and perspective taking, emotional self-regulation, positive social attachments) prevent CSA-related motivations from emerging in the first place, or when they do emerge to be readily inhibited. A more positive and proactive primary prevention strategy would therefore be to build on the natural resilience in the general population by strengthening these internal controls.

We described this approach, known as developmental prevention, in Chapter 4. As we saw there, developmental prevention is supported by established theoretical principles and underpinned by a strong evidence base. Because of the empirical and theoretical links between general criminal conduct and CSA offending, and because the positive outcomes arising from developmental crime prevention projects have included reductions in problematic sexual behaviour, we would expect developmental interventions that are successful in reducing the prevalence of general offending to also be successful in reducing the prevalence of CSA offending. In practical terms this suggests that increasing investments in universal developmental crime prevention programmes would yield positive benefits for preventing sexual abuse. At a broader level, whole-of-government policy can contribute by striving to create the economic and social conditions necessary for families and communities to provide optimal care and support for children. Realising the full potential of developmental prevention programmes for reducing sexual abuse will require further knowledge about the specific developmental trajectories and risk factors associated with CSA offending. Current knowledge suggests four general points of focus: primary attachment relationships; the transition to school; the transition to high school; and the transition to parenthood or child-related employment (see Chapter 4).

Victim-focused approaches

Another popular assumption underpinning current approaches to CSA prevention is that children can and should be taught to prevent their own sexual victimisation. Whereas general deterrence strategies have been applied to all types of offending, teaching children to resist the attentions of potential offenders is unique to the field of sexual abuse. As we have previously observed, there is no similar assumption that children could or should be taught to resist adults who may be disposed to neglect, physically or emotionally abuse, or otherwise harm or exploit them. In any event, despite their obvious popularity there is little convincing evidence for the effectiveness of child-focused personal safety programmes for actually preventing sexual abuse (see Chapter 7). If these programmes are to remain part of a broader prevention strategy, revisions are needed to better align their aims and content with knowledge concerning CSA offender modus operandi (e.g. grooming and detection avoidance strategies) and with the reality that sexual abuse often involves complex emotional connections with the potential offender. Because boys and girls are generally at risk at different ages and in different settings, different approaches may be needed for each.

An alternative approach may be to shift the focus from the 'resistance-training' model suggested by personal safety programmes to a 'resilience-building' model. Although we would usually be inclined to argue for an increased specificity in the targeting of preventive interventions, in this case we would argue for a more general approach. There is substantial overlap in the individual, family and community risk factors for CSA and other forms of child abuse and neglect, and interventions that reduce general psychological and emotional vulnerabilities (e.g. low self-esteem and excessive emotional neediness), and that provide children with more effective guardianship and safer environments, are therefore likely to reduce risks for many kinds of maltreatment, including CSA.

Situation-focused approaches

Situational interventions are no doubt already very widely employed in informal, everyday efforts to prevent CSA: parents and other capable guardians naturally take many common sense precautions to reduce children's exposure to situations that may present an increased risk of sexual abuse, just as they do to reduce children's exposure to a wide array of other environmental hazards (e.g. by monitoring the whereabouts of their children). Increasingly, those responsible for the care of children in institutional (e.g. educational, recreational and religious) settings are taking more formal steps to reduce risks for sexual (and other) abuse within their sphere of influence. However, we suspect that these efforts are rarely informed by a systematic and detailed analysis of specific situational risk and protective factors; instead, everyday situational prevention activities are likely to be based on popular assumptions about CSA, potentially including any number of misconceptions (e.g. that the greatest risk is from strangers; that offenders are likely to look 'sleazy' or odd in some other way; or that criminal history checks on prospective employees will make child-related organisations safe). For its part, formal CSA prevention policy has given virtually no attention to the systematic implementation of situational prevention methods.

Situational prevention has very wide applicability, and the design of situational interventions will vary from one set of circumstances to the next. Situational prevention in domestic settings may be supported by universal education strategies designed to better inform the general public about specific risk and protective factors and how to create natural situational barriers to CSA. In public settings, 'place managers' (e.g. shop keepers, security personnel) and other responsible adults could potentially be encouraged and assisted to provide extended guardianship for children they encounter in their routine activities. In many cases the physical design of buildings and other places could assist with these efforts, for example by increasing formal and natural surveillance. Although situational techniques can be applied across the spectrum of domestic, institutional and public settings, it is in institutional settings that the conditions for situational prevention are most conducive (see Chapter 8). Any child-related organisation could potentially be assisted to undertake situational risk assessments and to implement sensible situational interventions. At a broader policy level, requiring the systematic assessment of risks and the development of risk management plans within child-related organisations could extend the scope of situational prevention across whole jurisdictions.

Community-focused approaches

Universal awareness and education strategies are the mainstay of current community-focused approaches to primary prevention.

Awareness campaigns may be led or supported by government policy, but the most sustained campaigns seem to have been organised by politically and socially engaged advocacy groups (e.g. Stop It Now!). Awareness and concern will no doubt vary from community to community. Evaluations of awareness campaigns suggest that the targeted communities were already very aware that sexual abuse is a serious social problem, but that there is much less awareness of how CSA might be defined or recognised, and what might be done to reduce the risk (Chasan-Taber and Tabachnick 1999).

Awareness and education campaigns can take many forms, and it is not always clear whether they are aimed at potential or actual offenders, potential or actual victims, some other specific group (e.g. people who may suspect abuse) or the general community. These campaigns should be based on a clear rationale that specifies intended outcomes and controls for unintended outcomes. Different formats (e.g. scheduling, medium, style and content) will be required for each target group. Particular care needs to be taken to avoid engendering unnecessary fears and suspicions in the general public, and to avoid exposing children (and particularly sexual abuse victims) to messages that highlight harmful consequences.

Although awareness and education campaigns often make use of sophisticated mass media technologies and thereby can reach a very wide audience, efforts to convey useful information are likely to be overshadowed by routine public exposure to more pervasive (and often much less helpful) messages about sexual abuse. News media reporting of CSA, for example, tends to be highly selective, focusing on the most serious offences and emphasising the most serious and alarming aspects of those offences (Wilczynski and Sinclair 1999). Offenders themselves tend to be portrayed in ways that reinforce popular stereotypes of offenders as persistent, aggressive, predatory, mentally disturbed and untreatable (Cheit 2003). Other than this focus on strange and dangerous offenders, CSA itself is portrayed as a mysterious, inexplicable phenomenon. Since news media communicate a heightened but unspecified threat, without a concerted effort to provide accurate and helpful information, the public is likely to be left with increased anxiety but without any apparent means to protect itself.

An alternative approach to community-focused primary prevention is universal community capacity-building. As we saw in Chapter 9, community-focused approaches to crime and child maltreatment prevention have tended to favour direct community engagement over universal awareness and education strategies. These strategies are based on evidence that crime and child maltreatment can be prevented by intervening at multiple levels of potential offenders' and victims' social ecologies. While direct engagement strategies have generally concentrated on at-risk families and communities, and thus constitute secondary rather than primary prevention, we think there is a strong case for the universal provision of services designed to increase the capacity of communities and families to protect and care for children. These may include universal parenthood education, neighbourhood family support services and home visiting programmes.

Secondary prevention

Concentrating prevention efforts on at-risk individuals, groups and places promises a far greater efficiency than is possible with universal (primary) prevention programmes, since in secondary prevention resources are hypothetically directed to where they are most needed. However, because risk denotes the probability of some future outcome, and because there can be no certainty about the future, risk assessment inevitably involves prediction error. False-positive error (when individuals, groups or places are incorrectly identified as at-risk) not only introduces unwanted inefficiencies, but may also unfairly stigmatise and involve unnecessary intrusions into people's lives and liberties. False-negative error (when individuals, groups or places are incorrectly identified as 'safe') may place potential offenders and victims at avoidable risk. The magnitude of error associated with these risk judgements will vary according to the reliability and validity of prediction models and methods, and on the quality of information available for the assessment task. However it is the consequences, perhaps more than the magnitude, of these errors that present the most pressing ethical and practical problems. Secondary prevention interventions that are likely to produce positive or neutral effects for unintended targets, and of course that produce positive effects for intended targets, are the most desirable. Secondary interventions that result in negative outcomes for unintended targets should of course be avoided where possible.

Offender-focused approaches

In contrast to prevention activities targeting other forms of child maltreatment, which have devoted considerable effort to developing methods of identifying and assisting those at risk of abusing or neglecting children, current approaches to CSA prevention seem to give virtually no attention to identifying and assisting those who may be at increased risk of committing CSA offences but who have not yet done so. Instead, as we have repeatedly noted, apart from general deterrence strategies current CSA prevention efforts are generally organised to respond only after individuals have already committed these offences. An important exception, albeit on a rather small scale (and largely independent of government policy), has been the provision of telephone helplines which, among other things, offer information and advice to persons who may see themselves at risk of sexually abusing a child. While the effectiveness of these helplines remains to be demonstrated, evaluations do show that at least some potential offenders will call and ask for assistance. We think this is a very important development, and that telephone helplines should be much more widely available. These helplines need to be widely advertised and linked to follow-up services, which may include the provision of written or other self-help materials but should also include confidential face-to-face counselling and treatment services. We think a rational, informed debate is needed about whether this confidentiality should be extended to those who admit to having already committed an offence and who request assistance to prevent further offending.

An additional strategy for offender-focused secondary prevention is to direct developmental interventions more specifically to at-risk individuals and groups. As we have noted, developmental risk factors for CSA offending appear to be much the same as for general offending, so developmental interventions targeting at-risk groups for delinquency and general offending are likely to also reduce CSA offending (see Chapter 4). Developmental interventions aimed specifically at preventing CSA offending should target both adolescence-onset and adult-onset offending. Adolescence-onset CSA offending is associated with contemporaneous family-of-origin, internalising and peer isolation problems. Although general (nonsexual) abuse seems more prevalent than sexual abuse among CSA offenders, many persistent offenders report having begun sexual offending soon after having themselves been sexually abused. Counselling and support services for sexually abused boys may therefore play an important secondary prevention role. In practice, local education, health, child protection and youth justice agencies are probably best placed to identify and remediate emergent problems among at-risk youth.

'Early-in-life' interventions (e.g., home-based and school-based services) are also likely to contribute to the prevention of adult-onset CSA offending, but additional opportunities for secondary prevention are likely to be presented in adolescence and adulthood. Since many adult CSA offenders already have a history of nonsexual offending, youth justice and adult correctional programmes targeting general problems with empathy and perspective taking, emotional self-regulation, antisocial attitudes, intimate relationships, responsible parenting, and so forth, may play a role in interrupting the transition from nonsexual to sexual offending. Because the circumstances from which CSA arises are typically very private, even if specific risk factors were unambiguously present it would be very difficult to identify those most at risk of CSA offending (which is why programmes to encourage self-identified potential offenders, such as telephone helplines, are so important). One set of opportunities is presented in child-related institutional settings, where it is possible to screen prospective employees and volunteers. The usual system of criminal history checks may identify a proportionately small number of obvious cases (e.g. when applicants have a history of CSA offences), but employment screening and workplace supervision present further opportunities to identify, and either exclude or assist, those who may be drawn to establishing 'special' relationships with children, or who may demonstrate general self-restraint and interpersonal-boundary problems. Marshall (in press) has outlined how this might be done in the particular case of selection, training and supervision of priests, and similar approaches could be designed to apply to a very wide range of organisational settings.

Victim-focused approaches

Current CSA prevention policy has also neglected to invest in developing methods of identifying and assisting children at increased risk of being sexually abused. In fact there is a considerable body of research that identifies characteristics of children, and of their family and social circumstances, that may increase the risks of sexual victimisation. Most estimates indicate that girls are generally at greater risk than boys. As we have noted, girls are more at risk at a younger age and in familial settings, whereas boys are more at risk at an older age and in nonfamilial settings. For both girls and boys, general psychological vulnerabilities (e.g. low self-esteem, emotional neediness) seem to increase risk, as do general difficulties (including neglect and other forms of abuse) in the home. While individual offenders may be attracted to specific physical and psychological features, offenders generally are more likely to target children who are alone, have family problems and lack confidence, and who the offender regards as physically attractive, innocent, curious and trusting. Victims (and their families) are very likely to know the offender, and indeed the potential victim is likely to have established a close relationship with the offender, prior to the onset of the abuse.

These risk factors can be separated into two distinct types. The first involves otherwise positive individual (e.g. innocence, curiosity, trustfulness) and interpersonal characteristics (e.g. dependence on and emotional closeness with adults). Since the whole point of preventing sexual abuse is to preserve children's innocence, curiosity, trustfulness and capacity for emotional closeness, it would seem prudent to avoid interventions that may diminish these qualities in children. The second type of risk factors involves unambiguously negative features (e.g. low confidence and self-esteem, excessive emotional neediness, family problems), and it is these factors that would be the most appropriate targets for secondary-level victim-focused interventions. Since these negative risk factors are also associated with a wide range of other negative developmental outcomes, the benefits of secondary interventions are likely to extend beyond reducing the risks of sexual abuse. Apart from capable guardians themselves, schools, child protection services and general and mental health services are probably best placed to identify risk factors and to deliver secondary, child-focused interventions.

Situation-focused approaches

At a secondary prevention level, situational interventions would generally target at-risk places. Secondary situational interventions in domestic settings would require either self-identification or third-party identification of adolescents or adults who are at risk of sexually abusing a child, of children who are at risk of sexual victimisation or of other circumstances that may introduce particular risks in the home (e.g. when other forms of maltreatment have been suspected or substantiated). In any of these circumstances situational prevention methods could be used to guide the design and implementation of safety plans, which would involve an analysis of the specific physical features and routine activities associated with the home environment, and of the strengths and limitations of available guardians. In cases of third-party identification, child protection or other authorities could assist in the development, implementation and monitoring of safety plans, and in removing barriers to capable guardianship.

In public settings, secondary situational interventions may be employed in places where particular situational risk factors may be present. These are likely to be places where adolescent or adult males are in routine, unsupervised contact with children, such as parks, playgrounds, beaches, public swimming pools, shopping centres, game parlours and the like. Authorities responsible for the management of these places may employ situational assessment methods to undertake risk audits, and to introduce simple measures to strengthen formal surveillance, improve natural surveillance, utilise place managers for extending guardianship, and so on (see Chapter 8). However, once again, it is in institutional settings where secondary situational interventions may be particularly suited. Situational risks are generally increased in organisations where adult males are in employment or other roles that involve authority and care-giving activities in relation to children (especially vulnerable children), and particularly where it is likely that adults will form emotional attachments to, or are involved in intimate activities (e.g. bathing, dressing, massaging) with, children in their care. These are likely to be places such as residential institutions, organisations that provide care for vulnerable children, pastoral care settings, sport and recreational organisations and schools. As a matter of policy, situational risk audits and risk management plans could be required in all such settings. Where presently the emphasis in these organisations is on identifying a very small number of risky people (e.g. through background checks on prospective employees), a situational approach emphasises instead the identification and management of risks situated within the workplace itself.

Community-focused approaches

In the broader field of child maltreatment prevention considerable efforts have been made to identify community-level risk factors and to concentrate services in communities where these risk factors have been identified. Similarly there has been a long history of targeting at-risk communities with community crime prevention programmes. An immediate problem with embarking on a similar course of action for targeting CSA is that less is currently known about community-level risk factors for sexual abuse than there is for general maltreatment and crime. There is some US research that suggests that community risk factors for sexual abuse are similar to those for other forms of maltreatment, and that some social conditions (e.g. low socioeconomic conditions, proportion of single mother households) may be associated specifically with CSA, but much more detail is needed to give a clearer picture of the broader social ecology of sexual abuse. Moving forward will clearly require investments in further research investigating community-level and other ecological risk factors associated specifically with CSA. Drawing from the related fields of crime prevention and child maltreatment prevention, the present knowledge-base would support investments in local community initiatives modelled on programmes such as Communities That Care, and in programmes that concentrate the provision of neighbourhood family support and home visiting services in socially disadvantaged areas (see Chapter 9). Until more detailed information about the ecological risk factors for sexual abuse becomes available, these services could initially be directed to communities where child protection records or victimisation surveys indicate an increased prevalence of sexual abuse.

Tertiary prevention

Tertiary prevention involves interventions with individuals, groups or places after CSA has occurred. Because of the wide variations in the circumstances and outcomes for victims, in the risks and needs of offenders and in the capacity of families, organisations and communities to properly protect children in their care, a 'one size fits all' approach would be inefficient and in many cases ineffective. At a policy level, it is necessary to develop generic decision-making rules and guidelines. At a practice level, complex and difficult judgements often need to be made on a case-by-case basis: what is the best response to an initial disclosure or a formal report? How should investigations be prioritised? What is the most appropriate and effective response to the offender? These and many other questions require careful and informed risk and needs assessments which, as with secondary prevention, present inevitable problems with prediction error. The shift from secondary to tertiary prevention generally involves a lower tolerance for false-negative prediction error and a higher tolerance of false-positive error: the odds for tertiary-level predictions may be no better, but the stakes are often much higher.

Offender-focused approaches

By far the greatest share of current prevention resources is directed towards formal responses to CSA offenders. There are four main offender-focused tertiary prevention strategies: 1) detection and investigation; 2) specific deterrence; 3) general and selective incapacitation; and 4) offender rehabilitation. We discussed each of these in some detail in Chapters 5 and 6, and so make only a few concluding comments here.

Although some CSA offenders presumably desist of their own accord, in most cases bringing sexual abuse incidents to the attention of a responsible third party (i.e. someone other than the offender and victim who is willing and capable of intervening) seems to be a critical element of prevention. This may not always require a formal response, but the involvement of police or child protection authorities will be needed in circumstances where the third party (e.g. a non-offending parent, the workplace supervisor of the offender) cannot, for a variety of reasons, ensure the immediate and permanent cessation of the abuse, or when the offender may go on to commit further offences in a different setting. In most cases little can be done by police or other authorities until a notification or formal complaint is received, although in recent years police in particular have adopted more proactive investigation strategies. These have tended to concentrate on 'high-profile' types of offences, such as international and other organised CSA-related activities, child pornography production and distribution, Internet grooming, and so on. Police remain very limited in their capacity to be proactive in their investigation of CSA offences in domestic and child-related organisational settings, which are by far the most common, and this is one important reason that CSA prevention policy needs to extend its reach beyond criminal justice and other formal interventions.

For offenders with positive personal and social attachments the shame and embarrassment of having their offending become known by others may be sufficiently aversive to deter further offending, and indeed the effects of formal criminal justice punishments may well be mediated by these informal social controls. Where we may otherwise expect that a formal response is needed particularly for compulsive or generally unrestrained offenders, or for those with weak or negative social attachments, unfortunately it is these offenders for whom formal punishments are least likely to be effective. In some cases, particularly for youth offenders, arrest and formal punishment may actually increase the risk of further offending. Less is known about the deterrent effects of formal punishments specifically on CSA offenders, but general research findings suggest that diversionary options for some youth CSA offenders should remain a part of a broader prevention policy. For both youth and adult CSA offenders, appropriately supervised community sentences are a much less expensive option than detention and imprisonment, and in many cases will be equally effective, provided of course that victims are properly protected from further victimisation.

Imprisonment has become an increasingly popular means of incapacitating CSA offenders, but there is also a range of alternative (and much less costly) means of incapacitation, including the judicious use of serious offender registers, intensive community supervision, residency and other restrictions, and in some cases pharmacological interventions. Although lengthy prison terms may satisfy public desires for retribution (and provide governments with a way of showing they are 'doing something'), low average sexual recidivism rates among CSA offenders suggest that mandatory or long-term imprisonment will unnecessarily consume enormous financial and other resources that could be directed to other, perhaps much more effective, prevention strategies. On the other hand, evidence that a small number of persistent offenders (usually nonfamilial offenders with male victims) are disproportionately responsible for a large number of victims presents a compelling case for the selective incapacitation of high-risk CSA offenders. A major practical problem with selective incapacitation lies in the limitations of screening and assessment methods designed to distinguish high-risk from low-risk offenders. Leaving aside well-documented problems with prediction error, current methods rely heavily on sexual offending histories as an indicator of future offending and so tend to identify high-risk offenders only after they already have a substantial history of offending. Because all persistent offenders were once first-time offenders, methods of risk assessment that do not over-rely on the presence of past sexual offences are clearly needed to support a more effective selective incapacitation approach.

Psychological treatment of adolescent and especially adult CSA offenders has occupied an increasingly prominent place in the broader prevention effort. In contrast to the paucity of research into the effectiveness of other CSA prevention strategies, there is now an extensive research literature on the treatment of CSA offenders. Evidence for the effectiveness of treatment with adult CSA offenders, in both prison and community settings, is generally stronger than it is for the effectiveness of programmes for adolescent offenders. Nevertheless it is clear that well-designed and carefully implemented programmes for both adult and adolescent offenders can produce significant reductions in both sexual and nonsexual recidivism. While a great deal of work remains to be done to further improve their effectiveness and efficiency, and in particular to extend the reach of best-practice treatment models, current knowledge supports increasing investments in these programmes and associated research and evaluation activities.

Victim-focused approaches

A longer duration of abuse is one of several factors that have consistently been shown to be associated with more negative outcomes for sexual abuse victims. Research has also shown that repeat victimisation is not uncommon among sexual abuse victims and that this is, unsurprisingly, also associated with more negative outcomes. It is therefore essential that prevention efforts include a focus on early detection and intervention, and on preventing further abuse for known victims.

We noted in Chapter 7 that the availability of a supportive parent or other responsible adult seems to be the most important condition for encouraging victims to make an initial disclosure. Similarly, expectations about how child protection authorities, police and the courts are likely to respond seem to be an important consideration in the decisions by adults about whether to on-report the abuse. Research indicates that there continues to be considerable reluctance by parents and other adults, including mental health and other professionals, to report sexual abuse, at least in part because of concerns that doing so may exacerbate rather than solve the problem. Mandatory reporting laws increase reporting rates, but mandatory reporting can also introduce new problems (e.g. an increase in unsubstantiated cases) and does not of itself increase positive outcomes for victims. Instead, the main emphasis of victim-focused tertiary prevention policy needs to be on: 1) creating the conditions in which victims are most likely to disclose the abuse and receive appropriate support; 2) informing those most likely to discover abuse (e.g. teachers, general and mental health professionals), as well as the general public, about how best to respond to an initial disclosure or discovery, how to report sexual abuse and what to expect after doing so; 3) continuing to improve the ways in which child protection and criminal justice systems and personnel play their part in responding to the abuse; and 4) providing appropriate resources for high-quality, evidence-based victim counselling and support services.

Situation-focused approaches

At a tertiary prevention level, situational prevention methods may be employed in safety plans for victims and their families, risk management plans for offenders, and interventions with organisations or places where sexual abuse has been uncovered. Recognition that risky situations play a critical role in sexual abuse is implied, if rarely expounded, in the common practice of designing safety plans for victims and in policies that impose restrictions on the residence or movement of sexual offenders. In the former case, effective safety plans are no doubt already often developed through careful assessment and a common-sense appreciation of situational factors relevant to sexual abuse, however safety plans developed with particular regard to situational prevention theory and intervention methods may ensure that important situational factors are not overlooked. In the latter case, there has been a tendency to apply broad, generic restrictions (e.g. prohibiting offenders from living within a certain distance of schools, even when many have never offended in a school setting and are very unlikely to do so). Generic approaches may require less effort, knowledge and expertise, but will almost certainly be less effective than carefully planned, individualised risk management plans. Because situational prevention involves highly specific interventions that can be tailored to individual circumstances, it is well suited to the design and implementation of both safety plans for victims and risk management plans for offenders.

Situational prevention methods are also well suited to intervening in organisational settings where it has been discovered that sexual abuse has occurred. In recent times many reports have emerged of sexual and other abuse, sometimes having gone undetected for years, in particular residential children's homes, hospitals, churches, schools, sporting and recreational clubs, childcare centres and other child-related organisations. Recent efforts to prevent further abuse in these organisations have concentrated on developing codes of conduct, improving reporting and response systems and more carefully screening employees and visitors. With its focus on creating safe places, rather than on identifying risky individuals, situational prevention has a great deal of potential to enhance tertiary (as well as primary and secondary) prevention efforts in child-related organisations.

Community-focused approaches

Tertiary-level community interventions may be required in unusual cases where a particularly high prevalence of sexual abuse has been observed in specific communities. Generally, official prevalence rates of sexual abuse are very low – lower than for emotional and physical abuse, for example. However there are some exceptional circumstances where it has become clear that sexual abuse has been occurring in epidemic proportions. For example, it has become very clear in Australia that there is an alarmingly high prevalence of sexual abuse in some remote Indigenous communities, with anecdotal accounts suggesting that sexual abuse is almost universal in some of these communities (Aboriginal and Torres Strait Island Task Force on Violence 1999).

In an extraordinary response to the latest of many reports into this problem, in 2007 the Australian federal government launched a major intervention that was explicitly focused on preventing CSA in Aboriginal communities in the Northern Territory. This has been a very controversial intervention, involving the military and police as well as health practitioners and Indigenous community leaders. The main focus has been on universal health checks of children, bans on alcohol and pornography, income management schemes and the deployment of additional police. While there is very wide public support for 'something to be done', critics claim that the intervention is ill-conceived, and in particular that it has lacked community consultation and involvement. Proponents in turn argue that the problem is now so serious that quick and decisive action is required.

In these circumstances established community crime prevention methods, perhaps modelled on Communities That Care (see Chapter 9), may be usefully employed (and indeed probably should have been employed long ago). While these methods may include formal criminal justice and child protection interventions, they offer a much more collaborative and comprehensive approach, including developmental, ecological and situational interventions. One advantage of this approach is that systematic, evidence-based, community-level assessments and interventions would be undertaken on a case-by-case basis, rather than assuming that each distinct community faces the same problems and therefore requires the same pre-conceived solution. Perhaps ironically, understanding why CSA is so rife in such terribly disadvantaged communities may lead to important new insights about the social ecology of the wider problem of sexual abuse.

Where to from here?

It seems clear that a great deal more could be done to prevent CSA than is currently being done. The main limitations of current prevention efforts, as we see them, are not due to a lack of public or political concern, nor to a profound lack of knowledge and expertise. Rather, the central problem seems to lie in the translation of current and emerging knowledge and expertise to evidence-based prevention policy. Moving forward to a more comprehensive and effective prevention strategy will require: 1) a wider integration of current knowledge and expertise; 2) a clearer focus on prevention-centred research; and 3) a firmer commitment to evidence-based, prevention-centred policy and practice. In drawing our analysis to a close, we comment very briefly on each of these issues.

A great deal of progress has been made, particularly since the 1980s, in bringing the problem of CSA to the attention of policy-makers, researchers, practitioners, child protection advocates and the general public. Perhaps as an unintended consequence, CSA seems to have become widely conceived of as a distinct and unique phenomenon, requiring its own unique explanations and responses. Efforts to understand and prevent CSA accordingly seem to have become increasingly specialised and compartmentalised. We think that although CSA prevention does indeed require specific kinds of knowledge and expertise, it is nevertheless essential that prevention policy and practice draws from a much wider pool of intellectual, professional and community resources. We have tried in this book to situate the problem of sexual abuse in the wider contexts of public health, crime and child maltreatment, and we think that much can be learned from these related fields about how to understand and prevent sexual abuse.

At the same time, sexual abuse prevention requires its own distinct knowledge base. Significant progress has been made in understanding the social ecology of CSA victimisation, but there remain important gaps in knowledge about the individual, ecological and situational factors associated particularly with the onset of sexual abuse, and about the risk and protective factors associated with abuse outcomes for children. A great deal of progress has also been made in research with sexual offenders, which in recent years has led to significant improvements in applied risk assessment and in the effectiveness of psychological treatment for both adult and adolescent CSA offenders. Extending the scope of research to support primary and secondary prevention will require new emphases on understanding the individual, ecological and situational factors associated with the onset of CSA offending and victimisation. Outcome evaluations of existing and new preventive interventions are also essential. There has been a great deal of work examining the effectiveness of psychological treatment for offenders and victims, although there remains a need to understand more about the effectiveness of the various components of these programmes. Very little is presently known about the effectiveness of various policing strategies, offender registers, residency restrictions, community notification, civil commitment, and prison versus community sentencing regimes. Outcome evaluation methodologies need to be 'built-in' to new prevention programmes (e.g. developmental, situational and community interventions), and evaluations of existing and new programmes should aim to measure both positive (intended) and negative (unintended) outcomes.

Public, political and media attention to CSA seems to be concentrated more on questions about what to do with known offenders, than about what to do for children, their families and others directly and indirectly affected by the problem, or, least of all it seems, about how to prevent sexual abuse from occurring in the first place. Public policy responses have accordingly been aligned more closely with crime control policies than with public health, child protection and other social policies. The main response has been to increase efforts by criminal justice agencies to identify, punish and incapacitate offenders. It is patently the case that this 'back-end' approach cannot, by itself, solve the problem – today's offenders will be quickly replaced by others who have not yet committed their first CSA offence. The incentive for politicians to adhere to a punitive, back-end response is that it seems to align with public sentiments and expectations. Shifting the focus to an evidence-based, prevention-centred approach will require political leadership, involving a concerted effort to educate the public about its rationale and its benefits. For their part, researchers and practitioners must engage more effectively with policy-makers, and generate and disseminate the evidence that sexual abuse *can* be explained, and *is* preventable.

References

Abel, G.G., Becker, J.V., Mittelman, M., Cunningham-Rathner, J., Rouleau, J. and Murphy, W. (1987) 'Self-reported sex crimes of nonincarcerated paraphilics', *Journal of Interpersonal Violence*, 2(1): 3–25.

Abel, G.G., Blanchard, E.B. and Becker, J.V. (1978) 'An integrated treatment program for rapists', in R. Rada (ed.) *Clinical Aspects of the Rapist*. New York: Grune & Stratton, pp. 161–214.

Abel, G.G., Levis, D. and Clancy, J. (1970) 'Aversion therapy applied to taped sequences of deviant behavior in exhibitionism and other sexual deviations: A preliminary report', *Journal of Behavior Therapy and Experimental Psychiatry*, 1(1): 58–66.

Abel, G.G. and Osborn, C. (1992) 'The paraphilias: The extent and nature of sexually deviant and criminal behaviour', *Clinical Forensic Psychiatry*, 15(3): 675–687.

Abel, G.G., Osborn, C.A. and Twigg, D.A. (1993) 'Sexual assault through the lifespan: Adult offenders with juvenile histories', in W.L. Marshall, H.E. Barbaree and S.M. Hudson (eds) *The Juvenile Sex Offender*. New York: Guilford Press, pp. 104–117.

Abel, G.G. and Rouleau, J.L. (1990) 'The nature and extent of sexual assault', in W.L. Marshall, D.R. Laws and H.E. Barbaree (eds) *Handbook of Sexual Assault: Issues, Theories and Treatment of the Offender*. New York: Plenum Publishing, pp. 9–12.

Aboriginal and Torres Strait Island Task Force on Violence (1999) *The Aboriginal and Torres Strait Island Task Force on Violence Report*. Brisbane: Queensland Government.

Aftab, P. (2000) *The Parent's Guide to Protecting your Children in Cyberspace*. New York: McGraw-Hill.

AIDS Education and Research Trust (2005) *Age of Consent*. [Online]. Available at: http://www.avert.org/ageconsent.htm [accessed on 25 January 2008].

Ainsworth, M.D.S. (1991) 'Attachment and other affectional bonds across the life cycle', in C.M. Parkes, J. Stevenson-Hinde and P. Marris (eds) *Attachment Across the Life Cycle*. London: Routledge, pp. 33–51.

Ainsworth, M.D.S., Blehar, M.C., Waters, E. and Wall, S. (1978) *Patterns of Attachment*. Hillsdale, NJ: Erlbaum.

Alexander, M.A. (1999) 'Sexual offender treatment efficacy revisited', *Sexual Abuse: A Journal of Research and Treatment*, 11(2): 101–116.

Alexander, P.C. (1992) 'Application of attachment theory to the study of sexual abuse', *Journal of Consulting and Clinical Psychology*, 60(2): 185–195.

Aloysius, C. (2001) 'The media response: A journalist's view of the problem in Asia', in C.A. Arnaldo (ed.) *Child Abuse on the Internet: Ending the Silence*. New York: Berghahn Books.

American Academy of Child and Adolescent Psychiatry (2000) 'Summary of the practice parameters for the assessment and treatment of children and adolescents who are sexually abusive to others', *Journal of the American Academy of Child and Adolescent Psychiatry*, 39(1): 127–130.

Andenaes, J. (1968) 'Does punishment deter crime?' *Criminal Law Quarterly*, 11: 76–93.

Anderson, E.M. and Levine, M. (1999) 'Concerns about allegations of child sexual abuse against teachers and the teaching environment', *Child Abuse and Neglect*, 23(8): 833–843.

Andrews, D.A. and Bonta, J. (1994) *The Psychology of Criminal Conduct*. Cincinnati, OH: Anderson.

Andrews, D.A. and Bonta, J. (1998) *The Psychology of Criminal Conduct* (2nd ed.). Cincinnati, OH: Anderson.

Andrews, D.A. and Bonta, J. (2003) *The Psychology of Criminal Conduct* (3rd ed.). Cincinnati, OH: Anderson.

Andrews, D.A., Zinger, I., Hoge, R.D., Bonta, J., Gendreau, P. and Cullen, F.T. (1990) 'Does correctional treatment work? A clinically relevant and informed meta-analysis', *Criminology*, 28(3): 369–404.

Antunes, G. and Hunt, A.L. (1973) 'The impact of certainty and severity of punishment on levels of crime in American states: An extended analysis', *The Journal of Criminal Law and Criminology*, 64(4): 486–493.

Arata, C.M. (1998) 'To tell or not to tell: Current functioning of child sexual abuse survivors who disclosed their victimization', *Child Maltreatment*, 3(1): 63–71.

Australian Developmental Crime Prevention Consortium (1999) *Pathways to Prevention: Developmental and Early Intervention Approaches to Crime in Australia (Full Report)*. Canberra: Australian Government Publishing Service.

Australian Government Task Force on Child Development, Health and Wellbeing (2003) *Towards the Development of a National Agenda for Early Childhood-consultation Paper*. Canberra: Department of Family and Community Services.

Australian Institute of Health and Welfare (2006) *Child Protection 2004–05.* Canberra: Australian Institute of Health and Welfare.

Axelrod, S. and Apsche, J. (eds) (1983) *The Effects of Punishment on Human Behavior.* New York: Academic Press.

Bachman, R. (1998) 'The factors related to rape reporting behavior and arrest: New evidence from the national crime victimization survey', *Criminal Justice and Behavior*, 25(1): 8–30.

Bagley, C., Thurston, W.E. and Tutty, L.M. (1996) *Understanding and Preventing Child Sexual Abuse, Vol. 1: Children: Assessment, Social Work and Clinical Issues.* Aldershot: Ashgate Publishing.

Baker, L.M. (2001) *Learning and Behavior: Biological, Psychological and Sociological Perspectives* (3rd ed.). Upper Saddle River, NJ: Prentice Hall.

Barbaree, H.E., Langton, C. and Peacock, E.J. (2004) 'The evaluation of sex offender treatment efficacy using samples stratified by levels of actuarial risk', *paper presented at the 23rd Annual Research and Treatment Conference of the Association for the Treatment of Sexual Abusers*, Albuquerque, NM, October 2002.

Barbaree, H.E., Langton, C.M. and Peacock, E.J. (2006) 'Different actuarial risk measures produce different risk rankings for sexual offenders', *Sexual Abuse: A Journal of Research and Treatment*, 18(4): 423–440.

Barlow, D.H. (1974) 'The treatment of sexual deviation: Toward a comprehensive behavioral approach', in K.S. Calhoun, H.E. Adams and K.M. Mitchell (eds) *Innovative Treatment Methods in Psychopathology.* New York: Wiley, pp. 121–147.

Baron, S.W. and Kennedy, L.W. (1998) 'Deterrence and homeless male street youths', *Canadian Journal of Criminology*, 40(1): 27–60.

Barrett, M., Wilson, R.J. and Long, C. (2003) 'Measuring motivation to change in sexual offenders from institutional intake to community treatment', *Sexual Abuse: A Journal of Research and Treatment*, 15(4): 269–283.

Baumeister, R.F. and Vohs, K.D. (eds) (2004) *Handbook of Self-regulation: Research, Theory, and Applications.* New York: Guilford Press.

BBC News (2003) *Police to Trap Online Paedophiles.* [Online]. Available at: http://news.bbc.co.uk/1/hi/uk/3329567.stm [accessed 24 January 2008].

Becker, J.V. and Hicks, S.J. (2003) 'Juvenile sexual offenders: Characteristics, interventions, and policy issues', *Annals of the New York Academy of Sciences*, 989: 387–410.

Becker, J.V. and Kaplan, M.S. (1993) 'Cognitive behavioral treatment of the juvenile sex offender', in H.E. Barbaree, W.L. Marshall and S.M. Hudson (eds) *The Juvenile Sex Offender.* New York: Guilford Press, pp. 264–277.

Beech, A.R. and Fordham, A.S. (1997) 'Therapeutic climate of sexual offender treatment programs', *Sexual Abuse: A Journal of Research and Treatment*, 9(3): 219–237.

Beech, A.R. and Hamilton-Giachritsis, C.E. (2005) 'Relationship between therapeutic climate and treatment outcome in group-based sexual offender treatment programs', *Sexual Abuse: A Journal of Research and Treatment*, 17(2): 127–140.

Belsky, J. (1980) 'Child maltreatment: An ecological integration', *American Psychologist*, 35(4): 320–335.

Berliner, L. and Conte, J.R. (1990) 'The process of victimization: The victim's perspective', *Child Abuse and Neglect*, 14(1): 29–40.

Berliner, L. and Conte, J.R. (1995) 'The effects of disclosure and intervention on sexually abused children', *Child Abuse and Neglect*, 19(3): 381–384.

Berliner, L. and Elliott, D. (1996) 'Sexual abuse of children', in J. Briere, L. Berliner, J. Bulkley, C. Jenny and T. Reid (eds) *The APSAC Handbook on Child Maltreatment*. Thousand Oaks, CA: Sage Publications, pp. 51–71.

Besharov, D.J. (1994) 'Responding to child sexual abuse: The need for a balanced approach', *The Future of Children*, 4(2): 135–155.

Bevc, I. and Silverman, I. (2000) 'Early separation and sibling incest: A test of the revised Westermarck theory', *Evolution and Human Behavior*, 21(3): 151–161.

Beyer, L. (1993) *Community Policing: Lessons from Victoria*. Canberra: Australian Institute of Criminology.

Bohm, R.M. (ed.) (1991) *The Death Penalty in America: Current Research*. Cincinnati, OH: Anderson.

Bond, I.K. and Evans, D.R. (1967) 'Avoidance therapy: Its use in two cases of underwear fetishism', *Canadian Medical Association Journal*, 96(16): 1160–1162.

Boney-McCoy, S. and Finkelhor, D. (1995) 'Prior victimization: A risk factor for child sexual abuse and for PTSD-related symptomatology among sexually abused youth', *Child Abuse and Neglect*, 19(12): 1401–1421.

Bor, W., Najman, J.M., O'Callaghan, M., Williams, G. and Anstey, K. (2001) *Aggression and the Development of Delinquent Behaviour in Children: Trends and Issues in Crime and Criminal Justice, No. 207.* Canberra: Australian Institute of Criminology.

Borack, J.I. (1998) 'An estimate of the impact of drug testing on the deterrence of drug use', *Military Psychology*, 10(1): 17–25.

Borduin, C.M. and Schaeffer, C.M. (2001) 'Multisystemic treatment of juvenile sexual offenders: A progress report', *Journal of Psychology and Human Sexuality*, 13(3/4): 25–42.

Bourke, M.L. and Donohue, B. (1996) 'Assessment and treatment of juvenile sex offenders: An empirical review', *Journal of Child Sexual Abuse*, 5(1): 47–71.

Bowlby, J. (1969) *Attachment and Loss, Vol. 1: Attachment*. New York: Basic Books.

Bradford, J.M.W. (1990) 'The antiandrogen and hormonal treatment of sex offenders', in W.L. Marshall, D.R. Laws and H.E. Barbaree (eds) *Handbook of Sexual Assault: Issues, Theories, and Treatment of the Offender.* New York: Plenum, pp. 297–310.

Bradford, J.M.W. (1995) 'Pharmacological treatment of the paraphilias', in J.M. Oldham and M. Riba (eds) *Review of Psychiatry, Vol. 14.* Washington, DC: American Psychiatric Press, pp. 755–778.

Bradford, J.M.W. (2000) 'The treatment of sexual deviation using a pharmacological approach', *Journal of Sex Research*, 37(3): 248–257.

Bradley, A.R. and Wood, J.M. (1996) 'How do children tell? The disclosure process in child sexual abuse', *Child Abuse and Neglect*, 20(9): 881–891.

Briere, J.N. and Elliott, D.M. (1994) 'Immediate and long-term impacts of child sexual abuse', *The Future of Children*, 4(2): 54–69.

Briere, J.N. and Elliot, D.M. (2001) 'Immediate and long-term impacts of child sexual abuse', in K. Franey, R. Geffner and R. Falconer (eds) *The Cost of Child Maltreatment: Who Pays? We All Do.* San Diego, CA: Family Violence and Sexual Assault Institute, pp. 121–136.

Bronfenbrenner, U. (1979) *The Ecology of Human Development.* Cambridge, MA: Harvard University Press.

Browne, A. and Finkelhor, D. (1986) 'Impact of child sexual abuse: A review of research', *Psychological Bulletin*, 99(1): 66–77.

Buchner, J.C. and Chesney-Lind, M. (1983) 'Dramatic cures for juvenile crime: An evaluation of a prisoner-run delinquency prevention program', *Criminal Justice and Behavior*, 10(2): 227–247.

Burt, M.R. (1980) 'Cultural myths and support for rape', *Journal of Personality and Social Psychology*, 38(2): 217–230.

Burton, D.L. and Smith-Darden, J. (2001) *North American Survey of Sexual Abuser Treatment and Models Summary Data.* Brandon, VT: Safer Society Press.

Burton, D.L., Smith-Darden, J. and Frankel, S.J. (2006) 'Research on adolescent sexual abuser treatment programs', in H.E. Barbaree and W.L. Marshall (eds) *The Juvenile Sex Offender* (2nd ed.). New York: Guilford Press, pp. 291–312.

Buss, D. (1994) *The Evolution of Desire.* New York: Basic Books.

Campbell, E. (1990) 'The psychopath and the definition of "mental disease or defect" under the Model Penal Code test of insanity: A question of psychology or a question of law?', *Nebraska Law Review*, 69: 190–229.

Canadian Center for Justice Statistics (1999) *Sex Offenders* (Juristat Catalogue No. 85-002-xie, Vol. 19, No. 3). Ottawa, ON: Statistics Canada.

Carroll, J.S. (1982) 'The decision to commit the crime', in J. Konecni and E.B. Ebbesen (eds) *The Criminal Justice System.* San Francisco, CA: Freeman, pp. 49–67.

Carroll, J. and Weaver, F. (1986) 'Shoplifters' perceptions of crime opportunities: A process-tracing study', in D.B. Cornish and R.B. Clarke (eds) *The Reasoning Criminal: Rational Choice Perspectives on Offending.* New York: Springer-Verlag, pp. 19–38.

Cashmore, J. (1995) 'The prosecution of child sexual assault: A survey of NSW DPP solicitors', *Australian and New Zealand Journal of Criminology*, 28(1): 32–54.

Catalano, R.F. and Hawkins, F.D. (1995) *Risk-focused Prevention: Using the Social Development Strategy*. Seattle, WA: Developmental Research and Programs, Inc.

Ceci, S.J. and Bruck, M. (1993) 'The suggestibility to the child witness: A historical review and synthesis', *Psychological Bulletin*, 113(3): 403–439.

Chaffin, M. and Bonner, B. (1998) 'Don't shoot, we're your children: Have we gone too far in our response to adolescent sexual abusers and children with sexual behavior problems?', *Child Maltreatment*, 3(4): 314–316.

Chandy, J.M., Blum, R.W. and Resnick, M.D. (1997) 'Sexually abused male adolescents: How vulnerable are they?', *Journal of Child Sexual Abuse*, 6(1): 1–16.

Chasan-Taber, L. and Tabachnick, J. (1999) 'Evaluation of a child sexual abuse prevention program', *Sexual Abuse: A Journal of Research and Treatment*, 11(4): 279–292.

Cheit, R.E. (2003) 'What hysteria? A systematic study of newspaper coverage of accused child molesters', *Child Abuse and Neglect*, 27(6): 607–623.

Cicchetti, D., Rogosch, M.L., Lynch, M. and Holt, K.D. (1993) 'Resilience in maltreated children: Processes leading to adaptive outcome', *Development and Psychopathology*, 5(4): 626–647.

Clarke, R.V. (1992) *Situational Crime Prevention: Successful Case Studies*. Albany, NY: Harrow and Heston.

Clarke, R.V. (1997) *Situational Crime Prevention: Successful Case Studies* (2nd ed.). Guilderland, NY: Harrow and Heston.

Clarke, R.V. and Eck, J.E. (2003) *Become a Problem-solving Crime Analyst: In 55 Small Steps*. Cullompton: Willan Publishing.

Clarke, R.V. and Mayhew, P. (1988) 'The British gas suicide story and its criminological implications', in M. Tonry and N. Morris, *Crime and Justice: A Review of Research Vol. 10*. Chicago, IL: University of Chicago Press, pp. 79–116.

Cockfield, C. and Moss, K. (2002) 'Sex, drugs and broken bowls: Dealing with problems of crime reduction in public conveniences', *Community Safety Journal*, 1(1): 37–43.

Cohen, L.E. and Felson, M. (1979) 'Social change and crime rate trends: A routine activity approach', *American Sociological Review*, 44(4): 588–608.

Colton, M., Vanstone, M. and Walby, C. (2002) 'Victimization, care and justice: Reflections on the experiences of victims/survivors involved in large-scale historical investigations of child sexual abuse in residential institutions', *British Journal of Social Work*, 32(5): 541–551.

Communities That Care (UK) (1997) *Building Safer Communities Where Children and Young People are Valued*. London: Communities That Care, pp. 3–27.

Conte, J., Wolfe, S. and Smith, T. (1989) 'What sexual offenders tell us about prevention strategies', *Child Abuse and Neglect*, 13(2): 293–302.

Cook, S.L., Reppucci, N.D. and Small, M.A. (2002) 'The nature and efficacy of child-centered, neighborhood-based child protection programs: The record thus far', in G.B. Melton, R.A. Thompson and M.A. Small (eds) *Toward a Child-centered, Neighborhood-based Child Protection System: A Report of the Consortium on Children, Families and the Law*. Westport, CT: Praeger Publishers, pp. 67–88.

Cornish, D.B. and Clarke, R.V. (eds) (1986) *The Reasoning Criminal*. New York: Springer-Verlag.

Cornish, D.B. and Clarke, R.V. (2003) 'Opportunities, precipitators and criminal decisions: A reply to Wortley's critique of situational crime prevention', in M. Smith and D.B. Cornish (eds) *Theory for Situational Crime Prevention, Crime Prevention Studies, Vol. 16*. Monsey, NY: Criminal Justice Press.

Corsini, R.J. and Wedding, D. (eds) (1995) *Current Psychotherapies* (5th ed.). Itasca, IL: F.E. Peacock Publishing.

Cortoni, F. and Hanson, R.K. (2005) *A Review of the Recidivism Rates of Adult Female Sexual Offenders, Research Report No. R-169*. Ottawa, ON: Correctional Service of Canada.

Cullen, F.T. and Gendreau, P. (2000) 'Assessing correctional rehabilitation: Policy, practice, and prospects', in J. Horney (ed.) *NIJ Criminal Justice 2000: Changes in Decision Making and Discretion in the Criminal Justice System*. Washington, DC: US Department of Justice, National Institute of Justice, pp. 109–175.

Dadds, M.R., Smallbone, S.W., Nisbet, I. and Dombrowski, J. (2003) 'Willingness, confidence, and knowledge to work with adolescent sex offenders: An evaluation of training workshops', *Behaviour Change*, 20(2): 117–123.

Daly, K. (2002) 'Sexual assaults and restorative justice', in H. Strang and J. Braithwaite (eds) *Restorative Justice and Family Violence*. Cambridge: Cambridge University Press, pp. 62–68.

Daly, K. (2006) 'Restorative justice and sexual assault: An archival study of court and conference cases', *British Journal of Criminology*, 46(2): 334–356.

Darkness to Light (2005) *7 Steps to Protecting Our Children*. [Online]. Available at: http://www.darkness2light.org/7steps/7steps.asp [accessed 24 January 2008].

Darkness to Light (2006) *Public Awareness about Child Sexual Abuse*. [Online]. Available at: http://www.darkness2light.org [accessed 24 January 2008].

Daro, D. and Salmon-Cox, S. (1994) *Child Sexual Abuse Prevention Programs: Do They Work?* Englewood, CO: National Resource Center on Child Abuse and Neglect.

Davenport, W. (1965) 'Sexual patterns and their regulation in a society of the South-west Pacific', in F.A. Beach (ed.) *Sex and Behaviour*. New York: Wiley, pp. 164–207.

Davidson, W., Gottschalk, R., Gensheimer, L. and Mayer, J. (1984) *Interventions with Juvenile Delinquents: A Meta-analysis of Treatment Efficacy*. Washington, DC: National Institute of Juvenile Justice and Delinquency Prevention.

De Jong, A.R., Hervada, A.R. and Emmett, G.A. (1983) 'Epidemiologic variations in childhood sexual abuse', *Child Abuse and Neglect*, 7(2): 155–162.

De Jong, C. (1997) 'Survival analysis and specific deterrence: Integrating theoretical and empirical models of recidivism', *Criminology*, 35(4): 561–575.

DeLamater, J. and Friedrich, W.N. (2002) 'Human sexual development', *The Journal of Sex Research*, 39(1): 10–14.

Department of Families Community Services and Indigenous Affairs (2007) *Family Relationships Services Program (FRSP)*. [Online]. Available at: http://www.facs.gov.au/frsp [accessed 24 January 2008].

Dinsmoor, J.A. (1998) 'Punishment', in W. O'Donohue (ed.) *Learning and Behavior Therapy*. Boston, MA: Allyn & Bacon, pp. 188–204.

Dishion, T.J., McCord, J. and Poulin, F. (1999) 'When interventions harm', *American Psychologist*, 54(9): 755–764.

Dodge Reyome, N. (1994) 'Teacher ratings of the achievement-related classroom behaviors of maltreated and non-maltreated children', *Psychology in the Schools*, 31(4): 253–260.

Domjan, M. (1998) *The Principles of Learning and Behavior* (4th ed.). Pacific Grove, CA: Brooks/Cole Publishing.

Donnelly, A.C. (1997) 'An overview of prevention of physical abuse and neglect', in M.E. Helfer, R.S. Kempe and R.D. Krugman (eds) *The Battered Child* (5th ed.). Chicago, IL: The University of Chicago Press.

Doob, A.N., Sprott, J.B., Marinos, V. and Varma, K.N. (1998) *An Exploration of Ontario Residents' Views of Crime and the Criminal Justice System* (C98-931656-4). Toronto, ON: Centre of Criminology, University of Toronto.

Doob, A. and Webster, C.M. (2003) 'Sentence severity and crime: Accepting the null hypothesis', in M. Tonry (ed.) *Crime and Justice: A Review of Research Vol. 30*. Chicago, IL: University of Chicago Press, pp. 143–195.

Doren, D.M. (2002) *Evaluating Sex Offenders: A Manual for Civil Commitments and Beyond*. Thousand Oaks, CA: Sage Publications.

Doren, D.M. (2006) 'Recidivism risk assessments: Making sense of controversies', in W.L. Marshall, Y.M. Fernandez, L.E. Marshall and G.A. Serran (eds) *Sexual Offender Treatment: Controversial Issues*. Chichester: Wiley, pp. 3–15.

Dowden, C. and Andrews, D.A. (1999) 'What works in young offender treatment: A meta-analysis?', *Forum on Corrections Research*, 11(2): 21–24.

Dowden, C., Antonowicz, D. and Andrews, D.A. (2003) 'The effectiveness of relapse prevention with offenders: A meta-analysis', *International Journal of Offender Therapy and Comparative Criminology*, 47(5): 516–528.

Drake, B. and Pandey, S. (1996) 'Understanding the relationship between neighborhood poverty and specific types of child maltreatment', *Child Abuse and Neglect*, 20(11): 1003–1018.

Drapeau, M. (2005) 'Research on the processes involved in treating sexual offenders', *Sexual Abuse: A Journal of Research and Treatment*, 17(2): 117–125.

Dunne, E.A. (2004) 'Clerical child sex abuse: The response of the Roman Catholic Church', *Journal of Community and Applied Social Psychology*, 14(6): 490–494.

Dunne, M.P., Purdie, D.M., Cook, M.D., Boyle, F.M. and Najman, J.M. (2003) 'Is child sexual abuse declining? Evidence from a population-based survey of men and women in Australia', *Child Abuse and Neglect*, 27(2): 141–152.

Eastwood, C. (2003) 'The experiences of child complainants of sexual abuse in the criminal justice system', *Trends and Issues in Crime and Criminal Justice, No. 250*. Canberra: Australian Institute of Criminology.

Eastwood, C., Patton, W. and Stacy, H. (2000) 'Children seeking justice: Surviving child sexual abuse and the criminal justice system', *Queensland Journal of Educational Research*, 16(2): 158–182.

Eckenrode, J., Laird, M. and Doris, J. (1993) 'School performance and disciplinary problems among abused and neglected children', *Developmental Psychology*, 29(1): 53–62.

Egeland, B., Carlson, E. and Sroufe, L.A. (1993) 'Resilience as process', *Development and Psychopathology*, 5(4): 517–528.

Egeland, B., Jacobvitz, D. and Sroufe, L.A. (1988) 'Breaking the cycle of abuse', *Child Development*, 59(4): 1080–1088.

Elliot, A.N. and Carnes, C.N. (2001) 'Reactions of nonoffending parents to the sexual abuse of their children: A review of the literature', *Child Maltreatment*, 6(4): 314–331.

Elliott, M., Browne, K. and Kilcoyne, J. (1995) 'Child sexual abuse prevention: What offenders tell us', *Child Abuse and Neglect*, 19(5): 579–594.

Emmons, R.A. (1996) 'Striving and feeling: Personal goals and subjective well-being', in P.M. Gollwitzer and J.A. Bargh (eds) *The Psychology of Action: Linking Cognition and Motivation to Behavior.* New York: Guilford Press, pp. 313–337.

Ernst, J. (2000) 'Mapping child maltreatment: Looking at neighborhoods in a suburban county', *Child Welfare*, 79(5): 555–572.

Erwin, B. (1986) 'Turning up the heat on probationers in Georgia', *Federal Probation*, 50(2): 17–24.

Everill, J. and Waller, G. (1994) 'Disclosure of sexual abuse and psychological adjustment in female undergraduates', *Child Abuse and Neglect*, 19(1): 93–100.

Farrington, D.P. (1994) 'Early developmental prevention of juvenile delinquency', *Criminal Behavior and Mental Health*, 4(3): 209–227.

Fehrenbach, P., Smith, W., Monastersky, C. and Deischer, R. (1986) 'Adolescent sexual offenders: Offender and offense characteristics', *American Journal of Orthopsychiatry*, 56(2): 225–233.

Fergusson, D.M., Horwood, L.J. and Lynskey, M.T. (1997) 'Childhood sexual abuse, adolescent sexual behaviors and sexual revictimization', *Child Abuse and Neglect*, 21(8): 789–803.

Ferrara, M.L. and McDonald, S. (1996) *Treatment of the Juvenile Sex Offender: Neurologic and Psychiatric Impairments*. Northvale, NJ: Jason Aronson.

Finkelhor, D. (1979) *Sexually Victimized Children*. New York: Free Press.

Finkelhor, D. (1980) 'Sex among siblings: A survey on prevalence, variety, and effects', *Archives of Sexual Behavior*, 9(3): 171–194.

Finkelhor, D. (1984) *Child Sexual Abuse: New Theory and Research.* New York: Free Press.

Finkelhor, D. (1994) 'The international epidemiology of child sexual abuse', *Child Abuse and Neglect*, 18(5): 409–417.

Finkelhor, D. (2003) 'The legacy of the clergy abuse scandal', *Child Abuse and Neglect*, 27(11): 1225–1229.

Finkelhor, D. and Baron, L. (1986) 'Risk factors for child sexual abuse', *Journal of Interpersonal Violence*, 1(1): 43–71.

Finkelhor, D. and Daro, D. (1997) 'Prevention of child sexual abuse', in M. Helfer, R. Kempe and R. Krugman (eds) *The Battered Child* (5th ed.). Chicago, IL: The University of Chicago Press, pp. 615–626.

Finkelhor, D. and Dziuba-Leatherman, J. (1994) 'Children as victims of violence: A national survey', *Pediatrics*, 94(4): 413–420.

Finkelhor, D. and Dziuba-Leatherman, J. (1995) 'Victimization of children', *American Psychologist*, 49(3): 173–183.

Finkelhor, D. and Dziuba-Leatherman, J. (2001) 'Victimization of children', in R. Bull (ed.) *Children and the Law: The Essential Readings.* Oxford: Blackwell Publishing, pp. 5–28.

Finkelhor, D., Hotaling, G., Lewis, I.A. and Smith, C. (1990) 'Sexual abuse in a national survey of adult men and women: Prevalence, characteristics and risk factors', *Child Abuse and Neglect*, 14(1): 19–28.

Finkelhor, D. and Kendall-Tackett, K. (1997) 'A developmental perspective on the childhood impact of crime, abuse, and violent victimization', in D. Cicchetti and S.L. Toth (eds) *Rochester Symposium on Developmental Psychopathology Vol. 3 Trauma: Perspectives on Theory, Research and Intervention.* Rochester, NY: University of Rochester Press, pp. 1–32.

Finklehor, D., Mitchell, K.J. and Wolak, J. (2000) *Online Victimization: A Report on the Nation's Youth.* [Online]. Available at: http://www.missingkids.com [accessed on 24 January 2008].

Finklehor, D., Moore, D., Hamby, S.L. and Straus, M.A. (1997) 'Sexually abused children in a national survey of parents: Methodological issues', *Child Abuse and Neglect*, 21(1): 1–8.

Finkelhor, D. and Ormrod, R.K. (2001) 'Factors in the underreporting of crimes against juveniles', *Child Maltreatment*, 6(3): 219–229.

Finkelhor, D., Ormrod, R., Turner, H. and Hamby, S.L. (2005) 'The victimization of children and youth: A comprehensive national survey', *Child Maltreatment*, 10(1): 5–25.

Finkelhor, D., Wolak, J. and Berliner, L. (2001) 'Police reporting and professional help seeking for child crime victims: A review', *Child Maltreatment*, 6(1): 17–30.

Fischer, D.G. and McDonald, W.L. (1998) 'Characteristics of intrafamilial and extrafamilial child sexual abuse', *Child Abuse and Neglect*, 22(9): 915–929.

Fisher, H.E., Aron, A., Mashek, D., Li, H. and Brown, L.L. (2002) 'Defining the brain systems of lust, romantic attraction, and attachment', *Archives of Sexual Behavior*, 31(5): 413–419.

Fleming, J., Mullen, P. and Bammer, G. (1997) 'A study of potential risk factors for sexual abuse in childhood', *Child Abuse and Neglect*, 21(1): 49–58.

Forde, L. (1999) *Commission of Inquiry into Abuse of Children in Queensland Institutions*. Brisbane: Goprint.

Forrester, D., Frenz, S., O'Connell, M. and Pease, K. (1990) *The Kirkholt Burglary Prevention Project: Phase 2*. London: Home Office.

Freeman-Longo, R.E. (2003) 'Emerging issues, policy changes and the future of treating children with sexual behavior problems', *Annals of the New York Academy of Sciences*, 989: 502–514.

Freisthler, B., Merritt, D.H. and LaScala, E.A. (2006) 'Understanding the ecology of child maltreatment: A review of the literature and directions for future research', *Child Maltreatment*, 11(3): 263–280.

Fryer, G.E., Kerns Kraizer, S.K. and Miyoshi, T.J. (1987) 'Measuring actual reduction of risk to child abuse: A new approach', *Child Abuse and Neglect*, 11(2): 173–179.

Fryer, G.E. and Miyoshi, T.J. (1994) 'A survival analysis of the revictimization of children: The case of Colorado', *Child Abuse and Neglect*, 18(12): 1063–1071.

Gabriel, R.M. (1996) *Self-enhancement, Inc. Violence Prevention Program*. Portland, OR: RMC Research.

Gallagher, B. (2000) 'The extent and nature of known cases of institutional child sexual abuse', *British Journal of Social Work*, 30(6): 795–817.

Gallagher, C.A., Wilson, D.B., Hirschfield, P., Coggeshall, M.B. and MacKenzie, D.L. (1999) 'A quantitative review of the effects of sexual offender treatment on sexual re-offending', *Corrections Management Quarterly*, 3(4): 19–29.

Gallagher, P., Hickey, J. and Ash, D. (1997) *Child Sexual Assault: An Analysis of Matters Determined in the District Court of New South Wales During 1994*. Sydney: Judicial Commission of NSW.

Garbarino, J. (1977) 'The human ecology of child maltreatment: A conceptual model for research', *Journal of Marriage and the Family*, 39(4): 721–735.

Garcia, J. and Koelling, R.A (1966) 'Relation of cue to consequence in avoidance learning', *Psychonomic Science*, 4: 123–124.

Garrett, C.J. (1985) 'Effects of residential treatment of adjudicated delinquents: A meta-analysis', *Journal of Research in Crime and Delinquency*, 22(4): 287–308.

Gartner, R.B. (2004) 'Predatory priests: Sexually abusing fathers', *Studies in Gender and Sexuality*, 5(1): 31–56.

Gendreau, P. and Goggin, C. (1996) 'Principles of effective correctional programming', *Forum on Corrections Research*, 8(3): 38–41.

Gendreau, P., Goggin, C. and Cullen, F.T. (1999) *The Effects of Prison Sentences on Recidivism: Report to the Corrections Research and Development and Aboriginal Policy Branch*. Ottawa, ON: Solicitor General of Canada.

Gendreau, P., Goggin, C., Cullen, F.T. and Andrews, D.A. (2001) 'The effects of community sanctions and incarceration on recidivism', in L.L. Motiuk and R.C. Serin (eds) *Compendium 2000 on Effective Correctional Programming*. Ottawa, ON: Correctional Service Canada, pp. 18–21.

Gendreau, P., Goggin, C., French, S. and Smith, P. (2006) 'Practicing psychology in correctional settings', in I.B. Weiner and A.K. Hess (eds) *The Handbook of Forensic Psychology* (3rd ed.). Hoboken, NJ: Wiley, pp. 722–750.

Gendreau, P., Goggin, C. and Fulton, B. (2001) 'Intensive supervision in probation and parole', in C.R. Hollin (ed.) *Handbook of Offender Assessment and Treatment*. Chichester: Wiley, pp. 195–204.

Gendreau, P., Paparozzi, M., Little, T. and Goddard, M. (1993) 'Does "punishing smarter" work? An assessment of the new generation of alternative sanctions in probation', *Forum on Corrections Research*, 5(3): 31–34.

Gibson, L.E. and Leitenberg, H. (2000) 'Child sexual abuse prevention programs: Do they decrease the occurrence of child sexual abuse?', *Child Abuse and Neglect*, 24(9): 1115–1125.

Gittler, J. (2002) 'Efforts to reform child and family services: The political context and lessons to be learned', in G.B. Melton, R.A. Thompson and M.A. Small (eds) *Toward a Child-centered, Neighborhood-based Child Protection System: A Report of the Consortium on Children, Families and the Law*. Westport, CT: Praeger, pp. 115–141.

Glaser, W. (2003) 'Integrating pharmacological treatments', in T. Ward, D.R. Laws and S.M. Hudson (eds) *Sexual Deviance: Issues and Controversies*. Thousand Oaks, CA: Sage Publications, pp. 262–279.

Goddard, C.R. (1988) *A Child Sexual Abuse Police Tracking Project*. Victoria, BC: Law Reform Commission of Victoria.

Goddard, C.R. and Hiller, P. (1992) *Tracking Physical and Sexual Abuse Cases from a Hospital Setting into Victoria's Criminal Justice and Child Protection Systems, Vol. 1*. Melbourne: Department of Social Work, Monash University.

Goffman, E. (1959) *The Presentation of Self in Everyday Life*. Garden City, NY: Doubleday.

Goffman, E. (1961) *Asylums: Essays on the Social Situation of Mental Patients and Other Inmates*. Oxford: Aldine.

Gold, S.N., Elhai, J.D., Lucenko, B.A., Swingle, J.M. and Hughes, D.M. (1998) 'Abuse characteristics among childhood sexual abuse survivors in therapy: A gender comparison', *Child Abuse and Neglect*, 22(10): 1005–1012.

Goldstein, S. (1999) *The Sexual Exploitation of Children: A Practical Guide to Assessment Investigation and Intervention* (2nd ed.). Boca Raton, FA: CRC Press.

Gollwitzer, P.M. and Bargh, J.A. (eds) (1996) *The Psychology of Action: Linking Cognition and Motivation to Behavior*. New York: Guilford Press.

Goodman, G.S. and Aman, C. (1990) 'Children's use of anatomically detailed dolls to recount an event', *Child Development*, 61(6): 1859–1871.

Gottfredson, D. (1986) 'An empirical test of school-based environmental and individual intervention to reduce the risk of delinquent behaviour', *Criminology*, 24(4): 705–732.

Gottfredson, D.C. and Gottfredson, G.D. (1992) 'Theory-guided investigation: Three field experiments', in J. McCord and R.E. Tremblay (eds) *Preventing Antisocial Behavior: Interventions from Birth through Adolescence*. New York: Guilford.

Gottfredson, M. and Hirschi, R. (1990) *A General Theory of Crime*. Palo Alto, CA: Stanford University Press.

Grasmick, H.G. and Bryjak, G.J. (1980) 'The deterrent effect of perceived severity of punishment', *Social Forces*, 59(2): 471–491.

Green, R. (1995) 'Psycho-educational modules', in B.K. Schwartz and H.R. Cellini (eds) *The Sex Offender: Corrections, Treatment and Legal Practice*. Kingston, NJ: Civic Research Institute, s. 13.1–13.10.

Greenberg, D.M. and Bradford, J.M.W. (1997) 'Treatment of the paraphilic disorders: A review of the role of the selective serotonin reuptake inhibitors', *Sexual Abuse: A Journal of Research and Treatment*, 9(4): 349–360.

Greenberg, M.S. and Ruback, R.B. (1992) *After the Crime: Victim Decision Making*. New York: Plenum.

Greenland, P. and Hayman, L.L. (1997) 'Making cardiovascular disease prevention a reality', *Annals of Behavioral Medicine*, 19: 193–196.

Gross, J.J. (2007) *Handbook of Emotion Regulation*. New York: Guilford Press.

Gur, R.C., Mozley, L.H., Mozley, P.D., Resnick, S.M., Karp, J.S., Alavi, A., Arnold, S.E. and Gur, R.E. (1995) 'Sex differences in regional cerebral glucose metabolism during a resting state', *Science*, 267: 528–531.

Hall, G.C. (1995) 'Sexual offender recidivism revisited: A meta-analysis of recent treatment studies', *Journal of Consulting and Clinical Psychology*, 63(5): 802–809.

Hall, G.C. and Hirschman, R. (1992) 'Sexual aggression against children: A conceptual perspective of etiology', *Criminal Justice and Behavior*, 19(1): 8–23.

Haney, C., Banks, C. and Zimbardo, P. (1973) 'Interpersonal dynamics in a simulated prison', *International Journal of Criminology and Penology*, 1(1): 69–97.

Haney, C. and Zimbardo, P. (1998) 'The past and future of US prison policy: Twenty-five years after the Stanford prison experiment', *American Psychologist*, 53(7): 709–727.

Hanson, R.F., Resnick, H.S., Saunders, B.E., Kilpatrick, D.G. and Best, C. (1999) 'Factors related to the reporting of childhood rape', *Child Abuse and Neglect*, 23(6): 559–569.

Hanson, R.K. (2000) 'Treatment outcome and evaluation problems (and solutions)', in D.R. Laws, S.M. Hudson and T. Ward (eds) *Remaking Relapse Prevention: A Sourcebook*. Thousand Oaks, CA: Sage, pp. 485–499.

Hanson, R.K. (2002) 'Recidivism and age: Follow-up data from 4,673 sexual offenders', *Journal of Interpersonal Violence*, 17(10): 1046–1062.

Hanson, R.K. and Bussière, M.T. (1998) 'Predicting relapse: A meta-analysis of sexual offender recidivism studies', *Journal of Consulting and Clinical Psychology*, 66(2): 348–362.

Hanson, R.K., Gordon, A., Harris, A.J.R., Marques, J.K., Murphy, W.D., Quinsey, V.L. and Seto, M.C. (2002) 'First report of the collaborative outcome data project on the effectiveness of psychological treatment of sex offenders', *Sexual Abuse: A Journal of Research and Treatment*, 14(2): 169–195.

Hanson, R.K. and Harris, A.J.R. (2000) 'Where should we intervene? Dynamic predictors of sex offender recidivism', *Criminal Justice and Behavior*, 27(1): 6–35.

Hanson, R.K. and Morton-Bourgon, K. (2004) *Predictors of Sexual Recidivism: An Updated Meta-analysis* (Catalogue No. P53-1/2004-2E-PDF). Ottawa, ON: Public Works and Government Services Canada.

Harris, D., Smallbone, S.W., Dennison, S. and Knight, R. (in press) *Offense Specialization and Versatility in the Criminal Histories of Adult Male Sexual Offenders Referred for Civil Commitment*. Manuscript submitted for publication.

Harvey, J.H., Orbuch, T.L., Chwalisz, K.D. and Garwood, G. (1991) 'Coping with sexual assault: The roles of account-making and confiding', *Journal of Traumatic Stress*, 4(4): 515–531.

Haugaard, J. (2000) 'The challenge of defining child sexual abuse', *American Psychologist*, 55(9): 1036–1039.

Hawkins, J.D. and Catalano, R.F. (1992) *Communities That Care: Action for Drug Abuse Prevention*. San Francisco, CA: Jossey-Bass.

Hawkins, J., Catalano, R., Kosterman, R., Abbot, R. and Hill, K. (1999) 'Preventing adolescent health-risk behaviors by strengthening protection during childhood', *Archives of Pediatrics and Adolescent Medicine*, 153(3): 226–234.

Hawkins, J.D., Catalano, R.F., Morrison, D.M., O'Donnell, J., Abbott, R.D. and Day, L.E. (1992) 'The Seattle Social Development Project: Effects of the first four years on protective factors and problem behaviors', in J. McCord and R.E. Tremblay (eds) *The Prevention of Antisocial Behavior in Children*. New York: Guilford Press.

Hawkins, J.D., Herrenkohl, T.I., Farrington, D.P., Brewer, D.D., Catalano, R.F. and Harachi, T.W. (1998) 'A review of predictors of youth violence', in R. Loeber and D.P. Farrington (eds) *Serious and Violent Juvenile Offenders: Risk Factors and Successful Intervention*. Thousand Oaks, CA: Sage Publications.

Hawkins, J.D., Smith, B.H., Hill, K.G., Kosterman, R., Catalano, R.F. and Abbot, R.D. (2003) 'Understanding and preventing crime and violence: Findings from the Seattle Social Development Project', in T.P. Thornberry and M.D. Krohn (eds) *Taking Stock of Delinquency: An Overview of Findings from Contemporary Longitudinal Studies*. New York: Kluwer.

Hawkins, J.D. and Weis, J.G. (1985) 'The social development model: An integrated approach to delinquency prevention', *The Journal of Primary Prevention*, 6(2): 73–97.

Hazan, C. and Shaver, P. (1987) 'Romantic love conceptualized as an attachment process', *Journal of Personality and Social Psychology*, 52(3): 511–524.

Hazan, C., Zeifman, D. and Middleton, K. (1994) 'Adult romantic attachment, affection and sex', *paper presented at the 7th International Conference on Personal Relationships*, Groningen, The Netherlands, July 1994.

Hebert, M., Parent, N., Daignault, I.V. and Tourigny, M. (2006) 'A typological analysis of behavioral profiles of sexually abused children', *Child Maltreatment*, 11(3): 203–216.

Heeren, J. and Shichor, D. (1984) 'Mass media and delinquency prevention: The case of "scared straight"', *Deviant Behavior*, 5(4): 375–386.

Heller, S.S., Larrieu, J.A., D'Imperio, R.D. and Boris, N.W. (1999) 'Research on resilience to child maltreatment: Empirical considerations', *Child Abuse and Neglect*, 23(4): 321–338.

Henggeler, S.W., Cunningham, P.B., Pickrel, S.G. and Schoenwald, S.K. (1995) 'Multisystemic therapy for serious juvenile offenders and their families', in R.R. Ross, D.H. Antonowicz and G.K. Dhaliwal (eds) *Going Straight: Effective Delinquency Prevention and Offender Rehabilitation*. Ottawa, ON: Air Training & Publications, pp. 109–133.

Henggeler, S.W., Schoenwald, S.K., Borduin, C.M., Rowland, M.D. and Cunningham, P.B. (1998) *Multisystemic Treatment of Antisocial Behavior in Children and Adolescents*. New York: Guilford Press

Henry, J. (1997) 'System intervention trauma to child sexual abuse victims following disclosure', *Journal of Interpersonal Violence*, 12(4): 499–512.

Herdt, G. (1982) *Rituals of Manhood*. Berkeley, CA: University of California Press.

Heriot, J.K. (1996) 'Maternal protectiveness following the disclosure of intrafamilial child sexual abuse', *Journal of Interpersonal Violence*, 11(2): 181–194.

Herrenkohl, R.C. (2005) 'The definition of child maltreatment: From case study to construct', *Child Abuse and Neglect*, 29(5): 413–424.

Hershkowitz, I., Lamb, M.E., Sternberg, K.J. and Esplin, P.W. (1997) 'The relationships among interviewer utterance type, CBCA scores, and the richness of children's responses', *Legal and Criminological Psychology*, 2: 169–176.

Hertzman, C. (2002) *An Early Child Development Strategy for Australia? Lessons from Canada.* Queensland Government: Commission for Children and Young People.

Higgins, D., Bromfield, K. and Richardson, N. (2007) *Mandatory Reporting of Child Abuse.* [Online]. Available at: http://www.aifs.gov.au/nch/pubs/sheets/rs3/rs3.html [accessed 24 January 2008].

Himelein, M.J. and McElrath, J.A.V. (1996) 'Resilient child sexual abuse survivors: Cognitive coping and illusion', *Child Abuse and Neglect*, 20(8): 747–758.

Hirschi, T. and Stark, R. (1969) 'Hellfire and delinquency', *Social Problems*, 17(2): 202–214.

Hodson, L.P. (2007) *Onset of Offending in Child Sexual Abuse.* Unpublished raw data.

Holden, E.W. and Black, M.M. (1999) 'Theory and concepts of prevention science as applied to clinical psychology', *Clinical Psychology Review*, 19(4): 391–401.

Hollin, C.R. (ed.) (2001) *Handbook of Offender Assessment and Treatment.* Chichester: Wiley.

Homel, R. (2005) 'Developmental crime prevention', in N. Tilley (ed.) *Handbook of Crime Prevention and Community Safety.* Cullompton: Willan Publishing, pp. 71–106.

Homel, R., Lincoln, R. and Herd, B. (1999) 'Risk and resilience: Crime and violence prevention in aboriginal communities', *The Australian and New Zealand Journal of Criminology*, 32(2): 182–196.

Home Office (1993) *Digest 2: Information on the Criminal Justice System in England and Wales.* London: Home Office Research and Statistics Department.

Hood, M. and Boltje, C. (1998) 'The progress of 500 referrals from the child protection response system to the criminal court', *Australian and New Zealand Journal of Criminology*, 31(2): 182–195.

Hope, T. (1995) 'Community crime prevention', in M. Tonry and D.P. Farrington (eds) *Building a Safer Society: Strategic Approaches to Crime Prevention.* Chicago, IL: University of Chicago Press.

Hunter, J.A. (1991) 'A comparison of the psychosocial maladjustment of adult males and females sexually molested as children', *Journal of Interpersonal Violence*, 6(2): 205–217.

Hunter, J.A. and Figueredo, A.J. (1999) 'Factors associated with treatment compliance in a population of juvenile sexual offenders', *Sexual Abuse: A Journal of Research and Treatment*, 11(1): 49–67.

Insel, T.R. (1997) 'A neurobiological basis of social attachment', *American Journal of Psychiatry*, 154(6): 726–735.

Janus, E.S. and Meehl, P.E. (1997) 'Assessing the legal standard for predictions of dangerousness in sex offender commitment proceedings', *Psychology, Public Policy, and Law*, 3(1): 33–64.

Johnson, T.C. and Doonan, R. (2005) 'Children with sexual behaviour problems: What have we learned in the last two decades?', in M.C. Calder (ed.) *Children and Young People Who Sexually Abuse: New Theory, Research and Practice Developments*. Lyme Regis: Russell House, pp. 32–58.

Jones, L.M., Finkelhor, D. and Kopiec, K. (2001) 'Why is sexual abuse declining? A survey of state child protection administrators', *Child Abuse and Neglect*, 25(9): 1139–1158.

Kamerman, S.B. (2000) 'Early childhood intervention policies: An international perspective', in J.P. Shonkoff and S.J. Meisels (eds) *Handbook of Early Childhood Intervention* (2nd ed.) Cambridge: Cambridge University Press, pp. 613–629.

Kansas v. Hendricks, 117 S. Ct. 2072 (US Supreme Court) (1997).

Katz, J. (1988) *Seductions of Crimes*. New York: Blackwell Publishing.

Kaufman, K.L., Hilliker, D.R. and Daleiden, E.L. (1996) 'Subgroup differences in the modus operandi of adolescent sexual offenders', *Child Maltreatment*, 1(1): 17–24.

Kaufman, K.L., Holmberg, J.K., Orts, K.A., McCrady, F.E., Rotzien, A.L., Daleiden, E.L. and Hilliker, D.R. (1998) 'Factors influencing sexual offenders' modus operandi: An examination of victim–offender relatedness and age', *Child Maltreatment*, 3(4): 349–361.

Kaufman, K.L., Mosher, H., Carter, M. and Estes, L. (2006) 'An empirically based situational prevention model for child sexual abuse', in R.K. Wortley and S.W. Smallbone (eds) *Situational Prevention of Child Sexual Abuse, Crime Prevention Studies Vol. 19*. Monsey, NY: Criminal Justice Press.

Kebbell, M.R., Hurren, E.J. and Mazerolle, P. (2006) 'Sex offenders perceptions of how they were interviewed', *Canadian Journal of Police and Security Services*.

Kelley, S.J., Brant, R. and Waterman, J. (1993) 'Sexual abuse of children in day care centers', *Child Abuse and Neglect*, 17(1): 71–89.

Kelling, G.L. (2005) 'Community crime reduction: Activating formal and informal control', in N. Tilley (ed.) *Handbook of Crime Prevention and Community Safety*. Cullompton: Willan Publishing, pp. 107–142.

Kellogg, N.D. and Hoffman, T.J. (1995) 'Unwanted and illegal sexual experiences in childhood and adolescence', *Child Abuse and Neglect*, 19(9): 1457–1468.

Kellogg, N.D. and Hoffman, T.J. (1997) 'Child sexual revictimization by multiple perpetrators', *Child Abuse and Neglect*, 21(10): 953–964.

Kendall-Tackett, K. and Simon, A. (1992) 'A comparison of the abuse experiences of male and female adults molested as children', *Journal of Family Violence*, 7(1): 57–62.

Kendall-Tackett, K., Williams, L. and Finkelhor, D. (1993) 'The impact of sexual abuse on children: A review and synthesis of recent empirical studies', *Psychological Bulletin*, 113(1): 164–180.

Kendrick, A. and Taylor, J. (2000) 'Hidden on the ward: The abuse of children in hospitals', *Journal of Advanced Nursing*, 31(3): 565–573.

Kershaw, C., Goodman, J. and White, S. (1999) *Reconviction of Offenders Sentenced or Released from Prison in 1995, Research Findings No. 101*. London: Home Office Research and Statistics Department.

Ketring, S.A. and Feinauer, L.L. (1999) 'Perpetrator–victim relationship: Long-term effects of sexual abuse for men and women', *The American Journal of Family Therapy*, 27(2): 109–120.

Kilpatrick, D. and Saunders, B. (1997) *Prevalence and Consequences of Child Victimization: Results from the National Survey of Adolescents, Final Report*. Washington, DC: US Department of Justice, Office of Justice Programs, National Institute of Justice.

Koss, M.P., Bachar, K. and Hopkins, C.Q. (2006) 'Disposition and treatment of juvenile sex offenders from the perspective of restorative justice', in H.E. Barbaree and W.L. Marshall (eds) *The Juvenile Sex Offender* (2nd ed.) New York: Guilford Press, pp. 336–357.

Koss, M., Gidycz, C. and Wisniewski, N. (1987) 'The scope of rape: Incidence and prevalence of sexual aggression in a national sample of higher education students', *Journal of Consulting and Clinical Psychology*, 55(2): 162–170.

Kottler, J.A., Sexton, T.L. and Whiston, S.G. (1994) *The Heart of Healing: Relationships in Therapy*. San Francisco, CA: Jossey-Bass Publishers.

Krahé, B., Scheinberger-Olwig, R., Waizenhöfer, E. and Kolpin, S. (1999) 'Childhood sexual abuse and revictimization in adolescence', *Child Abuse and Neglect*, 23(4): 383–394.

Larner, M.B., Stevenson, C.S. and Behrman, R.E. (1998) 'Protecting children from abuse and neglect: Analysis and recommendations', *The Future of Children*, 8(1): 4–22.

Laws, D.R., Hudson, S.M. and Ward, T. (eds) (2000) *Remaking Relapse Prevention with Sex Offenders*. Thousand Oaks, CA: Sage Publications.

Laws, D.R. and Marshall, W.L. (1991) 'Masturbatory reconditioning with sexual deviates: An evaluative review', *Advances in Behaviour Research and Therapy*, 13(1): 13–25.

Laws, D.R. and Marshall, W.L. (2003) 'A brief history of behavioral and cognitive-behavioral approaches to sexual offender treatment: Part 1, Early developments', *Sexual Abuse: A Journal of Research and Treatment*, 15(2): 75–92.

Laws, D.R. and Ward, T. (2006) 'When one size doesn't fit all', in W.L. Marshall, Y.M. Fernandez, L.E. Marshall and G.A. Serran (eds) *Sexual Offender Treatment: Controversial Issues*. Chichester: Wiley, pp. 241–254.

Lawson, L. and Chaffin, M. (1992) 'False negatives in sexual abuse disclosure interviews: Incidence and influence of caretaker's belief in abuse in cases of accidental abuse discovery of STD', *Journal of Interpersonal Violence*, 7: 532–542.

Letourneau, E. and Miner, M. (2005) 'Juvenile sex offenders: A case against the legal and clinical status quo', *Sexual Abuse: A Journal of Research and Treatment*, 17(3): 293–311.

Levenson, J.S. (2004) 'Reliability of sexually violent predator civil commitment criteria', *Law and Human Behavior*, 28(4): 357–368.

Levy, H.B., Markovic, J., Chaudhry, U., Ahart, S. and Torres, H. (1995) 'Reabuse rates in a sample of children followed for 5 years after discharge from a child abuse inpatient assessment program', *Child Abuse and Neglect*, 19(11): 1363–1377.

Lewis, R.V. (1983) 'Scared straight: California style', *Criminal Justice and Behavior*, 10(3): 284–289.

Light, R., Nee, C. and Ingham, H. (1993) *Car Theft: The Offender's Perspective. Home Office Research Study No. 130*. London: HMSO.

Lipsey, M.W. (1992) 'Juvenile delinquency treatment: A meta-analytic inquiry into the variability of effects', in T. Cook, D. Cooper, H. Corday, H. Hartman, L. Hedges, R. Light, T. Louis and F. Mosteller (eds) *Meta-analysis for Explanation: A Casebook*. New York: Russell Sage Foundation, pp. 83–127.

Lipsey, M.W. (1995) 'What do we learn from 400 research studies on the effectiveness of treatment with juvenile delinquents?', in J. McGuire (ed.) *What Works: Reducing Re-offending*. Chichester: Wiley.

Lipsey, M. and Derzon, J. (1998) 'Predictors of violent or serious delinquency in adolescence and early adulthood: A synthesis of longitudinal research', in R. Loeber and D.P. Farrington (eds) *Serious and Violent Juvenile Offenders: Risk Factors and Successful Interventions*. Thousand Oaks, CA: Sage Publications, pp. 86–105.

Lipton, D.S., Pearson, F.S., Cleland, C.M., Yee, D. (2002) 'The effects of therapeutic communities and milieu therapy on recidivism', in J. McGuire (ed.) *Offender Rehabilitation and Treatment: Effective Programmes and Policies to Reduce Re-offending*. Chichester: Wiley, pp. 39–77.

Lloyd, C., Mair, G. and Hough, M. (1994) *Explaining Reconviction Rates: A Critical Analysis. Home Office Research Study No. 136*. London: HMSO.

Loeber, R. and Farrington, D.P. (eds) (1998) *Serious and Violent Juvenile Offenders: Risk Factors and Successful Interventions*. Thousand Oaks, CA: Sage Publications.

Loeber, R., Van Kammen, W.B. and Fletcher, M. (1996) *Serious, Violent and Chronic Offenders in the Pittsburgh Youth Study: Unpublished Data*. Pittsburgh, PA: Western Psychiatric Institute and Clinic.

London, K., Bruck, M., Ceci, S.J. and Shuman, D.W. (2005) 'Disclosure of child sexual abuse: What does the research tell us about the ways that children tell?', *Psychology, Public Policy, and Law*, 11(1): 194–226.

Long, P.J. and Jackson, J.L. (1991) 'Children sexually abused by multiple perpetrators: Familial risk factors and abuse characteristics', *Journal of Interpersonal Violence*, 6(2): 147–159.

Looman, J., Abracen, J. and Nicholaichuk, T.P. (2000) 'Recidivism among treated sexual offenders and matched controls: Data from the Regional Treatment Centre (Ontario)', *Journal of Interpersonal Violence*, 15(3): 279–290.

Lösel, F. (1995) 'The efficacy of correctional treatment: A review and synthesis of meta-evaluations', in J. McGuire (ed.) *What Works: Reducing Reoffending: Guidelines from Research and Practice*. Chichester: Wiley, pp. 79–111.

Lösel, F. and Schmucker, M. (2005) 'The effectiveness of treatment for sexual offenders: A comprehensive meta-analysis', *Journal of Experimental Criminology*, 1(1): 117–146.

Lothstein, L.M. (2004) 'Men of the flesh: The evaluation and treatment of sexually abusing priests', *Studies in Gender and Sexuality*, 5(2): 167–195.

Luster, T. and Youatt, J. (1989) 'The effects of pre-parenthood education on high school students', *paper presented at the annual meeting of the Society for Research in Child Development*. Kansas City, MO.

Lutzker, J.R., Wesch, D. and Rice, J.M. (1984) 'A review of project 12-ways: An ecobehavioral approach to the treatment and prevention of child abuse and neglect', *Advances in Behaviour Research and Therapy*, 6(1): 63–73.

Lyons-Ruth, K. (1996) 'Attachment relationships among children with aggressive behavior problems: The role of disorganized early attachment patterns', *Journal of Consulting and Clinical Psychology*, 64(1): 32–40.

MacIntyre, D. and Carr, A. (2000) 'Prevention of child sexual abuse: Implications of programme evaluation research'. *Child Abuse Review*, 9(3): 183–199.

MacKenzie, D.L. (2002) 'Reducing the criminal activities of known offenders and delinquents: Crime prevention in the courts and corrections', in L.W. Sherman, D.P. Farrington, B.C. Welsh and D.L. MacKenzie (eds) *Evidence-based Crime Prevention*. London: Routledge, pp. 330–404.

MacKenzie, D.L., Brame, R., McDowall, D. and Souryal, C. (1995) 'Boot camp prisons and recidivism in eight states', *Criminology*, 33(3): 327–357.

MacKenzie, D.L. and Souryal, C. (1994) *Multisite Evaluation of Shock Incarceration*. Washington, DC: National Institute of Justice.

MacMillan, H.L., Fleming, J.E., Trocmé, N., Boyle, M.H., Wong, M. and Racine, Y.A. (1997) 'Prevalence of child physical and sexual abuse in the community', *Journal of the American Medical Association*, 278(2): 131–135.

Maguire, M. and Brookman, F. (2005) 'Violent and sexual crime', in N. Tilley (ed.) *Handbook of Crime Prevention*. Cullompton: Willan Publishing.

Main, M. and Solomon, J. (1986) 'Discovery of an insecure-disorganized disoriented attachment pattern: Procedures, findings, and implications for the classification', in M. Yogman and T.B. Brazelton (eds) *Affective Development in Infancy.* Norwood, NJ: Ablex, pp. 95–124.

Malamuth, N.M. (1981) 'Rape proclivity among males', *Journal of Social Issues*, 37(4): 138–157.

Maletzky, B.M. (1991) *Treating the Sexual Offender.* Newbury Park, CA: Sage Publications.

Manion, I.G., McIntyre, J., Firestone, P., Ligezinska, M., Ensom, R. and Wells, G. (1996) 'Secondary traumatization in parents following the disclosure of extrafamilial child sexual abuse: Initial effects', *Child Abuse and Neglect*, 20(11): 1095–1109.

Manly, J.T. (2005) 'Advances in research definitions of child maltreatment', *Child Abuse and Neglect*, 29(5): 425–439.

Mann, R.E., Webster, S.D., Schofield, C. and Marshall, W.L. (2004) 'Approach versus avoidance goals in relapse prevention with sexual offenders', *Sexual Abuse: A Journal of Research and Treatment*, 16(1): 65–75.

Marlatt, G.A. (1982) 'Relapse prevention: A self-control program for the treatment of addictive behaviours', in R.B. Stuart (ed.) *Adherence, Compliance and Generalization in Behavioral Medicine.* New York: Brunner/ Mazel, pp. 329–378.

Marques, J.K. (1982) 'Relapse prevention: A self-control model for the treatment of sex offenders', *paper presented at the 7th Annual Forensic Mental Health Conference*, Asilomar, CA, March 1982.

Marques, J.K., Day, D.M., Nelson, C. and Miner, M.H. (1989) 'The Sex Offender Treatment and Evaluation Project: California's relapse prevention program', in D.R. Laws (ed.) *Relapse Prevention with Sex Offenders.* New York: Guilford Press, pp. 247–267.

Marquis, J.N. (1970) 'Orgasmic reconditioning: Changing sexual object choice through controlling masturbation fantasies', *Journal of Behavior Therapy and Experimental Psychiatry*, 1(3): 263–271.

Marshall, W.L. (1971) 'A combined treatment method for certain sexual deviations', *Behaviour Research and Therapy*, 9(3): 292–294.

Marshall, W.L. (1973) 'The modification of sexual fantasies: A combined treatment approach to the reduction of deviant sexual behavior', *Behaviour Research and Therapy*, 11(4): 557–564.

Marshall, W.L. (1979) 'Satiation therapy: A procedure for reducing deviant sexual arousal', *Journal of Applied Behavior Analysis*, 12(3): 377–389.

Marshall, W.L. (1988) 'The use of explicit sexual stimuli by rapists, child molesters and nonoffender males', *Journal of Sex Research*, 25(2): 267–288.

Marshall, W.L. (1997) 'Pedophilia: Psychopathology and theory', in D.R. Laws and W. O'Donohue (eds) *Handbook of Sexual Deviance: Theory and Application.* New York: Guilford Press, pp. 152–174.

Marshall, W.L. (2006) 'Diagnostic problems with sexual offenders', in W.L. Marshall, Y.M. Fernandez, L.E. Marshall and G.A. Serran (eds)

Sexual Offender Treatment: Controversial Issues. Chichester: Wiley, pp. 33–60.

Marshall, W.L. (2007) 'Diagnostic issues, multiple paraphilias, and comorbid disorders in sexual offenders: Their incidence and treatment', *Aggression and Violent Behavior: A Review Journal*, 12(1): 16–35.

Marshall, W.L. (in press) 'A proposal for the prevention and treatment of child molestation by Catholic clergy'.

Marshall, W.L. and Barbaree, H.E. (1988) 'The long-term evaluation of a behavioral treatment program for child molesters', *Behaviour Research and Therapy*, 26(6): 499–511.

Marshall, W.L. and Barbaree, H.E. (1990) 'An integrated theory of the etiology of sexual offending', in W.L. Marshall, D.R. Laws and H.E. Barbaree (eds) *Handbook of Sexual Assault: Issues, Theories and Treatment of the Offender.* New York: Plenum, pp. 257–275.

Marshall, W.L., Earls, C.M., Segal, Z.V. and Darke, J. (1983) 'A behavioral program for the assessment and treatment of sexual aggressors', in K. Craig and R. McMahon (eds) *Advances in Clinical Behavior Therapy.* New York: Brunner/Mazel, pp. 148–174.

Marshall, W.L. and Eccles, A. (1991) 'Issues in clinical practice with sex offenders', *Journal of Interpersonal Violence*, 6(1): 68–93.

Marshall, W.L. and Fernandez, Y.M. (1998) 'Cognitive-behavioural approaches to the treatment of the paraphiliacs: Sexual offenders', in V.E. Caballo (ed.) *International Handbook of Cognitive and Behavioural Treatments for Psychological Disorders.* Oxford: Elsevier Science, pp. 281–312.

Marshall, W.L. and Fernandez, Y.M. (2003) *Phallometric Testing with Sexual Offenders: Theory, Research and Practice.* Brandon, VT: Safer Society Press.

Marshall, W.L. and Fernandez, Y.M. (2004) 'Treatment outcome with juvenile sexual offenders', in G. O'Reilly, W.L. Marshall, A. Carr, and R.C. Beckett (eds) *The Handbook of Clinical Intervention with Young People who Sexually Abuse.* New York: Brunner-Routledge, pp. 442–452.

Marshall, W.L., Fernandez, Y.M., Serran, G.A., Mulloy, R., Thornton, D., Mann, R.E. and Anderson, D. (2003a) 'Process variables in the treatment of sexual offenders: A review of the relevant literature', *Aggression and Violent Behavior*, 8(2): 205–234.

Marshall, W.L., Kennedy, P., Yates, P. and Serran, G.A. (2002) 'Diagnosing sexual sadism in sexual offenders: Reliability across diagnosticians', *International Journal of Offender Therapy and Comparative Criminology*, 46(6): 668–676.

Marshall, W.L. and Laws, D.R. (2003) 'A brief history of behavioral and cognitive behavioral approaches to sexual offender treatment: Part 2: The modern era', *Sexual Abuse: A Journal of Research and Treatment*, 15(2): 93–120.

Marshall, W.L., Marshall, L.E., Serran, G.A. and Fernandez, Y.M. (2006) *Treating Sexual Offenders: An Integrated Approach.* New York: Routledge.

Marshall, W.L. and Serran, G.A. (2004) 'The role of the therapist in offender treatment', *Psychology, Crime and Law*, 10(3): 309–320.

Marshall, W.L., Serran, G.A., Fernandez, Y.M., Mulloy, R., Mann, R.E. and Thornton, D. (2003b) 'Therapist characteristics in the treatment of sexual offenders: Tentative data on their relationship with indices of behaviour change', *Journal of Sexual Aggression*, 9(1): 25–30.

Marshall, W.L., Serran, G.A., Marshall, L.E. and O'Brien, M.D. (in press) The Rockwood Treatment program for sexual offenders.

Marshall, W.L., Serran, G.A., Moulden, H., Mulloy, R., Fernandez, Y.M., Mann, R.E. and Thornton, D. (2002) 'Therapist features in sexual offender treatment: Their reliable identification and influence on behaviour change', *Clinical Psychology and Psychotherapy*, 9(6): 395–405.

Marshall, W.L., Ward, T., Mann, R.E., Moulden, H., Fernandez, Y.M., Serran, G.A. and Marshall, L.E. (2005) 'Working positively with sexual offenders: Maximizing the effectiveness of treatment', *Journal of Interpersonal Violence*, 20(1): 1–19.

Maurer, H. (1994) *Sex: Real People Talk About What They Really Do*. New York: Penguin Books.

McCabe, J. (1983) 'For marriage: Further support for the Westermarck hypothesis of the incest taboo', *American Anthropologist*, 85(1): 50–69.

McCain, M.N. and Mustard, J.F. (1999) *Reversing the Real Brain Drain: Early Years Study: Final Report*. Toronto, ON: Government of Ontario.

McCold, P. and Wachtel, T. (2002) 'Restorative justice theory validation', in E.G.M. Weitekamp and H.J. Kerner (eds) *Restorative Justice: Theoretical Foundations*. Cullompton: Willan Publishing, pp. 110–142.

McCord, J. (2006) 'Punishments and alternate routes to crime prevention', in I.B. Weiner and A.K. Hess (eds) *The Handbook of Forensic Psychology*. Hoboken, NJ: Wiley, pp. 701–721.

McGloin, J. and Widom, C. (2001) 'Resilience among abused and neglected children grown up', *Development and Psychopathology*, 13(4): 1021–1038.

McGrath, R.J., Cumming, G.F. and Burchard, B.L. (2003) *Current Practices and Trends in Sexual Abuser Management: Safer Society 2002 Nationwide Survey*. Brandon, VT: Safer Society Press.

McGuire, J. (2002) 'Criminal sanctions versus psychologically-based interventions with offenders: A comparative empirical analysis', *Psychology, Crime and Law*, 8(2): 183–208.

McGuire, R.J., Carlisle, J.M. and Young, B.G. (1965) 'Sexual deviations as conditioned behaviour: A hypothesis', *Behaviour Research and Therapy*, 3(3): 185–190.

McKillop, N., Smallbone, S.W. and Wortley, R.K. (unpublished) *Associations Between Victim–Offender Relationships and the Frequency and Duration of Child Sexual Abuse*. Unpublished manuscript.

McMahon, P.M. and Puett, R.C. (1999) 'Child sexual abuse as a public health issue: Recommendations of an expert panel', *Sexual Abuse: A Journal of Research and Treatment*, 11(4): 257–266.

Meier, R.F. and Johnson, W.T. (1977) 'Deterrence as social control: The legal and extralegal production of conformity', *American Sociological Review*, 42(2): 292–304.

Melella, J.T., Travin, S. and Cullen, K. (1989) 'Legal and ethical issues in the use of antiandrogens in treating sex offenders', *Bulletin of the American Academy of Psychiatry and Law*, 17(3): 223–231.

Memon, A. and Vartoukian, R. (1996) 'The effect of repeated questioning on young children's eyewitness testimony', *British Journal of Psychology*, 87(3): 403–415.

Messman-Moore, T.L. and Brown, A.L. (2004) 'Child maltreatment and perceived family environment as risk factors for adult rape: Is child sexual abuse the most salient experience?', *Child Abuse and Neglect*, 28(10): 1019–1034.

Mian, M., Wehrspann, W., Klajner-Diamond, H., LeBaron, D. and Winder, C. (1986) 'Review of 125 children 6 years of age and under who were sexually abused', *Child Abuse and Neglect*, 10(2): 223–229.

Miethe, T.D., Olson, J. and Mitchell, O. (2006) 'Specialization and persistence in the arrest histories of sex offenders: A comparative analysis of alternative measures and offense types', *Journal of Research in Crime and Delinquency*, 43(3): 204–229.

Mischel, W. (1968) *Personality and Assessment*. Chichester: Wiley.

Moffit, T.E. (1990) 'Juvenile delinquency and attention deficit disorder: Boys' developmental trajectories from age 3 to age 15', *Child Development*, 61(3): 893–910.

Moffit, T.E. (1997) 'Adolescence-limited and life-course-persistent offending: A complementary pair of developmental theories', in T. Thornberry (ed.) *Developmental Theories of Crime and Delinquency: Advances in Criminological Theory, Vol. 7*. New Brunswick: Transaction Publishers, pp. 11–54.

Molnar, B.E., Buka, S.L. and Kessler, R.C. (2001) 'Child sexual abuse and subsequent psychopathology: Results from the national comorbidity survey', *American Journal of Public Health*, 91(5): 753–760.

Moore, M.H. (1992) 'Problem-solving and community policing', in M. Tonry and N. Morris (eds) *Crime and Justice: A Review of Research Vol. 15*. Chicago, IL: University of Chicago Press.

Moran, P.B. and Eckenrode, J. (1992) 'Protective personality characteristics among adolescent victims of maltreatment', *Child Abuse and Neglect*, 16(5): 743–754.

Morrison, S. and O'Donnell, I. (1994) *Armed Robbery: A Study in London*. Oxford: Centre for Criminological Research.

Murphy, M.R., Seckl, J.R., Burton, S., Checkley, S.A. and Lightman, S.L. (1987) 'Changes in oxytocin and vasopressin secretion during sexual activity in men', *Journal of Clinical Endocrinology and Metabolism*, 65(4): 738–741.

Myers, J.E.B. (1994) 'Adjudication of sexual abuse cases', *The Future of Children*, 4(2): 84–101.

Nagin, D.S. (1998) 'Criminal deterrence research at the outset of the twenty-first century', in M. Tonry (ed.) *Crime and Justice: A Review of Research Vol. 23*. Chicago, IL: University of Chicago Press, pp. 1–42.

NAPN (1993) 'The revised report from the National Task Force on Juvenile Sexual Offending', *Juvenile and Family Court Journal*, 44: 1–120.

Newman, O. (1972) *Defensible Space: People and Design in the Violent City*. London: Architectural Press.

New South Wales Commission for Children and Young People (2008) *Our Work for Kids* [online]. Available at: http://www.kids.nsw.gov.au/kids/ourwork/researchkids/completedresearch.cfm [accessed on 4 March 2008].

Nisbet, I., Wilson, P. and Smallbone, S.W. (2004) 'A prospective longitudinal study of sexual recidivism among adolescent sexual offenders', *Sexual Abuse: A Journal of Research and Treatment*, 16(4): 223–234.

NRC (1993) *Understanding Child Abuse and Neglect*. Washington DC: National Academy Press.

O'Connor, L. (1990) 'Education for parenthood and the national curriculum: Progression or regression?', *Early Child Development and Care*, 57(1): 85–88.

O'Donohue, W.T., Regev, L.G. and Hagstron, A. (2000) 'Problems with the DSM-IV diagnosis of pedophilia', *Sexual Abuse: A Journal of Research and Treatment*, 12(2): 95–105.

Olds, D. (2002) 'Prenatal and infancy home visiting by nurses: From randomised trials to community replication', *Prevention Science*, 3(3): 153–172.

Olds, D.L. and Kitzman, H. (1990) 'Can home visitation improve the health of women and children at environmental risk?', *Pediatrics*, 86(1): 108–116.

O'Reilly, G. and Carr, A. (2006) 'Assessment and treatment of criminogenic needs', in H.E. Barbaree and W.L. Marshall (eds) *The Juvenile Sex Offender* (2nd ed.). New York: Guilford Press, pp. 189–218.

Orpinas, P., Parcel, G.S., McAlister, A. and Frankowski, R. (1995) 'Violence prevention in middle schools: A pilot study', *Journal of Adolescent Health*, 17(6): 360–371.

Orsagh, T. and Chen. J.R. (1988) 'The effect of time served on recidivism: An interdisciplinary theory', *Journal of Quantitative Criminology*, 4(2): 155–171.

Otterbein, K.F. (1979) 'A cross-cultural study of rape', *Aggressive Behavior*, 5(4): 425–435.

Panksepp, J. (1998) *Affective Neuroscience: The Foundations of Human and Animal Emotions*. New York: Oxford University Press.

Paradise, J.E., Rose, L., Sleeper, L. and Nathanson, M. (1994) 'Behavior, family function, school performance, and predictors of persistent disturbance in sexually abused children', *Pediatrics*, 93(3): 452–459.

Parker, H. and Parker, S. (1986) 'Father–daughter sexual abuse', *American Journal of Orthopsychiatry*, 56(4): 531–549.

Parkinson, P.N., Shrimpton, S., Swanston, H.Y., O'Toole, B.I. and Oates, R.K. (2002) 'The process of attrition in child sexual assault cases: A case flow analysis of criminal investigations and prosecutions', *Australian and New Zealand Journal of Criminology*, 35(3): 347–362.

Paternoster, R., Saltzman, L.E., Waldo, G.P. and Chiricos, T.G. (1983) 'Causal ordering in deterrence research', in J. Hagan (ed.) *Deterrence Reconsidered.* Beverly Hills, CA: Sage Publications, pp. 55–70.

Patterson, G.R., Reid, J.B. and Dishion, T.J. (1992) *Antisocial Boys.* Eugene, OR: Castalia.

Pence, D.M. and Wilson, C.A. (1994) 'Reporting and investigating child sexual abuse', *The Future of Children*, 4(2): 70–83.

Petersilia, J. (1990) 'When probation becomes more dreaded than prison', *Federal Probation*, 54(1): 23–27.

Petrosino, A., Turpin-Petrosino, C., Buehler, J. (2003) 'Scared straight and other juvenile awareness programs for preventing juvenile delinquency: A systematic review of the randomized experimental evidence', *Annals of the American Academy of Political and Social Science*, 589: 41–62.

Pietromonaco, P.R., Feldman, L. and Barrett, P. (2000) 'The internal working models concept: What do we really know about the self in relation to others?', *Review of General Psychology*, 4(2): 155–175.

Pithers, W.D., Marques, J.K., Gibat, C.C. and Marlatt, G.A. (1983) 'Relapse prevention with sexual aggressors: A self-control model of treatment and maintenance of change', in J.G. Greer and I.R. Stuart (eds) *The Sexual Aggressor: Current Perspectives on Treatment.* New York: Van Nostrand Reinhold, pp. 214–239.

Powers, E. and Witmer, H. (1951) *An Experiment in the Prevention of Delinquency: The Cambridge–Somerville Youth Study.* New York: Columbia University Press.

Prentky, R. and Righthand, S. (2003) *Juvenile Sex Offender Assessment Protocol (J-SOAP).* Bridgewater, MA: Justice Resource Institute.

Print, B. and O'Callaghan, D. (2004) 'Essentials of an effective treatment programme for sexually abusive adolescents', in G. O'Reilly, W.L. Marshall, A. Carr and R.C. Beckett (eds) *The Handbook of Clinical Intervention with Young People Who Sexually Abuse.* New York: Brunner-Routledge, pp. 237–274.

Queensland Police Service (2005) *Statistical Review 2004–2005.* [Online]. Available at: http://www.police.qld.gov.au/statsnet.htm [accessed 25 January 2008].

Rayment, S., Shumack, D. and Smallbone, S.W. (in press) 'Treatment with youth sexual offenders: Extending the scope of systemic interventions through collaborative partnerships', *Clinical Psychologist*.

Redondo, S., Sánchez-Meca, J. and Garrido, V. (1999) 'The influence of treatment programmes on the recidivism of juvenile and adult offenders: A European-meta-analytic review', *Psychology, Crime and Law*, 5(3): 251–278.

Redondo, S., Sánchez-Meca, J. and Garrido, V. (2002) 'Crime treatment in Europe: A review of outcome studies', in J. McGuire (ed.) *Offender Rehabilitation and Treatment: Effective Programmes and Policies to Reduce Re-offending*. Chichester: Wiley, pp. 113–141.

Reitzel, L.R. and Carbonell, J.L. (2006) 'The effectiveness of sexual offender treatment for juveniles as measured by recidivism: A meta-analysis', *Sexual Abuse: A Journal of Research and Treatment*, 18(4): 401–421.

Righthand, S. and Welch, C. (2001) *Juveniles who have Sexually Offended: A Review of the Professional Literature*. Washington, DC: Office of Juvenile Justice and Delinquency Prevention.

Rind, B., Tromovitch, P. and Bauserman, R. (1998) 'A meta-analytic examination of assumed properties of child sexual abuse using college samples', *Psychological Bulletin*, 124(1): 22–53.

Risin, L.I. and Koss, M.P. (1987) 'The sexual abuse of boys: Prevalence and descriptive characteristics of childhood victimizations', *Journal of Interpersonal Violence*, 2(3): 309–323.

Rispens, J., Aleman, A. and Goudena, P. (1997) 'Prevention of child sexual abuse victimization: A meta-analysis of school programs', *Child Abuse and Neglect*, 21(10): 975–987.

Roberts, J.A. and Miltenberger, R.G. (1999) 'Emerging issues in the research on child sexual abuse prevention', *Education and Treatment of Children*, 22(1): 84–102.

Rolls, E.T. (2005) *Emotion Explained*. Oxford: Oxford University Press.

Romans, S.E., Martin, J.L., Anderson, J.C., O'Shea, M.L. and Mullen, P.E. (1995) 'Factors that mediate between child sexual abuse and adult psychological outcome', *Psychological Medicine*, 25(1): 127–142.

Roodman, A.C. and Clum, G.A. (2001) 'Revictimization rates and method variance: A meta-analysis', *Clinical Psychology Review*, 21(2): 183–204.

Ross, H.L. (1992) *Confronting Drunk Driving Social Policy for Saving Lives*. New Haven, CT: Yale University Press.

Russell, D.E.H. (1983) 'The incidence and prevalence of intrafamilial and extrafamilial sexual abuse of female children', *Child Abuse and Neglect*, 7(2): 133–146.

Russell, D.E.H. (1984) *Sexual Exploitation*. Beverly Hills, CA: Sage Publications.

Russell, G., Barclay, L.G., Edgecombe, G.A., Donovan, J., Habib, G. and Pawson, Q. (1999) *Fitting Fathers into Families: Men and the Fatherhood Role in Contemporary Australia*. Canberra: Department of Family and Community Services.

Salcido, R.M., Ornelas, V. and Garcia, J.A. (2002) 'A neighbourhood watch program for inner-city school children', *Children and Schools*, 24(3): 175–187.

Sampson, R.J. and Laub, J.H. (1993) *Crime in the Making: Pathways and Turning Points through Life*. Cambridge, MA: Harvard University Press.

Sampson, R.J. and Laub, J.H. (2006) 'A general age-graded theory of crime: Lessons learned and the future of life-course criminology', in D.P. Farrington (ed.) *Advances in Criminological Theory: Testing Integrated Developmental/Life Course Theories of Offending Vol. 13*. New Brunswick, NJ: Transaction Publishers.

Sanday, P.R. (1981) 'The socio-cultural context of rape: A cross-cultural study', *Journal of Social Issues*, 37(4): 5–27.

Sanders, M. (1999) 'Triple P-Positive Parenting Program: Towards an empirically validated multilevel parenting and family support strategy for the prevention of behaviour and emotional problems in children', *Clinical Child and Family Psychology Review*, 2(2): 71–90.

Sanderson, J. (2004) 'Child-focussed sexual abuse prevention programs: How effective are they in preventing child abuse?', *Research and Issues Paper Series, No. 5*. Brisbane: Crime and Misconduct Commission.

Saradjian, A. and Nobus, D. (2003) 'Cognitive distortions of religious professionals who sexually abuse children', *Journal of Interpersonal Violence*, 18(8): 905–923.

Sarno, J.A. and Wurtele, S.K. (1997) 'Effects of a personal safety program on preschoolers' knowledge, skills, and perceptions of child sexual abuse', *Child Maltreatment*, 2(1): 35–46.

Sas, L.D., Hurley, P., Hatch, A., Mall, S. and Dick, T. (1993) *Three Years after the Verdict: A Longitudinal Study of the Social and Psychological Adjustment of Child Witnesses Referred to the Child Witness Project*. London, ON: London Family Court Clinic.

Sas, L.D., Wolfe, D.A. and Gowdey, K. (1996) 'Children and the courts in Canada', *Criminal Justice and Behavior*, 23(2): 338–357.

Sauzier, M. (1989) 'Disclosure of child sexual abuse: For better or worse', *Psychiatric Clinics of North America*, 12(2): 455–469.

Schaeffer, B. (2008) *Therapeutic engagement with youth who have committed sexual offences*. Unpublished Doctoral Dissertation: Griffith University, Australia.

Schiff, M. and Bazemore, S.G. (2002) 'Resotrative conferencing for juveniles in the United States: Prevalence, process, and practice', in E.G.M. Weitekamp and H.J. Kerner (eds) *Restorative Justice: Theoretical Foundations*. Cullompton: Willan Publishing, pp. 177–203.

Schlank, A. (2006) 'The civil commitment of sexual offenders: Lessons learned', in W.L. Marshall, Y.M. Fernandez, L.E. Marshall and G.A. Serran (eds) *Sexual Offender Treatment: Controversial Issues*. Chichester: Wiley, pp. 45–60.

Schmauk, F.J. (1970) 'Punishment, arousal and avoidance learning in sociopaths', *Journal of Abnormal Psychology*, 76(3): 325–335.

Schulz, W. (2000) 'Multiple reward signals in the brain', *Nature Reviews Neuroscience*, 1(3): 199–207.

Schweinhart, L.J. (2004) *The High/Scope Perry Preschool Study through Age 40: Summary, Conclusions and Frequently Asked Questions*. Ypsilanti, MI: High/Scope Educational Research Foundation.

Schweinhart, L.J., Barnes, H.V. and Weikhart, D.P. (1993) *Significant Benefits: The High/Scope Perry Preschool Study through Age 27*. Ypsilanti, MI: High/Scope Educational Research Foundation.

Serran, G.A., Fernandez, Y.M., Marshall, W.L. and Mann, R.E. (2003) 'Process issues in treatment: Application to sexual offender programs', *Professional Psychology: Research and Practice*, 34(4): 368–374.

Shaver, P. (1994) 'Attachment, caregiving and sex in adult romantic relationships', *paper presented at the American Psychological Association Annual Meeting*, Los Angeles, CA.

Shaw, T. and Funderburk, J. (1999) 'Civil commitment of sexual offenders as therapeutic jurisprudence – a rational approach to community protection', in A. Schlank and F. Cohen (eds) *The Sexual Predator: Law, Policy, Evaluation and Treatment Vol. 1.* Kingston, NJ: Civic Research Institute, s. 5.1–5.8.

Shaw, C.R. and McKay, H.D. (1942) *Juvenile Delinquency and Urban Areas*. Chicago, IL: University of Chicago Press.

Shaw, C.R. and McKay, H.D. (1969) *Juvenile Delinquency and Urban Areas*. Chicago, IL: University of Chicago Press.

Shepard, B. (2003) 'In search of a winning script: Moral panic vs institutional denial', *Sexualities*, 6(1): 54–59.

Shepher, J. (1971) 'Mate selection among second-generation kibbutz adolescents and adults: Incest avoidance and negative inprinting', *Archives of Sexual Behavior*, 1(4): 293–307.

Sherman, L.W. (1993) 'Defiance, deterrence, and irrelevance: A theory of the criminal sanction', *Journal of Research in Crime and Delinquency*, 30(4): 445–473.

Sherman, L.W. and Eck, J.E. (2002) 'Policing for crime prevention', in L.W. Sherman, D.P. Farrington, B.C. Welsh and D. Layton MacKenzie (eds) *Evidence-based Crime Prevention*. London: Routledge.

Sherman, L.W., Schmidt, J.D., Rogan, D.P., Smith, D.A., Gartin, P.R., Cohn, E.G., Collins, D.J. and Bacich, A.R. (1992) 'The variable effects of arrest on criminal careers: The Milwaukee domestic violence experiment', *The Journal of Criminal Law and Criminology*, 83(1): 137–170.

Shingler, J. and Mann, R.E. (2006) 'Collaboration in clinical work with sexual offenders: Treatment and risk assessment', in W.L. Marshall, Y.M. Fernandez, L.E. Marshall and G.A. Serran (eds) *Sexual Offender Treatment: Controversial Issues*. Chichester: Wiley, pp. 225–239.

Shonkoff, J.P. and Meisels, S.J. (2000) 'Preface', in J.P. Shonkoff and S.J. Meisels (eds) *Handbook of Early Childhood Intervention* (2nd ed.). New York: Cambridge University Press, pp. xvii–xviii.

Short, J.F. (1975) 'The natural history of an applied theory: Differential opportunity and mobilization for youth', in N.J. Demerath, O. Larson and K.F. Schuessler (eds) *Social Policy and Sociology*. New York: Academic Press.

Simon, L.M.J. and Zgoba, K. (2006) 'Sex crimes against children: Legislation, prevention and investigation', in R.K. Wortley and S.W. Smallbone (eds) *Situational Prevention of Child Sexual Abuse, Crime Prevention Studies Vol. 19*. Monsey, NY: Criminal Justice Press, pp. 65–100.

Sizonenko, P.C. (1978) 'Endocrinology in preadolescents and adolescents: Hormonal changes during normal puberty', *American Journal of Diseases of Childhood*, 132(7): 704–712.

Smallbone, S.W. (2006) 'An attachment theoretical revision of Marshall and Barbaree's integrated theory of the etiology of sexual offending', in W.L. Marshall, Y.M. Fernandez and L.E. Marshall (eds) *Sexual Offender Treatment: Controversial Issues*. Hoboken, NJ: Wiley, pp. 93–108.

Smallbone, S.W. and Dadds, M.R. (1998) 'Childhood attachment and adult attachment in incarcerated adult male sex offenders', *Journal of Interpersonal Violence*, 13(5): 555–573.

Smallbone, S.W. and Dadds, M.R. (2000) 'Attachment and coercive behavior', *Sexual Abuse: A Journal of Research and Treatment*, 12(1): 3–16.

Smallbone, S.W. and Milne, L. (2000) 'Associations between trait anger and aggression used in the commission of sexual offences', *International Journal of Offender Therapy and Comparative Criminology*, 44(5): 606–617.

Smallbone, S.W., Rayment, S. and Shumack, D. (unpublished) *Griffith Youth Forensic Service*. Unpublished raw data.

Smallbone, S.W. and Wortley, R.K. (2000) *Child Sexual Abuse in Queensland: Offender Characteristics and Modus Operandi*. Brisbane: Queensland Crime Commission.

Smallbone, S.W. and Wortley, R.K. (2001) *Child Sexual Abuse: Offender Characteristics and Modus Operandi. Trends and Issues in Crime and Criminal Justice, No. 193*. Canberra: Australian Institute of Criminology.

Smallbone, S.W. and Wortley, R.K. (2004a) 'Onset, persistence and versatility of offending among adult males convicted of sexual offences against children', *Sexual Abuse: A Journal of Research and Treatment*, 16(4): 285–298.

Smallbone, S.W. and Wortley, R.K. (2004b) 'Criminal diversity and paraphilic interests among adult males convicted of sexual offences against children', *International Journal of Offender Therapy and Comparative Criminology*, 48(2): 175–188.

Smallbone, S.W., Wortley, R.K. and Lancefield, K. (1999) *Sexual Offending by Aboriginal Men in Queensland*. Brisbane: Queensland Department of Corrective Services.

Smith, P., Goggin, C. and Gendreau, P. (2002) *The Effects of Prison Sentences and Intermediate Sanctions on Recidivism: General Effects and Individual Differences, Report 2002–01*. Ottawa, ON: Solicitor General of Canada.

Sorenson, T. and Snow, B. (1991) 'How children tell: The process of disclosure in child sexual abuse', *Child Welfare League of America*, 70(1): 3–15.

Spaccarelli, S. (1994) 'Stress, appraisal, and coping in child sexual abuse: A theoretical and empirical review', *Psychological Bulletin*, 116(2): 340–362.

Spaccareli, S. and Kim, S. (1995) 'Resilience criteria and factors associated with resilience in sexually abused girls', *Child Abuse and Neglect*, 19(9): 1171–1182.

Spelman, W. (1995) 'The severity of intermediate sanctions', *Journal of Research in Crime and Delinquency*, 32(2): 107–135.

Sroufe, L.A. (1988) 'The role of infant–caregiver attachment in development', in J. Belsky and T. Nezworski (eds) *Clinical Implications of Attachment*. Hillsdale, NJ: Erlbaum, pp. 18–38.

Sternberg, K.J., Lamb, M.E., Orbach, Y., Esplin, P.W. and Mitchell, S. (2001) 'Use of structured investigative protocol enhances young children's responses to free-recall prompts in the course of forensic interviews', *Journal of Applied Psychology*, 86(5): 997–1005.

Stewart, D.J. (1972) 'Effects of social reinforcement on dependency and aggressive responses of psychopathic, neurotic, and subculture delinquents', *Journal of Abnormal Psychology*, 79(1): 76–83.

Stirpe, T.S., Wilson, R.J. and Long, C. (2001) 'Goal attainment scaling with sexual offenders: A measure of clinical impact at post-treatment and at community follow-up', *Sexual Abuse: A Journal of Research and Treatment*, 13(2): 65–77.

Stop It Now! (2006) *The Campaign to Prevent Child Sexual Abuse*. [Online]. Available at: http://www.stopitnow.org/about.html [accessed on 25 January 2008].

Strang, H. (2002) *Repair or Revenge: Victims and Restorative Justice*. Oxford: Clarendon Press.

Strang, H., Barnes, G.C., Braithwaite, J. and Sherman, L.W. (1999) *Experiments in Restorative Policing: A Progress Report on the Canberra Reintegrative Shaming Experiments (RISE)*. Canberra: Australian National University.

Strang, H. and Braithwaite (eds) (2002) *Restorative Justice and Family Violence*. Cambridge: Cambridge University Press.

Sullivan, J. and Beech, A. (2004) 'A comparative study of demographic data relating to intra-familial and extra-familial child sexual abusers and professional perpetrators', *Journal of Sexual Aggression*, 10(1): 39–50.

Swanston, H.Y., Parkinson, P.N., Oates, R.K., O'Toole, B.I., Plunkett, A.M. and Shrimpton, S. (2002) 'Further abuse of sexually abused children', *Child Abuse and Neglect*, 26(2): 115–127.

Sykes, G. and Matza, D. (1957) 'Techniques of neutralization: A theory of delinquency', *American Sociological Review,* 22(6): 664–670.

Taal, M. and Edelaar, B. (1997) 'Positive and negative effects of a child sexual abuse prevention program', *Child Abuse and Neglect*, 21(4): 399–410.

Testa, M., Miller, B.A., Downs, W.R. and Paneck, D. (1992) 'The moderating impact of social support following childhood sexual abuse', *Violence and Victims*, 7(2): 173–186.

Thomas, J. (2004) 'Family intervention with young people with sexually abusive behaviour', in G. O'Reilly, W.L. Marshall, A. Carr and R.C. Beckett (eds) *The Handbook of Clinical Intervention with Young People who Sexually Abuse*. New York: Brunner-Routledge, pp. 315–342.

Thornton, D., Curran, L., Grayson, D. and Holloway, V. (1984) *Tougher Regimes in Detention Centres: Report of an Evaluation by the Young Offender Psychology Unit*. London: Home Office Research, Development and Statistics Directorate.

Tomison, A. and Wise, S. (1999) *Community-based Approaches in Preventing Child Maltreatment*. Melbourne: The Australian Institute of Family Studies.

Tong, L., Oates, K. and McDowell, M. (1987) 'Personality development following sexual abuse', *Child Abuse and Neglect*, 11(3): 371–383.

Tonry, M. and Farrington, D.P. (1995) 'Strategic approaches to crime prevention', in M. Tonry and D.P. Farrington (eds) *Building a Safer Society: Strategic Approaches to Crime Prevention*. Chicago: University of Chicago Press, pp. 1–20.

Toth, S.L. and Cicchetti, D. (1993) 'Child maltreatment: Where do we go from here in our treatment of victims?', in D. Cicchetti and S.L. Toth (eds) *Child Abuse, Child Development and Social Policy*. Norwood, NJ: Ablex, pp. 399–438.

Tremblay, P. (2006) 'Convergence setting for non-predatory "boy lovers"', in R.K. Wortley and S.W. Smallbone (eds) *Situational Prevention of Child Sexual Abuse, Crime Prevention Studies Vol. 19*. Monsey, NY: Criminal Justice Press.

Tremblay, R.E. and Craig, W.M. (1995) 'Developmental crime prevention', in M. Tonry and D.P. Farrington (eds) *Building a Safer Society: Strategic Approaches to Crime Prevention. Crime and Justice: A Review of Research Vol. 19*. Chicago, IL: University of Chicago Press, pp. 151–237.

Tremblay, R.E., Pagani-Kurtz, L., Masse, L.C. and Vitaro, F. (1995) 'A bimodal preventive intervention for disruptive kindergarten boys: It's impact through mid-adolescence', *Journal of Consulting and Clinical Psychology*, 63(4): 560–568.

Trivits, L.C. and Repucci, N.D. (2002) 'Application of Megan's Law to juveniles', *American Psychologist*, 57(9): 690–704.

Trocmé, N., Fallon, B., MacLaurin, B. and Copp, B. (2002) *The Changing Faces of Welfare Cases in Ontario: Ontario Incidence Studies of Reported Child Abuse and Neglect (OIS 1993–1998)*. Toronto, ON: Centre of Excellence for Child Welfare, Faculty of Social Work, University of Toronto.

Trocmé, N. and Schumaker, K. (1999) 'Reported child sexual abuse in Canadian schools and recreational facilities: Implications for developing effective prevention strategies', *Children and Youth Services Review*, 21(8): 621–642.

Tunstill, J., Allnock, D., Meadows, P. and McLeod, A. (2002) *Early Experiences of Implementing Sure Start*. London: London University.

US Department of Health and Human Services, Administration on Children, Youth and Families (2006) *Child Maltreatment 2004*. Washington, DC: US Government Printing Office.

US Department of Justice (2004) *Law Enforcement Initiative Targets Child Pornography over Peer-to-Peer Networks*. [Online]. Available at: http://www.usdoj.gov/opa/pr/2004/May/04_crm_331.htm [accessed on 25 January 2008].

Ussher, J.M. and Dewberry, C. (1995) 'The nature and long-term effects of childhood sexual abuse: A survey of women survivors in Britain', *British Journal of Clinical Psychology*, 34(2): 177–192.

Utting, W. (1997) *People Like Us: The Report on the Review of Residential Child Care*. London: Department of Health.

Valentine, L. and Feinauer, L.L. (1993) 'Resilience factors associated with female survivors of child sexual abuse', *The American Journal of Family Therapy*, 21(3): 216–224.

Van Bruggen, L.K., Runtz, M.G. and Kadlec, H. (2006) 'Sexual revictimization: The role of sexual self-esteem and dysfunctional sexual behaviors', *Child Maltreatment*, 11(2): 131–145.

van Dijk, J.J.M., Mayhew, P. and Killias, M. (1991) *Experiences of Crime Across the World: Key Findings of the 1989 International Crime Survey* (2nd ed.). Deventer: Kluwer Law and Taxation Publishers.

van Ijzendoorn, M.H. (1997) 'Attachment, emergent morality, and aggression: Toward a developmental socioemotional model of antisocial behaviour', *International Journal of Behavioral Development*, 21(4): 703–727.

Veneziano, C. and Veneziano, L. (2002) 'Adolescent sex offenders: A review of the literature', *Trauma, Violence, and Abuse: A Review Journal*, 3(4): 247–260.

von Hirsch, A., Bottoms, A.E., Burneu, E. and Wikström, P.O. (1999) *Criminal Deterrence and Sentencing Severity: An Analysis of Recent Research*. Oxford: Hart.

Wallis, A. and Ford, D. (eds) (1980) *Crime Prevention through Environmental Design: The Commercial Demonstration in Portland, Oregon*. Washington, DC: US Department of Justice.

Ward, T. (1999) 'A self-regulation model of the relapse process in sexual offenders', in B.K. Schwartz (ed.) *The Sex Offender: Theoretical Advances, Treating Special Populations and Legal Developments Vol. III*. Kingston, NJ: Civic Research Institute, s. 6.1–6.8.

Ward, T. and Hudson, S.M. (1996) 'Relapse prevention: A critical analysis', *Sexual Abuse: A Journal of Research and Treatment*, 8(3): 177–200.

Ward, T. and Hudson, S.M. (2000) 'A self-regulation model of relapse prevention', in D.R. Laws, S.M. Hudson and T. Ward (eds) *Remaking Relapse Prevention with Sex Offenders: A Sourcebook.* Thousand Oaks, CA: Sage Publications, pp. 79–101.

Ward, T., Hudson, S.M. and Marshall, W.L. (1994) 'The abstinence violation effect in child molesters', *Behaviour Research and Therapy*, 32(4): 431–437.

Ward, T., Hudson, S.M. and Siegert, R.J. (1995) 'A critical comment on Pithers' relapse prevention model', *Sexual Abuse: A Journal of Research and Treatment*, 7(3): 167–175.

Ward, T. and Marshall, W.L. (2004) 'Good lives, aetiology and the rehabilitation of sex offenders: A bridging theory', *Journal of Sexual Aggression*, 10(2): 153–169.

Ward, T. and Marshall, W.L. (2007) 'Narrative identity and offender rehabilitation', *International Journal of Offender Therapy and Comparative Criminology*, 51(3): 279–297.

Ward, T. and Stewart, C.A. (2003a) 'Good lives and the rehabilitation of sexual offenders', in T. Ward, D.R. Laws and S.M. Hudson (eds) *Sexual Deviance: Issues and Controversies.* Thousand Oaks, CA: Sage Publications, pp. 12–44.

Ward, T. and Stewart, C. A. (2003b) 'Criminogenic needs or human needs: A theoretical critique', *Psychology, Crime and Law*, 9(2): 125–143.

Wasserman, G.A. and Miller, L. (1998) 'The prevention of serious and violent offending', in R. Loeber and D.P. Farrington (eds) *Serious and Violent Juvenile Offending: Risk Factors and Successful Interventions.* Thousand Oaks, CA: Sage Publications, pp. 197–247.

Webster, C.D., Harris, G.T., Rice, M.E., Cormier, C. and Quinsey, V.L. (1994) *The Violence Prediction Scheme: Assessing Dangerousness in High Risk Men.* Toronto, ON: Centre of Criminology, University of Toronto.

Weikart, D.P. and Schweinhart, L.J. (1992) 'High/Scope preschool program outcomes', in J. McCord and R.E. Tremblay (eds) *Preventing Antisocial Behavior: Interventions from Birth to Adolescence.* New York: Guilford Press, pp. 67–86.

Weisburd, D., Sherman, L.W. and Petrosino, A.J. (1990) *Registry of Randomized Criminal Justice Experiments in Sanctions.* Unpublished report, Rutgers University, University of Maryland and Crime Control Institute.

Wekerle, C. and Wolfe, D.A. (1991) *An Empirical Review of Prevention Strategies for Child Abuse and Neglect*: Unpublished manuscript, University of Western Ontario.

Welsh, B.C. and Hoshi, A. (2002) 'Communities and crime prevention', in L.W. Sherman, D.P. Farrington, B.C. Welsh and D. Layton MacKenzie (eds) *Evidence-based Crime Prevention.* London: Routledge.

Westermarck, E.A. (1889) *The History of Human Marriage.* London: Macmillan and Co.

Whiting, J.W.M. and Child, I.L. (1953) *Child Training and Personality: A Cross Cultural Study.* New Haven, CT: Yale University.

WHO (2006) *Preventing Child Maltreatment: A Guide to Taking Action and Generating Evidence.* Geneva: World Health Organisation.

Wilczynski, A. and Sinclair, K. (1999) 'Moral tales: Representations of child abuse in the quality and tabloid media', *The Australian and New Zealand Journal of Criminology*, 32(3): 262–283.

Williams, L.M. and Farrell, R.A. (1990) 'Legal response to child sexual abuse in day care', *Criminal Justice and Behavior*, 17(3): 284–302.

Williams, L.M. and Finkelhor, D. (1995) 'Paternal caregiving and incest: Test of a biosocial model', *American Journal of Orthopsychiatry*, 65(1): 584–586.

Wilson, J.Q. and Kelling, G. (1982) 'Broken windows: The police and neighborhood safety', *Atlantic Monthly*, March: 29–38.

Wolak, J., Finkelhor, D. and Mitchell, K.J. (2004) 'Internet-related sex crimes against minors: Implications for prevention based on findings from a national study', *Journal of Adolescent Health*, 35(5): 424.

Wolf, A.P. (1995) *Sexual Attraction and Childhood Association: A Chinese Brief for Edward Westermarck.* Stanford, CA: Stanford University Press.

Worling, J.R. (2004) 'Essentials of a good intervention programme for sexually abusive juveniles', in G. O'Reilly, W.L. Marshall, A. Carr, and R.C. Beckett (eds) *The Handbook of Clinical Intervention with Young People who Sexually Abuse.* New York: Brunner-Routledge, pp. 275–296.

Worling, J.R. and Curwen, T. (2000) 'Adolescent sexual offenders recidivism: Success of specialized treatment and implications for risk prediction', *Child Abuse and Neglect*, 24(7): 965–982.

Wortley, R.K. (2001) 'A classification of techniques for controlling situational precipitators of crime', *Security Journal*, 14(4): 63–82.

Wortley, R.K. and Smallbone, S.W. (2006a) 'Applying situational principles to sexual offending against children', in R.K. Wortley and S.W. Smallbone (eds) *Situational Prevention of Child Sexual Abuse, Crime Prevention Studies Vol. 19*. Monsey, NY: Criminal Justice Press.

Wortley, R.K. and Smallbone, S.W. (2006b) *Child Pornography on the Internet: Problem-oriented Guides for Police Series.* Washington DC: US Department of Justice.

Wurr, J.C. and Partridge, I.M. (1996) 'The prevalence of a history of childhood sexual abuse in an acute adult inpatient population', *Child Abuse and Neglect*, 20(9): 867–872.

Wurtele, S.K. (1986) *Teaching Young Children Personal Body Safety: The Behavioral Skills Training Program.* Colorado Springs, CO: Author.

Wyatt, G.E. (1985) 'The sexual abuse of afro-American and white American women in childhood', *Child Abuse and Neglect*, 9(4): 507–519.

Wyatt, G.E. and Newcomb, M. (1990) 'Internal and external mediators of women's sexual abuse in childhood', *Journal of Consulting and Clinical Psychology*, 58(6): 758–767.

Wyles, P. (1988) *Missing Children: Advice, Information and Preventative Action for Parents, Teachers and Counsellors.* Canberra: Australian Institute of Criminology.

Zielinski, D.S. and Bradshaw, C.P. (2006) 'Ecological influences on the sequelae of child maltreatment: A review of the literature', *Child Maltreatment*, 11(1): 49–62.

Zimbardo, P.G. (1970) 'The human choice: Individuation, reason, and order, vs deindividuation, impulse, and chaos', in W.J. Arnold and D. Levine (eds) *Nebraska Symposium on Motivation 1969*. Lincoln, NE: University of Nebraska Press.

Index

Abel, G.G. 6, 7
abuse, definitions of 3
acceptance of responsibility 120
adolescence-onset offenders
    deterrence 102–3
    estimates of 81
    needs principle 126–8
    persistence 5–7
    recidivism rates 8
    responsivity principle 128–30
    risk principle 124–6
    treatment 123–30
    treatment outcomes 131–2
adult offenders
    criminal versatility 9
    needs principle 117–20
    onset offences 6
    responsivity principle 120–3
    risk factors 82
    risk principle 116–17
    transition to parenthood 84
    treatment 115–23, 130–1
    treatment outcomes 130–1
age
    offender characteristics 5–7
    victim characteristics 12–13
age of consent 3
    aggression

developmental factors 32
high school transition 81
integrated theory 24–5
overview 44
school transition 79
situational factors 43
alcoholism 38
Aman, C. 147
American Academy of Child and
    Adolescent Psychiatry 129
Andrews, D.A. 103, 114
androgens 28
anti-social conduct 23–4
antisocial predators 40–1
Antunes, G. 100
approach plans 123
arranged marriages 27
arrest 92–3
attachment
    biological foundations 24–6
    developmental factors 30–3
    developmental prevention 74–6,
      87
    maltreatment prevention 187–8
    needs principle 127
    overview 44
    self-restraint 30–1
    sexual development and 72–3

situational factors 42–3
transition to parenthood 85–6
attrition rates 129–30
Australia
developmental prevention 66
indigenous communities 214
institutional settings 168
maltreatment 186–7
transition to parenthood 85–6
treatment 124–6
Australian Developmental Crime
Prevention Consortium 69
authorities, reporting to 145–6
avoidance attachment 32, 74–5
avoidance plans 123

Barbaree, H.E. 22, 24, 29, 108
Baron, L. 17
Baron, S.W. 99
Beccaria, Cesare 97
Beech, A. 10, 121
Behavioural Skills Training (BST)
138–9
behavioural specificity 156–7
Bentham, Jeremy 97
Berliner, L. 146, 149
Besharov, D.J. 145
biological foundations 22, 23–9,
55–6
Blum, R.W. 38
Boney-McCoy, S. 150
Bonta, J. 114
boot camps 101–2
Borack, J.J. 99
Bowlby, J. 22, 26, 31, 43
Bradford, J.M.W. 105
Bradley, A.R. 147
brain reward systems 28
British Gas Study (Clarke) 159
Bruck, M. 143, 147
Bryjak, G.J. 99
Bussiere, M.T. 8, 9

Cambridge-Somerville Youth Study
70–1

Canada
dangerous sexual offender laws
106
risk principle 116–17
treatment 133
Canadian Institute for Advanced
Research 66
capable guardians 40
Carbonell, J.L. 132
Carr, A. 138–9
Carroll, J.S. 98
castration 104–5
Catalano, R.F. 179
Ceci, S.J. 147
celerity principle 97
Chaffin, M. 143
Chandy, J. M. 38
chemical castration 104–6
Chicago Area Project (CAP) 177
child, definitions of 2–3
child pornography 94, 164
child protection agencies 91
child protection resources 36–9
childcare workers 10
chronic attachment 32, 127
Cicchetti, D. 153
Clarke, R.V. 40–2, 159
Clun, G.A. 14
Cockfield, C. 166
cognitive-behavioural therapy (CBT)
113–16, 133
Cohen, L.E. 165
committed offenders 41, 161, 162t,
163
Communities That Care 179–80,
209, 214
community capacity-building 203–4
community defence approaches 178
community development crime
prevention 51–2
community-focused approaches 199t
crime prevention 176–80, 194–5
to CSA 180–3
effectiveness 114
integrated theory 62

to maltreatment 183–8
of maltreatment to CSA 185–8
overview 194–6
primary prevention 202–4
risk principle 117
secondary prevention 208–9
sexual abuse prevention 188–94
tertiary prevention 213–14
community organising approach 177
community policing 93
community sentences 101, 211
complaints procedures 169
conditioning model 115
confidentiality 191–2
Conte, J. 135, 146, 149
control models 29, 40, 160
controlling prompts 173–4
controlling tools/weapons 164
Cook, S.L. 183–5
coping skills 118–19
Cornish, D.B. 40–2, 159
Correctional Service of Canada (CSC) 116–17, 133
Cortoni, F. 5
counselling 205
courtroom practices 148–9
crime prevention *see also* developmental prevention
community-focused approaches 176–80, 194–5
situational prevention 39–42, 50, 51, 155, 157–9
crime prevention model 50–2, 64
Crime Prevention through Environment Design (CPTED) 178
crime reduction hypotheses 90
criminal justice interventions
crime prevention model 52
detection and investigation 90–4, 111
deterrence 97–104, 111
incapacitation strategies 104–10, 111

legislation 106–7, 198–200
primary prevention 198–200
psychology of punishment 94–7
criminal versatility 9–10, 20, 23–4, 160
criminogenic needs 114, 117–20
Cullen, F.T. 97
cultural norms 35–6
current approaches 46–54
child maltreatment prevention 52–4
crime prevention 50–2
future of 214–16
public health model 47–50

Dangerous Offender 106, 110
dangerous sexual offender laws 106–7
Darkness to Light 190, 192
Daro, D. 52–3, 83, 86, 186
decline in CSA 19
defensible spaces 165–6
definitions of CSA 2–4
DeLamater, J. 72
delinquency studies
developmental prevention 67–9, 86–7
high school transition 81
transition to school 77
denial, by victims 147
Derzon, J. 67–8, 81
detection and investigation 210
detection, increasing risks 165–6
deterrence 92–3, 97–104, 111, 198–204
developmental factors 22, 29–33, 44, 56–7
developmental prevention
conceptual and empirical foundations 65–71
current approaches 50–1
early attachment relationships 74–6
integrated theory and 71–2
overview 86–8

primary prevention 200–1
secondary prevention 205
sexual development 72–4
transition to high school 80–4
transition to parenthood 84–6
transition to school 76–80
Dewberry, C. 143
dimensions of CSA
see offender characteristics; victim characteristics
disclosure
see reporting of CSA
Dishion, T.J. 71
diversion 210
domestic settings
familial offenders 16–17
offender characteristics 162t
primary prevention 202
secondary prevention 207
situational prevention 171–4
tertiary prevention 212–13
domestic violence 92–3, 116
Doob, A. 100
Doonan, R. 79
Doren, D.M. 107–8
Dowden, C. 103
Drake, B. 37
Drapeau, M. 121
dynamic risk factors 114, 118
Dziuba-Leatherman, J. 12, 15, 138, 139–40

early attachment relationships 74–6, 87
early intervention 70–1, 205–6
Eastwood, C. 146
Eck, J.E. 90, 93–4
ecosystemic factors 22, 33–9, 44–5, 57–8, 193
Edelaar, B. 139
education programmes
community programmes 53–4, 195–6, 202–3
parenthood education 172–3, 184, 195

school-based 53, 83
ego control 153
Elliott, M. 135, 163
Elmira Prenatal/Early Infancy Project 75
Ernst, J. 37
estrogens 28
evidence, providing 147–8
evolutionary foundations 22, 23
extending guardianship 165–6, 169, 172

false allegations 147–8
false positives/negatives 204
familial offenders
see domestic settings
family factors 30–1, 38, 127–8
Family Relationships Services Program (FRSP) 85–6
family support approaches 184–5, 195, 209
Farrington, D.P. 50
Felson, M. 165
Fernandez, Y.M. 131
Ferrrara, M.L. 79
Finkelhor, D.
decline in CSA 19
educational approaches 83
gender 12
maltreatment 52–3, 186
offence settings 17
personal safety programmes 137–8, 139–40
prevalence 18, 28–9
re-victimisation 150
reporting of CSA 15
situation-focused approaches 62–3
transition to parenthood 86
victimisation process 136
victimisation surveys 145
Fischer, D.G. 12–13
Fisher, H.E. 28
Forde, L. 171
Friedrich, W.N. 72

Fryer, G.E. 150
fundamental attributional error 156

Gallagher, B. 169
gender
    gender-role norms 73
    offender characteristics 5, 24
    personal safety programmes 140
    victim characteristics 7, 11–12,
        18, 20
Gendreau, P. 97, 100, 101
general deterrence 98–100
Gibson, L.E. 140
Gittler, J. 91
Goffman, E. 170
Goggin, C. 101
Goodman, G.S. 147
Gottfredson, M. 24
Grasmick, H.G. 99
Greater Newark Safer Cities
    Initiative 180
Griffith Youth Forensic Service
    (GYFS) 124–30
grooming 11, 25, 136–7
group-based treatment 121, 129, 133
guardianship, extending 165–6, 169,
    172
Gzoba, K. 160

handlers 40
Hanson, R.K. 5, 8, 9, 109, 118, 131
harm reduction model 142
Harris, A.J.R. 118
Haugaard, J. 3
Hawkins, J.D. 68, 77, 179
Head Start 66
Heller, S.S. 152
helplines 190–2, 205
Henry, J. 146
Heriot, J.K. 144
Hertzman, C. 76
high school, transition to 76–80
High/Scope Perry Pre-School project
    66–7, 77
Himelein, M.J. 153

Hirschi, R. 24
Hodson, L.P. 17
Hoffman, T.J. 150
Home Office statistics 96
home visiting programmes 185,
    186, 195, 209
Homel, Ross 69, 70, 182–3
homosexuality, illegality of 3
Hope, T. 177
hormonal treatments 119–20
hot spots 92
Hotaling, G. 18
Hudson, S.M. 115
Hunt, A.L. 100

imprisonment 211
incapacitation strategies 104–10,
    111, 210–11
incest 6, 27, 131
increasing effort 163–5, 167–9, 172
increasing risks 165–6, 170–1, 172–3
indicated prevention 47–8
indigenous communities 182–3, 214
infant attachment 74–5
institutional programmes 114
institutional settings 16
    offender characteristics 162t
    primary prevention 202
    secondary prevention 206, 208
    strategies for prevention 166–71
    tertiary prevention 213
integrated theory
    biological foundations 23–9
    community-focused approaches
        62
    developmental factors 29–33
    ecosystemic factors 33–9
    implications of 54–60
    offender-focused approaches
        61–2
    overview 44–5
    situation-focused approaches
        62–3
    situational factors 39–44
    victim-focused approaches 62

Intensive Supervision Programming
(ISP) 102
International Crime Survey 14–15
International Society for the
Prevention of Child Abuse and
Neglect (IPSCAN) 3–4
Internet grooming 136–7, 164–5
Internet Service Providers (ISPs)
164–5
interviewing 147–8

Jackson, J.L. 149
Johnson, T.C. 79
Jones, L.M. 19

Kellog, N.D. 150
Kendall-Tackett, K. 12
Kennedy, L.W. 99
Kershaw, C. 102
Kitzman, H. 185
known victims 142–53

Langton, C. 108
Laub, J.H. 69, 74, 84
Lawson, L. 143, 147
learning theory 173
legislation 106–7, 198–200
Leitenberg, H. 140
Levenson, J.S. 110
Levy, H.B. 150
life-course approach 69–70, 72, 80,
84, 87
Lincoln, R. 182–3
Lipsey, M. 67–8, 81
Lloyd, C. 101
locations of CSA
see offence settings
locus of control 152–3
London, K. 143
Long, P.J. 149
Lösel, F. 131
low risk offenders 113–14

McCord, J. 71
McDonald, S. 79

McDonald, W.L. 12–13
McElrath, J.A.V. 153
McGuire, J. 101
MacIntyre, D. 138–9
MacKenzie, D.L. 101
maltreatment
community-focused approaches
183–8, 195
definitions of 2
prevention 52–4
scope of 18
Mann, R.E. 123
Markovic, J. 150
Marshall, W.L.
institutional settings 206
integrated theory 21–2, 24, 29
responsivity principle 120–2
treatment 112
treatment outcomes 131
treatment targets 118–20
Mayhew, P. 159
media reporting 174, 188, 193–4,
203, 216
Miethe, T.D. 9
Mischel, W. 156
mixed-type offenders 16
Miyoshi, T.J. 150
Mobilisation for Youth (MFY)
Project 178
modus operandi 10–11
Moffit, T.E. 80
Morton-Bourgon, K. 109
Moss, K. 166
motivation 3, 10, 22, 40–1, 127 see
also attachment; nurturance
multisystemic therapy (MST) 124
mundane offenders 41

National Adolescent Perpetrator
Network 129–30
National Crime Victimisation Survey
(NCVS) 14, 18
needs principle 114, 117–20, 126–8,
132
neighbourhood characteristics 37

Newman, O. 165–6
nightclubs 157–9
nurturance
  biological foundations 24–6
  developmental factors 31–3
  high school transition 81–2
  situational factors 42–3

OECD 66
offence pathways 120
offence settings
  see domestic settings; institutional
    settings; public settings
offender characteristics
  age 5–7, 19, 159–60
  criminal versatility 9–10, 20, 160
  gender 5, 24
  modus operandi 10–11, 20
  offence settings and 162t
  persistence 7–8, 19–20
  situational typologies 40–2
  stereotypes 153–4
offender-focused approaches 199t
  integrated theory 61–2
  primary prevention 198–204
  secondary prevention 204–6
  tertiary prevention 209–12
Olds, D.L. 185
Olson, J. 9
onset and progression 60
onset offences 42–4
opportunistic offenders 10–11, 31,
  41–2, 161, 162t
optimism 153
oxytocin 25–6

Pandey, S. 37
parenthood education 184, 195
parenthood, transition to 84–6
Parkinson, P.N. 150
Paternoster, R. 104
Patton, W. 146
peer influences 37–8, 128, 129
permissibility, reducing 170–1
persistence 5–8, 19–20, 41, 211

personal safety programmes 137–
  42, 201
personalising victims 171
physical violence 11
place managers 40
policing 90–4, 111, 210
pornography 94, 164
potential offenders 204–5
potential victims 134–42
pre-arrest persistence 7–8
pre-occupied attachment 32
preserving order 178
primary prevention 47–8, 198–204,
  199t
principles of effective offender
  treatment 113–14
prior convictions 9
problem-oriented policing 94
professions of offenders 10–11
proof 147–8
prosecution 148–9
protecting the vulnerable 178–9
provoked offenders 42, 159
psychology of punishment 94–7
psychopaths 95–6
public health model
  primary prevention 198–204
  secondary prevention 47–9, 199t,
    204–9
  target identification 47–50,
    63–4
  tertiary prevention 47–8, 49,
    199t, 209–14
public policy
  future of 214–16
  primary prevention 198–204
  secondary prevention 204–9
  tertiary prevention 209–14
public settings 16–17, 162t, 163–6,
  202, 208
punishment, deterrence and 97–104,
  111
punishment, psychology of 94–7

Queensland 124–6

rape 36, 160
Rational Choice theory 62
re-victimisation 13–14, 149–53, 154
recantation, by victims 147
recidivism rates *see also* treatment
   adolescence-onset offenders 8
   criminal versatility 9–10
   onset offences 8
   specific deterrence 100–1
   treatment outcomes 9, 130–2
reducing permissibility 170–1
reducing provocations 159
reinforcement principle 114
Reitzel, L.R. 132
relationship skills 118
religious institutions 10, 35–6
removing excuses 170–1
repeat victimisation 149–53, 154, 212
reporting of CSA
   to authorities 145–6
   initial disclosure 143–5
   mandatory reporting 212
   prevention and 210
   victimisation process 136
   victimisation surveys 14–16
residential programmes 114
resilience 38, 151–3, 201
resource mobilisation initiatives 178
responsivity principle 114, 120–3, 128–30, 132–3
restorative justice 95
retribution 89
Rind, B. 13
risk assessments 204, 211
   increasing effort 167–9
risk factors, victim 135
risk management plans 213
risk measurement 107–10
risk principle 113, 116–17, 124–6, 132
Rispens, J. 139
Roodman, A.C. 14
routine activities 39, 62, 134–5
rule setting 170–1

Russell, G. 186–7

Safer Cities 180
safety plans 212
Sampson, R.J. 69, 74, 84
Sanderson, J. 137
Scared Straight 103, 113
Schmauk, F.J. 95–6
Schmucker, M. 131
schools 37–8, 53
schools, transition to 76–84
scope of CSA 17–19
Seattle Social Development Project 70, 77–8
secondary prevention
   community-focused approaches 208–9
   developmental prevention 205
   domestic settings 207
   institutional settings 206, 208
   offender-focused approaches 204–6
   public health model 47–9, 199t, 204–9
selected prevention 47–8
selective serotonin reuptake inhibitors (SSRIs) 120
self-disclosure 143–5
self-esteem 152
self-management skills 118, 119
self-regulation model 115
self-restraint 30–1, 85
serotonin 120
sexual attraction 27–9
sexual, definitions of 3
sexual development 72–4
sexual harassment 81
sexual interests modification 118, 119–20
Sexually Violent Predator (SVP) 106–7, 109–10
Sherman, L.W. 90, 92, 93–4, 101
sibling abuse 10, 172
Simon, A. 12
Simon, L.M.J. 160, 172

single mothers 10, 86, 162t, 171, 172
situation-focused approaches 199t
  assessment 127
  integrated theory 62–3
  primary prevention 201–2
  secondary prevention 207–8
  tertiary prevention 212–13
situational bases 23, 39–44
situational prevention 161–74
  conceptual and empirical
    foundations 156–61
  crime prevention 39–42, 50, 51,
    155, 157–9
  domestic settings 16–17, 162t,
    171–4
  institutional settings 16–17, 162t,
    166–71
  integrated theory 58–60
  public settings 16–17, 162t,
    163–6
  situational bases 159–61
Smallbone, S.W.
  domestic settings 171
  institutional settings 168
  modus operandi 10–11
  offence settings 16
  offender characteristics 6, 8
  policing 94
  situational factors 40
  treatment 112, 124
  victimisation process 136
Snow, B. 147
Sorenson, T. 147
Souryal, C. 101
specific deterrence 100–2, 210
Sroufe, L.A. 74
STABLE 118
step fathers 55, 66, 172
Stewart, D.J. 96
Stop It Now! 11, 54, 190–1, 192,
  195–6
strangers 17
subcultural norms 35
suicides 159
Sullivan, J. 10

supportive adults 143–4, 145, 146,
  152, 154, 212
Sure Start 66
surveillance 165–6, 169
Swanston, H.Y. 150

Taal, M. 139
target hardening 164
target identification
  community-focused approaches
    63
  current approaches 46–54, 63–4
  integrated theory 54–60
  offender-focused approaches
    61–2
  situation-focused approaches
    62–3
victim-focused approaches 62
teachers 10
tenant involvement approach 177–8
territoriality 166
tertiary prevention 47–8, 49, 199t,
  209–14
testifying 148–9
testosterone 24–5, 28, 104–5
therapist characteristics
  see responsivity principle
Thornton, D. 102
Tomison, A. 186
Tonry, M. 50
total institutions 170
transition points
  early attachment relationships
    74–6
  to high school 80–4
  to parenthood 84–6
  to school 76–80
treatment
  adolescent offenders 123–30,
    131–2
  adult offenders 115–23, 130–1
  effectiveness 211–12
  general principles 113–15
  outcomes 9, 130–2, 215–16
Tremblay, P. 39

Tromovitch, P. 13

UNICEF 66
universal prevention 47–8
unsubstantiated cases 145–6
USA
  community-focused approaches
    177–8, 190–1
  dangerous sexual offender laws
    106–7
  deterrence 102–3
  developmental prevention 66,
    70, 77–8
  maltreatment 186
  National Research Council (NRC)
    2
  personal safety programmes 137–8
  specific deterrence 101–2
  treatment 129
Ussher, J.M. 143

vasopressin 25–6
versatility 9–10
victim characteristics
  age 12–13
  gender 7, 11–12, 18, 20, 206
  outcomes 13–14
  overview 135, 206–7
  reporting of CSA 14–16
  target hardening 164
victim-focused approaches 199t
  integrated theory 62
  known victims 142–53
  potential victims 134–42
  primary prevention 200–1
  restorative justice 95
  secondary prevention 206–7

tertiary prevention 212
victimisation process 136–7, 149–53
victimisation surveys 18–19, 20,
  145
Violence Risk Appraisal Guide (VRAG)
  109

Ward, T. 115, 122
Webster, C.D. 109
Webster, C.M. 100
Weis, J.G. 77
Weisburd, D. 101
Westermarck, E.A,. 27
Wise, S. 186
Wolak, J. 136
Wood, J.M. 147
World Bank 66
World Health Organisation (WHO)
  2, 3–4, 186
Wortley, R.K.
  domestic settings 171
  institutional settings 168
  modus operandi 10–11
  offence settings 16
  offender characteristics 6, 8
  opportunistic offenders 41
  policing 94
  situational crime prevention 158
  situational factors 40
  situational offenders 42
  victimisation process 136

youth offenders, deterrence and
  102–3

Zgoba, K. 172
Zimbardo, P.G. 170